APPLIED PUBLIC RELATIONS

Cases in Stakeholder Management

LEA's Communication Series
Jennings Bryant/Dolf Zillmann, General Editors

For a complete list of titles in LEA's Communication Series,
please contact Lawrence Erlbaum Associates, Publishers
at www. erlbaum.com

APPLIED PUBLIC RELATIONS

Cases in Stakeholder Management

Larry F. Lamb
University of North Carolina–Chapel Hill

Kathy Brittain McKee
Berry College

LAWRENCE ERLBAUM ASSOCIATES, PUBLISHERS

2005   Mahwah, New Jersey   London

ON THE COVER: Albuquerque news media heard Sandia National
Laboratories experts describe the use of its counter-terrorism technol-
ogy in disabling explosives that an airline passenger allegedly con-
cealed in his shoes before boarding a transatlantic flight in London in
December 2001. (Source: Sandia National Laboratories. Photo by
Randy Montoya.)

Lawrence Erlbaum Associates, Inc., Publishers
10 Industrial Avenue
Mahwah, New Jersey 07430

Cover design by Kathryn Houghtaling Lacey

Library of Congress Cataloging-in-Publication Data

Lamb, Larry F.
    Applied public relations : cases in stakeholder management / Larry
    F. Lamb, Kathy Brittain McKee.
        p. cm. — (LEA's communication series)
Includes bibliographical references and index.
ISBN 0-8058-4606-9 (cloth : alk. paper)
ISBN 0-8058-4607-7 (pbk. : alk. paper)
1. Public relations—Case studies. I. McKee, Kathy Brittain. II. Title.
    III. Series.
HD59.L36   2004
659.2—dc22   2004047061
                                                            CIP

Printed in the United States of America
10 9 8 7 6 5 4 3 2 1

Contents

5 Stakeholders: Media

6 Stakeholders: Investors

List of Cases

Preface

Applied Public Relations: Cases in Stakeholder Management offers readers the opportunity to observe and analyze the manner in which contemporary businesses and organizations interact with key groups and influences. A basic assumption of the text is that principles of best practice may best be learned through examining how real organizations have chosen to develop and maintain relationships in a variety of industries, locations and settings.

We seek to offer readers insights into contemporary business and organizational management practices. Some of the cases detail positive, award-winning practices, while others provide an overview of practices that may have been less successful. Some target specific public relations campaigns; others offer evidence of broader business and organizational practices that had public image or public relations implications. Readers should be prompted not only to consider the explicit public relations choices but also to analyze and assess the impact of all management decisions on relationships with key stakeholders, whether they were designed or implicit or even accidental.

Preprofessional programs in schools of business, law, and medicine commonly include case-study courses because they encourage students to use both deductive and inductive reasoning to sort through the facts of situations, propose alternatives, and recommend treatments or solutions. For the same reason, academic programs in public relations usually offer courses that teach reputation and relationship management through the case-study method. In fact, the Commission on Public Relations Education specifically recommended the use of case-study teaching to provide undergraduates with a bridge between theory and application.

The strategic use of public relations is expanding in business, government, cultural institutions, and social service agencies. According to the U.S. Bureau of Labor Statistics, public relations is one of the fastest growing professional fields in the nation, and its practice is spreading rapidly throughout the rest of the world as well.

Paralleling this growth, the complexity of public relations has increased with globalization of corporate enterprise and the application of new communication technologies. Social movements and activist organizations now cross borders easily, using public relations strategies to influence publics connected everywhere by satellite and the Internet. Through case studies throughout the book, readers can examine these changing stakeholder relationships from several perspectives.

This book is appropriate for use as an undergraduate text for courses such as public relations management, public relations cases and campaigns, or business management or integrated communication management. A commitment to the ethical practice of public relations underlies the book. Students are challenged not only to assess the effectiveness of the practices outlined but also to consider the ethical implications of those choices. We have placed special emphasis on public relations as a strategic management function that must coordinate its planning and activities with several organizational units—human resources, marketing, legal counsel, finance, operations, and others.

The first chapter provides a review of the public relations landscape, the basic principles underlying effective practice. It also offers a method for case analysis, pointing not only to an understanding of the particular case but also leading students to assess the more comprehensive implications for best practices and ethical practices the case offers.

This chapter is followed by nine chapters, each of which offers an overview of principles associated with relations with the particular stakeholder group and supplemented with suggestions for additional readings. Then, within each chapter, four or five case studies are presented, offering sufficient information for analysis but also providing opportunities for students to engage in additional research that would support their conclusions. Reflection questions are offered to help prompt thinking and focus discussion.

Chapter 2 examines relationships with employees, posing such questions as why is employee satisfaction vital to customer service, financial results, recruiting, and what are the most important predictors of employee satisfaction? How do high-performing organizations use employee communications?

The third chapter explores relationships with community stakeholders. What obligations or duties do organizations have to act as good citizens? What are the appropriate means of publicizing organizational activities as a community citizen?

Relationships with a key stakeholder group (consumers) are probed in chapter four. What are the most effective means of communicating with this group? How are new fusions of marketing, public relations, and advertising working together to reach this group? What duties do businesses owe their customers?

What is news and what motivates reporters to cover it are some of the concerns raised in chapter 5, which deals with media relations. Cases explore both planned and unplanned interactions with reporters and raise issues of both traditional and emerging media formats.

Chapter 6 focuses on a priority stakeholder group for public companies: shareholders and investors and those who offer advice to them. Examining the cases presented in this chapter yields insight into issues such as the importance of timely and truthful material disclosure and the implications management decisions have on subsequent stock values.

In contrast, chapter 7 focuses on building and maintaining relationships with the stakeholders of nonprofit organizations, their members, volunteers, and donors. The unending need to raise funds is addressed, as well as the ongoing need to keep members and volunteers satisfied and to attract new members and volunteers.

Relationships with government regulators are addressed in chapter 8. Cases examine how governments seek to influence their constituents and how organizations seek to influence regulation.

Chapter 9 examines activist stakeholder groups and how they use public relations strategies to grab attention, win adherents and motivate change. It also considers how targeted organizations may establish and maintain effective communication with them. The impact of public demonstrations and of media coverage is examined. Principles of cooperation are explored.

The final chapter looks at relationships within the global community, focusing on the ways in which media practice, cultural mores, and political differences may affect relationships that cross borders and languages.

Four guest commentaries are included, each answering a question about the best practices in contemporary public relations. We thank Lee Duffey, founder and president of Duffey Communications; Dr. James Grunig, professor at the University of Maryland; Mr. James E. Moody, executive director of the Georgia Society of Association Executives; and Louis M. Thompson, Jr., president and CEO, National Investor Relations Institute, for their thoughtful reflections based on years of expertise and experience.

Professors may approach the cases within the book in several ways. A focus on specific stakeholder groups would be easily possible, using the chapters as presented. However, one might also focus on particular issues, such as labor relations or crisis management, by selecting cases from within several chapters. One might highlight the operations of agencies, corporations, and nonprofits in the same manner. One might also select cases that contrast campaigns with ongoing programs or managerial behaviors.

The authors acknowledge the contribution of Dr. Carol J. Pardun of the University of North Carolina-Chapel Hill to the inception of this project. Amy Holcombe at Berry College and P. Andrew Sleeth in Chapel Hill offered research and editing support during the initial phases of writing. We also acknowledge the gracious support of our Lawrence Erlbaum Associates editors, Linda Bathgate and Karin Wittig Bates, who kept us on track and moving forward throughout the planning and production process.

ABOUT THE AUTHORS

Larry F. Lamb is assistant professor in the School of Journalism and Mass Communication at the University of North Carolina at Chapel Hill. He holds a BA in journalism and an MBA from Pennsylvania State University. He has held public relations and advertising management positions at AT&T, Dial Corporation, other public companies, and an international strategic communications firm.

Kathy Brittain McKee is associate provost and professor of communication at Berry College, Rome, Georgia. She holds a BA in communication and religion/philosophy from Shorter College and an MA in journalism and a PhD in mass communication from the Grady College of Journalism and Mass Communication at The University of Georgia. She is coauthor of *Media Ethics Cases and Moral Reasoning*.

1

Public Relations: Maintaining Mutually Beneficial Systems of Stakeholder Relationships

No formal organization is an island. Each is composed of an internal system of social networks, and each exists within a framework of interrelated systems of relationships with key stakeholders such as competitors, donors, consumers, regulators, the media, and so on. Some organizations may prefer to think of themselves as islands, however, or floating battleships equipped with all the resources necessary for their own sustenance. In reality, however, such a view is too short-sighted for success.

PRACTICING PUBLIC RELATIONS

The effective practice of public relations is integrally bound to the health of an organization or institution. As such, it provides the avenue for the organization to effectively monitor, interact, and react with other key groups within the organizational environment. Public relations is thought of here as *the communication and action on the part of an organization that supports the development and maintenance of mutually beneficial relationships between the organization and the groups with which it is interdependent.* This text is written overtly from a systems theory perspective, which suggests that without such adaptation, units within an environment will wither and fade as they will not be able to exchange vital information with other units within the environment. Such a balanced flow of information creates an *open system*, one that is responsive and adaptive to changes within the environment and its internal and external systems and subdivisions. In public relations terms, we think of this exchange as occurring through the building of mutually beneficial relationships based on a balanced flow of information from

1

and to the organization and its key publics. Thus, effective public relations practice underlies the maintenance of an open system. Conversely, when public relations is not an integral part of the organization and balancing internal and external communicating with the environment and other systems and subsystems is not a basic function for the organization and its management, then the system is described as *closed*, one subject to restriction and perhaps even death because it will not change or respond to its environment.

Clearly, for the practice of public relations to ensure openness, it requires the support and involvement of management. To use a crude human systems example, the nervous system within one's leg or arm cannot truly function without the support and direction from the brain. Some movement or reaction may occur, but the functioning of the limb is dependent on coordination with all other internal systems that is triggered by the brain through the central nervous system. Public relations practitioners may be assigned duties or activities, but unless these are coordinated with the "management brains" of the entire organization, these actions may produce little that is truly functional for the organization or its interrelated systems.

PUBLIC RELATIONS PROCESSES WITHIN SYSTEMS

With the assumption that effective public relations promotes a healthy, open system for an organization, and its interrelated systems and environment, however, comes certain other suppositions. First, an organization must be able and willing to identify who or what these key interrelated systems are. Because the health of other units within a system is also dependent on a mutually beneficial relationship and exchange, as is that of the central unit, they have a mutual stake in each other's well-being. Thus, these groups are often identified as *publics* or *stakeholders*. The process of coming to know and continuing to understand the concerns, needs, priorities, media habits, communication patterns, and social commitments of those key stakeholder groups requires effort, resources, and knowledge. And, although it may be sometimes frustrating, such research is an ongoing process; one never can "know" all one needs to know about a stakeholder. Thus, the practice of public relations requires continuing efforts at research, planning, executing, and evaluating in order for organizations to remain open for new input and output. This text seeks to explore how the relationships with those stakeholders may best be managed through appropriate public relations practices.

Although different writers and organizations may describe the process differently, systems theory suggests that the practice of public relations requires other ongoing environmental monitoring. Plans should be based on solid and thorough research that explores the internal and external situation of the organization and its systems. Such research should guide organizations in defining carefully the problem or opportunity within the environment that should be responded to. Setting a goal or goals that relate to the problem or opportunity establishes the environment for planning. In turn, plans are only as good as their execution, and systems theory again would suggest that such execution should be carried out at the same time environmental monitoring is maintained. Finally, input regarding successes and weaknesses should be sought out deliberately at the end of a program and plan. That way, important feedback may become part of the next system action or program and perhaps shared with other linked systems as appropriate to help foster their health.

It should be acknowledged that effective analysis, planning, executing, and evaluating of both the environment and relationship management may be approached from other theoretical perspectives, or other theories and constructs may inform the assumptions of systems theory. Practitioners and managers within organizations would be well advised to attend to the other dominant communication and social-psychological constructs, such as Maslow's hierarchy of needs and the theories and assumptions of social exchange, social learning, agenda setting, behaviorism, diffusion of innovations, classical rhetoric, and the elaboration-likelihood model. Knowledge of traditional business fields such as marketing and management provides a solid underpinning for communicating within and throughout organizations effectively. An understanding of contemporary media practices is also a vital tool for practitioners.

ETHICAL AND LEGAL PERSPECTIVES

A plethora of laws, regulations, and torts may govern the relationships of organizations with various publics. Within the United States, the framework of the First Amendment to the Constitution provides for the free practice of public relations, yet certain practices may be either restricted or required by statute or regulation. For example, businesses and organizations are as affected by concerns regarding libel and privacy as any individual or media group. Copyright and trademark regulation may, in fact, promote and protect the interests of organizations over the interest of individuals. Publicly traded companies face specific regulation of communication activity, ranging from required speech dealing with quarterly and annual statements to prohibited or premature information sharing among insiders. Clearly, the practitioner must consider the legal environment as a key component affecting relationships with stakeholder groups.

The social and economic power of public relations practices today should also be grounded in a foundation of social ethics. Professional associations such as the Public Relations Society of America (PRSA) and the International Association of Business Communicators (IABC) have endorsed principles that should underlie practice: advocacy of free speech and communication; commitment to disseminating truthful and accurate information; respect for the dignity and value of all individuals; and the maintenance of independence from undue conflicts of interest or allegiance. Again, systems theory suggests that the good of the whole is supported by the good of the parts, so behaviors that promote mutual benefit are not only ethical but perhaps essential for the ongoing growth and success of an organization or business. Practitioners must seek discernment about what is the *best* choice for behavior—that which most effectively promotes the principles of human dignity, social responsibility, and truth telling. As the communications conduit between and among systems that may have competing interests, determining what choices offer the most effective ethical alternatives requires reflection and introspection, rather than just reaction and response.

CASE-STUDY ANALYSIS

This book addresses nine key stakeholder groups with which many businesses and organizations interrelate, and proffers contemporary case studies for analysis. Some of these cases exemplify the very highest standards of public communication, mutual benefit, and business savvy. Others may raise questions about performance and benefit. Chapter 2 investigates relationships with employees as exemplified by national and international firms such as General Motors, Southwest Airlines, UPS, and the U.S. Postal Service. Chapter 3 presents examples of community stakeholders from the perspective of both a for-profit corporation such as Avon or the Chicago Bulls sports team and nonprofit groups such as Habitat for Humanity. The ways in which corporations seek to foster healthy relationships with consumers may be examined through cases in chapter 4 involving crisis communication, branding, and product publicity.

The important role played by media relations is explored in chapter 5 where health care, political, religious, and social issues aroused media coverage to which organizations had to react and respond. Chapters 6 and 7 address special stakeholder groups, investors, members, and volunteers. From crises of financial reporting to efforts to diversify memberships, these cases raise issues for publicly traded and nonprofit organizations.

Chapter 8 investigates the relationships between governmental organizations and their publics or organizations and regulatory agencies. Critical questions about the role of public relations within public affairs are explored. Chapter 9 addresses critical questions from another perspective—those raised by activist groups seeking to affect change in environmental or social practices. Last, chapter 10 raises the issue of the expanded international environment in which organizations and businesses now operate. How does one successfully build and maintain relationships in varied settings with diverse stakeholders?

Although there are many ways to approach case studies as a learning tool, we suggest the following as one method that may prove helpful. It suggests three layers of analysis that might be used:

- *Analyze the Problem:* How fully do you understand the situation described here? Through additional research you might conduct, what more can you learn about the organization in question, its publics, this situation, or other organizations that have faced similar situations? Articulate the public relations problem or opportunity faced by the organization and/or its key stakeholders in one or two sentences.

- *Understand the Practices:* Critique the actions or reactions undertaken by the organization and its publics described here. Are they in line with accepted best practices? Identify the phases of the communication or campaign cycle and the strengths and weaknesses of the plan and actions. In your opinion, were actions taken that were not necessary? Were other appropriate actions not included? Were there factors of timing and budgeting that impacted actions, or that could have been exploited to better advantage?
- *Identify the Principles:* What are the implications of this case for maintaining mutually beneficial relationships with the key stakeholder identified, or other strategic stakeholders? How does this case illustrate, either positively or negatively, common ethical principles for effective practice? What does this case suggest in terms of effective principles for public relations practitioners in other situations with the same stakeholder or others?

The following questions may help you clarify aspects of the cases as you analyze these levels:

- What goal(s) and objectives do you think this organization is attempting to achieve through its actions or reactions?
- What would characterize a mutually beneficial relationship with this public or stakeholder? What would motivate members of that stakeholder group to enter into or to maintain a relationship with this organization? What might be a liability or caution about an ongoing relationship?
- Does this organization's actions demonstrate open- or closed-system practices and philosophies? What type of research do you believe was used in order to develop this plan of action? What more should the organization have known in order to more effectively plan and execute its communication program or campaign?
- What ethical philosophies or precepts are demonstrated by the organization in this case?
- Are there other examples you can cite of organizations that have faced similar challenges? What do those examples tell you about how this organization might have improved its relationships and its outcomes?
- What style of internal management does this case illustrate? Does it appear that public relations practitioners within the organization are taken seriously? Is public relations a management function within this organization?

ADDITIONAL READINGS

Ault, Philip H., Warren K. Agee, Glen T. Cameron, & Dennis L. Wilcox. (2002). *Public relations: Strategies and tactics* (7th ed.). New York: Pearson, Allyn & Bacon.

Caywood, Clarke L. (Ed.). (1997). *The handbook of strategic public relations & integrated communication*. Boston: McGraw-Hill.

Cutlip, Scott M., Allen H. Center, & Glen M. Broom. (2000). *Effective public relations* (8th ed.). Upper Saddle River, NJ: Prentice Hall.

Grunig, James E. (Ed.). (1992). *Excellence in public relations and communications man-agement.* Hillsdale, NJ: Lawrence Erlbaum Associates.

Heath, Robert L. (Ed.). (2000). *Handbook of public relations.* Thousand Oaks, CA: Sage.

Lattimore, Dan, Otis Baskin, Suzette T. Heiman, Elizabeth T. Toth, & James K. Van Leuven. (2004). *Public relations: The profession and the practice.* Boston: McGraw-Hill.

Ledingham, J. A., & Stephen D. Bruning. (Eds.). (2001). *Public relations as relationship management: A relational approach to the study and practice of public relations.* Mahwah, NJ: Lawrence Erlbaum Associates.

Moore, Roy L., Ronald T. Farrar, & Erik L. Collins. (1999). *Advertising and public rela-tions law* (2nd ed.). Mahwah, NJ: Lawrence Erlbaum Associates.

Newsom, Doug. (2003). *This is PR: The realities of public relations.* New York: Wadsworth.

Toth, Elizabeth L., & Robert L. Heath. (Eds.). (1992). *Rhetorical and critical approaches to public relations.* Hillsdale, NJ: Lawrence Erlbaum Associates.

2

Stakeholders: Employees

The first day of a new job often includes an employee's initial contact with the public relations department, though the employee may not realize it. Part of the day is spent in the human resources office, completing paperwork and an orientation program, and part is spent with the employee's new supervisor. During these visits, a new employee may receive printed material about the organization, see an orientation video, and learn how to use the intranet to get news and information. The printed, visual, and online materials very likely were prepared by or with help from a public relations professional. Through a variety of media channels, this connection to public relations will continue, directly and indirectly, until the individual retires or leaves the organization.

Employee relations responsibilities cut across many departments. Human resources focuses mainly on recruiting, pay and benefits, training programs, employee appraisal systems, and similar concerns affecting all jobholders. The marketing department wants to keep employees up to date on products and services offered to customers. In every department, individual supervisors handle employee relations needs that are specific to the people in their work groups, such as linking an organization's overall mission and goals to the everyday reality of the job.

Public relations professionals work in close partnership with human resources managers, individual supervisors, and others to foster good employee relations. In fact, public relations professionals seldom undertake employee relations programs without input from human resources and other departments. This partnership aims to create conditions where all employees, individually and as a group, can get the greatest reward from the human capital they invest in the job and where the organization can gain the highest value from the resources it uses to reach its goals.

All of us invest varying amounts of *human capital* in work. Human capital is the combination of talents and skills, knowledge, behavior, effort, and time that an individual commits to the job. In turn, an organization pays its workers for their human capital and also provides capital of its own—machinery, office space, computers, and so on—for each of us to use on the job.

EMPLOYEE SATISFACTION PAYS MEASURABLE RETURNS

Everyone, individuals and the organization, will get the most from an enterprise when all commit as much human and hard capital to the endeavor as they can. And employees are most likely to invest more human capital when they are satisfied with their jobs. Satisfied employees care more about customer satisfaction, cooperate more with each other, and apply more effort. They are more productive.

Employee satisfaction has tangible benefits for all organizations, but the results may be most easily measured in for-profit businesses. Satisfied employees are associated with higher revenues (the dollars that businesses receive from their customers), lower costs (the dollars that businesses spend to provide customers with products or services), and greater profitability (the revenues that remain after all costs are met). The reasons for the positive payback from employee satisfaction are self-evident. Not only do they appeal to our common sense, but they also have been examined by researchers and found valid. Here are a few examples:

- *Employee retention:* Satisfied employees are less likely to look for or accept new jobs with other organizations, which might be competitors. As workers stay longer at one employer, they become more proficient, building up their human capital in ways that benefit both employee and employer. Turnover, replacing employees who quit, is expensive; some say it costs between 100% and 200% of an individual's base pay. It entails not only the visible costs of recruiting new workers but also the invisible costs of a lower level of human capital offered by a brand-new employee.
- *Customer satisfaction:* Each of us, as consumers, has encountered unhappy employees, surly or slow or sour. They can make a sales transaction or a meal away from home an experience to remember, which we vow never to repeat. On the other hand, satisfied employees create a detectable climate of care to which customers respond. It may lead to a bigger purchase and to repeat business. Similarly, customer satisfaction appears to have a reciprocal effect on employees. Imagine how much more pleasant a job can be when customers are happy.
- *Productivity:* Employees generally must interact with coworkers and managers to make a product or provide a service; few create output entirely on their own. When individuals actively cooperate with each other, more work gets done in less time, often using fewer resources. Similarly, satisfied em-

ployees put more "discretionary effort" into the job, making the difference between average and superior performance.

Considering the payoff that's available to employers from taking steps to assure employee satisfaction, what's surprising is how many organizations neglect the things they could be doing, big and little, to make employees happier.

EFFECTIVE LEADERS INSPIRE TRUST AND CONFIDENCE

Some things that might improve employee satisfaction are beyond the influence of public relations professionals—for example, better pay and benefits. Yet, there are many areas where public relations professionals, in partnership with others, can and should apply their expertise. These areas include feedback mechanisms that give employees a voice and an opportunity to raise questions, open-book management that shares details on current results, reports on goals and plans that are expressed in language everyone can understand, and more.

Perhaps the best place to begin is employees' desire to know where the organization is going, how it's going to get there, and when it will arrive—goals, strategies, and timetables. These subjects constitute leadership responsibilities, and there may be nothing more important to employees. Coincidentally, these subjects also give public relations professionals the opportunity to make their greatest contributions.

Research shows that employee satisfaction depends on the qualities of trust and integrity that bind individuals to organizations. Yet, investigators have learned that workers are most disappointed in employers' efforts to achieve open and honest communication. Also high on the list of disappointments are clarity of goals and directions, trust and respect, and management competence.

The Hay Group, international consultants on human resources, says that its studies have shown that trust and confidence in top leadership constitute the single most important predictor of employee satisfaction. Moreover, the Hay study found that leaders can get trust and confidence through effective communication programs that:

- Help employees understand the overall strategy of the organization.
- Help employees see their role in achieving key objectives.
- Update employees regularly on progress that's made toward the objectives.

SOURCE OF SATISFACTION:
OPEN AND HONEST COMMUNICATION

Because key indicators of an organization's success depend on employee satisfaction and, in turn, satisfaction depends on trust and confidence in leadership, public relations professionals should develop programs that help leaders win trust and confidence as well as show respect and appreciation for employees. In some cases, these programs will involve giving employees valid reasons to extend trust; in others, programs will help leaders earn it. In all cases, trust cannot exist without open and honest communication.

Of course, communication should be two-way—not simply the top-down, here's-what-you-need-to-know approach that's used in too many employee relations programs. Instead, it should provoke a dialogue that will both help employees gain satisfaction from their work life and support overall goals of the organization.

When Watson Wyatt Worldwide, a global human resources consulting firm, examined 914 companies to learn which communication policies typify successful organizations, they found that the high-performing companies integrated communications into business strategy. Working with the IABC and the IABC Research Foundation, Watson Wyatt found that employees in high-performing firms understood overall goals better as well as employees' roles in reaching them. The study learned that the high-performing organizations:

- Provide channels for upward communication and use employee input in decision making.
- Focus on helping employees understand the business, its values and culture, goals and progress, and ways for employees to improve performance.
- Give communications professionals a strategic role in business planning rather than pigeon-holing them as facilitators.
- Do better in explaining major changes to employees and winning support for change.

MEDIA CHANNELS FOR EMPLOYEES

Organizations use a variety of media to reach employees, including newsletters and employee newspapers, posters, bulletin boards, voice-mail announcements, e-mail messages, closed-circuit TV newscasts, kiosks, intranets, and more.

Intranet communication has been growing fastest because it offers the advantages of speed, flexibility, color, interactivity, and ease in updating. However, experts advise public relations professionals to use intranet communication for its special capabilities rather than treat it as if it were print projected on a screen. Intranets can offer multimedia, chats and bulletin boards, previews of ad campaigns and commercials, breaking news, and more, but people don't read intranet screens as if they were the printed page. In fact, the proliferation of office computers has led to a rising tide of electronic communication, but it is unsuitable where employees, such as assembly line workers or outdoor crews, have little or no access to a digital network.

Even with all the advanced technology that's available today, one of the most effective media channels is an old standby, used in offices and garages and on the plant floor for generations—the small-group meeting where the boss and team get together for a 10- or 20-minute discussion. There are two main reasons for the continued popularity of small-group meetings:

- Face-to-face discussion is the most effective form of communication.
- Employees prefer to get job-related news from their immediate supervisor.

Public relations professionals often play an important role in the success of small-group meetings even though they may not be present when the supervisor and team get together. To introduce major policy changes and the like, materials for small-group meetings are prepared in advance by public relations practitioners. The materials take the form of what's often called a meeting-in-a-box that includes a meeting outline, skeleton remarks for the supervisor to adapt, perhaps a short videotape, DVD or PowerPoint presentation, handouts for participants, feedback forms, and similar items. The purpose is to give the supervisor useful materials, minimize preparation time, keep the message consistent, and achieve communications objectives.

Proving that everything old is new again, each supervisor may obtain the PowerPoint presentation or visual portion of the meeting-in-a-box by downloading it from the intranet or receiving it as an e-mail attachment.

ADDITIONAL READINGS

Becker, Brian E., Mark A. Huselid, & Dave Ulrich. (2001). *The HR scorecard: Linking people, strategy, and performance*. Boston: Harvard Business School Press.

Beitler, Michael A. (2003). *Strategic organizational change*. Greensboro, NC: Practitioner Press International.

Catlette, Bill, & Richard Hadden. (2001). *Contented cows give better milk: The plain truth about employee relations & your bottom line*. Germantown, TN: Saltillo Press.

Koys, Daniel. (2001). "Effects of employee satisfaction, organizational citizenship behavior, and turnover on organizational effectiveness," *Personnel Psychology*, 101–114.

CASE 1.   A NEW KIND OF CAR, A NEW KIND OF TEAM: SATURN COMES TO TENNESSEE

In the 1980s, the world's largest car manufacturer faced a dilemma: Would it be possible for an American unionized traditional auto company to retool so it could compete with the Japanese manufacturers who were making huge inroads into the U.S. and world auto market? General Motors (GM) came up with one possible solution, developing the Saturn brand in a brand-new facility in a brand-new location for the automotive industry. Even its style of employee/management relations was brand-new for GM. They utilized a team approach to employee organization and found that it paid off in terms of productivity and satisfaction for employees and consumers. After only 2 years of production, Saturn became the leader in the J.D. Power and Associates Sales Satisfaction Index, a position it held for several consecutive years.

Spring Hill, Tennessee, Becomes Saturn's New Home

After gaining large tax concessions from the state of Tennessee, GM began building a new, $1.9 billion auto plant in a small town south of Nashville in April 1986. The 800-population town of Spring Hill soon became home to more than 6,800 employees of the plant, most of whom were newcomers. Most were GM employees laid off at other plants around the country who moved south for the job opportunity. The population swelled to more than 12,000, and it is expected to double again by 2020.

The small town felt the strains almost immediately. Although the influx of residents brought increased revenues with them, there was some resentment over the fact that so few employees were local. The local school system was strained by the influx of new students with no new tax dollars, and the town that had never needed a traffic light suddenly found itself fighting traffic jams and delays.

As for the newcomers, they found that property values quickly rose, so the real estate deals they had anticipated soon vanished. Because many had worked before in traditional unionized facilities, they found adjusting to the Japanese, team-style management at the plant a new experience, too. Saturn formed a community relations task force to help communicate with the townspeople and the new employees. To help ease the transitions, the company sought to match employees who had recently moved with similar employees who had been at the plant longer, and the corporation also sponsored recreational and social events and a spouse club for employees and their families. Job-hunting support was provided to spouses.

GM did seek to make itself known as a good community citizen. Land was donated for the county to build a new high school and a new fire station. GM helped support the building of a new City Hall complex.

The Employees Form Teams

When the brand was first conceptualized, a group of 99 labor and management leaders was asked to engineer the best organization for the new plant. After studying many other companies, they decided to adopt a team approach for every part of the new corporation, from those who would design and assemble the cars to those who would advertise them. According to the 1985 Memorandum of Agreement, the labor force would be organized as self-directed work teams. Decisions were to be arrived at through consensus, and the corporation would be run by joint labor–management committees at the corporate, manufacturing, plan, and department levels. The United Auto Workers would be a full partner in all business decisions. For example, groups of work teams were "advised" by two people, one a union member and the other not. The union remained active in the organization, holding weekly meetings of the leadership team, training elected team leaders, and holding biweekly meetings with members who had full-time management responsibilities.

According to the Saturn Web site, the plans have been carried out. Saturn's teams or *work units* now are composed of 9 to 15 employees who elect their own work leaders, called *work unit counselors*. The units then are accountable for their production, budgets, and other issues related to quality. The joint committees are known as *modules* and are composed of teams that do similar work, and all the modules within a plan make up the business unit. The two leaders of the modules, one labor and one management, represent the module at the plant-level unit.

Workers who joined the Saturn team received extensive training—some 320 hours of training in the first year and at least 92 hours after that—and rewards were based on meeting organizational and team goals. Saturn used an internal television network to send information continuously to their assemblers, and managers employed frequent meetings and practice an open-door policy to foster two-way communication.

The Saturn Web site describes the corporation's philosophy in meeting what it calls its "members'" or employees' needs:

- We will create a sense of belonging in an environment of mutual trust, respect, and dignity.
- We believe that all people want to be involved in decisions that affect them, care about their jobs and each other, take pride in themselves and in their contributions, and want to share in the success of their efforts.
- We will develop the tools, training, and education for each member, recognizing individual skill and knowledge.
- We believe that creative, motivated, responsible team members who understand that change is critical to success are Saturn's most important asset.

In 1992, 87% of Saturn workers voted to retain their innovative labor contract, and in 1998, they voted by a margin of nearly two to one to keep the system. The contract offers bonuses and incentive pay based on training, quality control, and production quotas, rather than the more conventional contracts found at most other auto-manufacturing plants. Saturn wages were typically about 88% of the other GM workers' hourly wage, but their bonuses often were considerably higher.

And the arrangement has expanded. In May 1999, Saturn production began at a GM plant in Wilmington, Delaware.

Customers, as Well as Employees, Join the Saturn Team

The Saturn introduced a new marketing strategy for car purchases: The price was fixed, so no haggling over price was needed, relieving buyers of the anxieties of wondering if someone else got a better deal for the same-style vehicle. Buyers were offered a money-back guarantee; within the first 30 days or 1,500 miles, the car could be returned for a full refund or a replacement auto. The buyers of the new cars were fiercely loyal.

GM supported the loyalty: In 1994, GM began sponsoring "Saturn Homecoming" events, where customers were invited to bring their vehicles back to Spring Hill where they would join together under large air-conditioned tents to hear speeches from Saturn managers and engineers, meet celebrities such as Olympic skater Dan Jansen and Gemini and Apollo astronauts Jim Lovell and Gene Cernan, and enjoy concerts from such musicians as Hootie and the Blowfish, Wynonna Judd, Blood, Sweat & Tears, Faith Hill, and Tim McGraw. The main event was a tour of the plant. In 1994, more than 38,000 Saturn owners came to Spring Hill, and more than 2,300 employees volunteered to serve as hosts at the Homecoming. In 1999, more than 20,000 tickets for the Homecoming were presold to Saturn owners, and thousands of others bought tickets on site. Clearly, these car owners believe they are a part of the Saturn team as well.

QUESTIONS FOR REFLECTION

1. GM faced a series of potential public relations issues while establishing this new brand and plant site. Identify at least two of those problems.
2. This case illustrates the multiple layers found among some stakeholder groups, such as employees and their families. What type of research is needed in order to understand more fully how to establish mutually beneficial relationships with such multifaceted publics?
3. How closely related are issues of community relations and employee relations? Public affairs and community relations? Employee relations and consumer relations?

4. What special threats emerge when corporations or organizations must relocate employees? What opportunities?
5. What communication principles are illustrated through Saturn's interactions with its unionized and nonunionized workforce?

Material for this case was drawn from the following: Saturn Web site at http://www.saturn.com/; Chappell, L. (9 January 1995), "Pact draws Saturn closer to GM," *Automotive News*, No. 5586, p. 37; Chappell, L. (24 November 1997), "Saturn workers get help with college tuition," *Automotive News*, p. 9; Compton, C. (3 November 2000), "Maintaining employee satisfaction and productivity during a relocation & redeployment," www3.best-in-class.com/bestp/; Convey, E. (2 March 2002), "Motor mouth; Taking a fresh look at Saturn's approach," *Boston Herald*, p. C12; Cummins, A. J. (12 March 1998), "Saturn workers vote to retain innovative labor pact with GM," *The Wall Street Journal*; Dessler, G. (September 1995), in "Enriching and empowering employees—the Saturn way," *Personnel Journal, 74*(9), 32; Dessler, G. (May 1999), "How to earn your employees' commitment," *The Academy of Management Executive, 13*(2), 58–67; Evanoff, T. (12 March 1998), "Saturn UAW workers vote to maintain cooperative labor agreement," *Detroit Free Press*; Goff, L. J. (24 January 2000), "What it's like to work at Saturn Corp.," *Computerworld*, www.computerworld.com; Kennen, T. (1 September 1999), "A hot time in Spring Hill," *Ward's Dealer Business*; Paul, P. T. (10 November 2002), "Sudden impact," *The Atlanta Journal-Constitution*, p. D1; Rubinstein, S. A. (January 2000), "The impact of co-management on quality performance: The case of the Saturn corporation," *Industrial & Labor Relations Review, 53*(2), 197–218; and (18 March 2003),"Spring Hill, Tenn., rode out rough patches in relations with GM auto plant," *Montgomery Advertiser*.

CASE 2.   FREDDIE MAC EMPLOYEES GET PROMPT REPORT ON SWEEPING CHANGES

Cloudy weather during the first June weekend of 2003 matched the mood of many employees at Freddie Mac's headquarters in McLean, Virginia. For 5 months, the financial institution had been wrestling with an internal investigation into accounting irregularities.

As a high-profile target of an accounting inquiry, Freddie Mac had some undistinguished company. Several large firms—Adelphi, Enron, Global Crossing, WorldCom, and more—had recently attracted the same kind of attention for the use of creative accounting to improve the appearance if not the reality of their financial results. Many employees at Freddie Mac were unsettled to see their employer standing in the same line-up.

Returning to the office on Monday, June 9, employees found an e-mail message waiting in their electronic mailboxes. It directed them to the company's intranet site, the *Home Front,* for an announcement concerning the institution's leadership.

The announcement was a shocker. The company's president had been fired; the chairman had retired; and the chief financial officer had resigned. The *Home Front* introduced a new leadership team that had been installed by the board of directors. The sweeping changes led to a tide of employee questions that would need quick answers.

A Leader in the Secondary Mortgage Market

Freddie Mac is a huge but somewhat obscure financial institution formerly known—but not well known—as the Federal Home Loan Mortgage Corporation. It was established by the U.S. Congress in 1970 to make home ownership an affordable dream for more families. Congress chartered Freddie Mac as an investor-owned and publicly traded corporation, though it remains a government-sponsored entity. Its trading symbol on the New York Stock Exchange (NYSE) is FRE.

Basically, Freddie Mac works like this. Financial institutions, such as banks and thrift associations, provide mortgage loans to individuals who want to purchase a home. A mortgage loan obligates a homebuyer to make monthly payments for a period of years—usually 15 or 30 years for a conventional mortgage. Freddie Mac buys the individual mortgage loans from the financial institutions and then bundles a number of them together in a package. The packages are sold to investors in the form of bonds and are known as mortgage-backed securities.

This process enables financial institutions to serve more homebuyers because Freddie Mac provides a stable and reliable source of capital. It gives Freddie Mac an opportunity to profit from its role as middleman, and it gives investors a chance a buy a safe, long-term income flow from mortgage-backed bonds.

By most measures, Freddie Mac was a big success. Ranked as one of the five largest diversified financial companies in the United States, it had financed homes for more than 30 million families—one of every six homes—since 1970 and had reported 31 consecutive years of profit. Its major competitors were Citigroup, Countrywide Financial, and Fannie Mae. Like Freddie Mac, the larger Fannie Mae is a government-sponsored entity in the secondary mortgage market. It formerly was known as the Federal National Mortgage Association.

On the Most-Admired List

Before the accounting questions surfaced in January 2003, Freddie Mac had a stellar reputation. It appeared on the *Fortune* magazine list of "America's Most Admired Companies" for six consecutive years, and it received high marks from others for more than its financial prowess.

Some described the institution as a progressive employer. For example, the *Washington Post* reported in 2001 on Freddie Mac's career transition program, which enabled employees from any department to apply for an intense 4-month course that provided a route into high-tech occupations. The program's goal, the *Post* said, was "to foster employee loyalty and avoid the turnover that plagues information technology departments in high-tech companies and other businesses." In 2002, *Computerworld* magazine listed Freddie Mac among the 100 best places to work for information technology professionals. Also, *Health* magazine's Web site, www.health.com, has complimented the company for helping employees achieve a balance between work and home responsibilities.

Freddie Mac's image in 2002 provided a bright contrast to the darkening mistrust of corporate governance. Beginning with Enron's disgrace in October 2001, a succession of corporate scandals lowered the public's estimation of big business, chief executives, auditors, and accountants. In fact, Freddie Mac fired its independent auditor, Arthur Andersen, in early 2002 after the accounting firm was implicated in Enron's debacle.

Accounting Questions Loom

Then, the new auditor raised troubling questions about the institution's own financial reports, and an internal investigation was opened in January 2003. The auditor said Freddie Mac's earnings in recent years appeared to have been higher than reported. Higher earnings generally are good news, but truth in accounting is valued even more than profits. Only from honest reports can investors judge whether to buy or sell a company's stock. Similarly, employees need honest financial feedback to know whether they're meeting objectives or slipping.

As the investigation progressed, Freddie Mac said it would restate its financial results for the three preceding years—2000, 2001, and 2002—after adjusting them to conform to generally accepted accounting principles. On the rainy Saturday of June 7, the Office of Federal Housing Enterprise Oversight (OFHEO), a regulatory agency that monitored Freddie Mac, sent a two-page fax to the board of directors telling them it was time to come clean.

"Freddie Mac will make available to OFHEO all communications to the board and management regarding deficiencies in accounting practices and an investigation of employee misconduct that was discovered on June 4, 2003," the fax said in part.

A Busy Monday for Public Relations

For Freddie, the big internal changes and the external scrutiny marked Monday as a day of communications challenges and risks. The company would need to:

- Tell investors about the new top-management team and the departure of the old one before the day's trading opened at 9:30 a.m. on the NYSE.
- Provide the news media with the details and background that they would need to report on the shake-up with fairness, accuracy, and perspective.
- Give Freddie's 3,900 employees the information they would need to understand what was happening, the reasons for it, how it would affect them, and what to expect in the future.

One of the oldest rules in public relations is *Tell employees first*, but following this rule in investor-owned companies is often impossible. The Securities and Exchange Commission (SEC), which regulates the flow of information to investors, requires companies to assure timely and fair disclosure of news that could influence any investor's decisions on stock ownership. Many employees are investors in their employer's securities, and they are not permitted to receive news before other investors do. However, they may be told at the same time.

To satisfy employees' desire for information and abide by SEC regulations, Freddie Mac sent an e-mail alert to all employees on Monday morning and referred them to the *Home Front* intranet. The company also issued a news release with wide distribution, reaching general and financial news media as well as investment analysts.

Announcement on the Intranet

On the intranet, employees saw a detailed report on the executive changes and brief biographies of the new corporate officers. It also reviewed the plans for restating prior years' financial results, the potential effect on future accounting periods, and cooperation with the OFHEO, SEC, and NYSE authorities.

Given such surprising news, employees buzzed with curiosity and speculation. Everyone knew that, for a short while at least, the pace of work would inevitably slow as people compared interpretations of the events, raised questions about the effects on Freddie Mac, and shared personal concerns.

As employees digested the news, Freddie Mac's leadership participated in a conference call for investors at 9 a.m. Eastern time. The conference call also was accessible live through the Freddie Mac Web site (www.freddiemac.com). Investors reacted to the news—or to the uncertainty it suggested—by driving the share price of FRE down 16% before the end of the day.

Face-to-Face Communication

At 10 a.m., Freddie Mac managers met with executives to discuss the announcement and the direction of the company, and then all employees were invited to meetings with the new leadership team at 11 a.m. and noon. At the McLean headquarters, more than 1,000 employees packed an amphitheater for the 11 a.m. meeting, overflowing into a lobby where video monitors carried the proceedings. Freddie Mac offices in Atlanta, Chicago, Dallas, Los Angeles, and New York joined the discussion and question-and-answer period through teleconference facilities.

An account of the meetings in the *Washington Post* indicated that Freddie Mac had scored a home run with most employees.

"And then, as the meetings started, something rather amazing, considering the news of the day, happened," the *Post* said. "The new executives were greeted with sustained applause."

The newspaper interviewed an Internet project manager who said: "Everyone was clapping. There was definitely a sense of excitement in the air—excitement for the future of what this will bring to Freddie and how it will affect us as a whole."

Later the same day, a number of managers met in smaller meetings or individually with employees in their work groups to address specific questions or personal worries.

A Memo to Employees

On June 25, the company sent the news media an update on the company's progress in restating its financial results. The release said the company expected the cumulative effect of the restatement to increase retained earnings, as of year-end 2002, by $1.5 billion to $4.5 billion. The size of the amount surprised many investors. At the same time, the company's chief executive sent a memo on the subject to all employees with a promise to keep them current on the difficult situation, which said:

> This morning, Freddie Mac issued a news release providing additional information about issues related to the restatement of our prior year's financial results. The information in this release reflects the new leadership team's strong commitment to candor and transparency in our financial and business reporting—even when the news reflects poorly on our company. Freddie Mac's board of directors shares that commitment.

I strongly encourage you to read today's news release. It identifies numerous issues that led to the need to restate our earnings for prior years. It also describes the significant actions under way to strengthen our internal controls and financial reporting.

QUESTIONS FOR REFLECTION

1. Freddie Mac's accounting troubles involved understating net income, but companies more often are accused of overstating net income. Why do both lead to a public relations crisis?
2. The SEC does not allow publicly traded companies to give employees any information on significant developments ahead of others. Why?
3. How did Freddie Mac accommodate the SEC rules on fair disclosure of significant information?
4. Freddie Mac has gone through more management changes since June 2003. What has happened?

Information for this case was drawn from the following: the Freddie Mac Web site at http://www.freddiemac.com/news/; Berenson, A. (10 June 2003), "Mortgage concern in broad shake-up," *The New York Times,* p. A1; Dugas, C., & Waggoner, J. (11 June 2003), "Criminal probe targets Freddie Mac," *USA Today,* p. 1; Falcon, A., Jr. (7 June 2003), Letter to Freddie Mac Board of Directors from Office of Federal Housing Enterprise Oversight (10 June 2003), "Freddie's market bomb," *The Wall Street Journal,* p. A18; Johnson, C. (8 April 2001), "Freddie Mac giving employees a chance to change fields," *The Washington Post,* p. L1; and Joyce, A. (15 June 2003), "Bad news, good practices: Prompt, thorough answers key to maintaining employee morale in crisis," *The Washington Post,* p. F6.

CASE 3.   SOUTHWEST AIRLINES FINDS A PAYOFF
IN AVOIDING EMPLOYEE LAYOFFS

Commercial aviation in the United States was grounded for 2 days following the terrorist tragedies of Tuesday, September 11, 2001. Planes sat idle at the gates; airport concourses stood quiet and empty; skies showed no trace of the contrails that follow passenger jets.

After planes were allowed back in the air at 11 a.m., Thursday, almost everyone began to wonder if the aviation business would ever recover. Fear kept some travelers on the ground; they drove, used the train, or simply stayed home. Strict security measures at airports, requiring travelers to get to the terminal 2 hours or more before departure, discouraged others from flying.

One-day business trips by air—between Philadelphia and Pittsburgh, for example, or Phoenix and Los Angeles—had been common before but now were difficult or impossible. Business people flew less. On most planes, more than half the seats were empty.

The impact on U.S. air carriers was devastating. In the first week after the terrorist attacks, Midway Airlines suspended operations and let go 1,700 employees. Continental Airlines announced plans to cut 12,000 jobs and reduce flights by 20%. Over the next 4 weeks, most U.S. carriers trimmed schedules and announced layoffs affecting about 100,000 workers altogether—20,000 at United Airlines, another 20,000 at American and Trans World Airlines, 10,000 at Northwest Airlines, and so on.

Never a Layoff

One carrier, Southwest Airlines, had been flying for 30 years but had never imposed a layoff. Respect for employees was written into the company's mission statement and ingrained in its culture.

The mission says, in part: "We are committed to provide our employees a stable work environment with equal opportunity for learning and personal growth. Creativity and innovation are encouraged for improving the effectiveness of Southwest Airlines. Above all, employees will be provided the same concern, respect, and caring attitude within the organization that they are expected to share externally with every Southwest customer."

One of the company's founders, Herb Kelleher, had explained the emphasis on employee relations for *Fortune* magazine just before stepping down as chief executive officer and president on June 19, 2001.

"The thing that would disturb me most to see after I'm no longer CEO [chief executive officer] is layoffs at Southwest. Nothing kills your company's culture like layoffs. Nobody has ever been furloughed here, and that is unprecedented in the airline industry" Mr. Kelleher told *Fortune*. "You want to show your people that you value them and you're not going to hurt them just to get a little bit more money in the short term."

Of course, Herb Kelleher could not have imagined at the beginning of the summer what his company would be facing in the fall—3 days on the ground and a frightened flying public.

Back in the Air

On Friday, September 14, Southwest returned to the air with a modified schedule. The same day, the company's leadership faced difficult decisions, described by new CEO James F. Parker in a *Fast Company* article:

> We had a $180-million profit-sharing payment due on September 14. Because of our limited resources, we had a tough time deciding whether to fund it. In the end, we chose to pay it out because it was the right thing to do for our employees.
>
> Next on the agenda was deciding not to furlough employees and to protect all employee jobs. We have a lot of people who have worked hard for more than 30 years so that they can have job security in hard times. It would have been breaking faith with our employees if our first reaction was to cut jobs. Cutting jobs should be the last thing a company does rather than the first thing.

Yet, Southwest could not adopt a business-as-usual attitude. No one knew when—or even if—fearful passengers would begin using air travel as they had before the attacks.

Mr. Parker said, "We did declare an immediate hiring freeze and cut capital spending across the board. We halted discretionary projects, including the expansion of our headquarters building. We also told Boeing that we needed to defer our next airplane deliveries, even though they were scheduled for the following week."

Southwest Airlines completed 30 consecutive years of profitable operations and earned employee loyalty with a policy of no layoffs. (Photo courtesy of Southwest Airlines.)

Looking everywhere to cut costs and keep employees on the payroll, the company found that even small changes could save money. For example, a switch from white to unbleached paper towels saved the airline $75,000 a year.

Full-Schedule Operations

Southwest returned to its full flight schedule on Monday, September 17, but the costs of operation exceeded ticket sales by a wide margin. Payrolls for the flight crew and ground operations, the cost of jet fuel, and expenses like utilities and rent were the same whether planes were three-quarters full or three-quarters empty. For at least 6 weeks after September 11, the airline lost money every day. A few outsiders were pessimistic about Southwest's ability to maintain its no-layoffs record.

For days after the September 11 attacks, the television networks and cable news channels carried nothing but news. Gradually, commercials began to reappear, and Southwest was the first major air carrier to resume advertising. The commercials began running Wednesday, September 19, on the company's Major League Baseball sponsorships in nine markets. One spot featured Southwest's president, Colleen Barrett, with a from-the-heart message about the conviction to prevail.

"As you know, our advertising is about the freedom to fly," Ms. Barrett told Southwest employees in the *LUVLines* employee newsletter. "But today I want us to reflect on that freedom in a different light. The airline industry is indispensable to our nation because, as Americans, we are blessed with the opportunity to travel throughout the country. At this important time, we have no competitors because we are all focused on one thing—restoring America's commerce. We must, and we will, restore this freedom and show those who doubt our resolve that we will provide safe, reliable and dependable transportation."

Encouraging the Urge to Travel

To get Americans flying again, Southwest launched a fare sale on Tuesday, September 25, that required an advance purchase of only 3 days and offered fares as low as $34 for travel on any day. Many passengers couldn't resist, and the airline's load factor—the percentage of available seats occupied by paying customers—improved significantly.

Southwest was able to recover quickly from September's tragedies because it was determined to use its resources—people, equipment, and reputation—to return to normal as soon as it could and as best as it could.

By keeping all its people, it could fly a full schedule. By flying a full schedule, it could give customers the same choice of flights that they'd had earlier and a level of service as good or better. By giving customers good service and lower fares, it underscored the key messages that had made the airline successful from the start.

Financial Results Turn Positive

In late October, the airline's chief financial officer, Gary Kelly, shared an encouraging report with Southwest employees:

> The traffic levels have been nicely stimulated by what is a very, very successful fare sale that we launched on September 25. Our load factors, as many of you know, are actually quite good. For the full week ended October 14, we actually had a 67 percent load factor. Not quite as high as last year, but last year was an all-time record load factor for us. Anything in the 60s, I think, we have to be pretty pleased with. We generated a lot of that traffic, though, with very, very deep discounts. And we're simply not making money at these sales. But understand, our first objective was to get people to fly, and we feel like we've accomplished that. So, now we'll be trying to move those fares up so that we can charge fares that we actually do make money at, and it remains to be seen what the travel demand will be like, because the economy is very weak.

At year-end, the company reported its 29th consecutive year of profitability. Fourth-quarter net income in 2001 was $64 million, down 59% from $155 million in the corresponding period of 2000.

In the earnings announcement issued in January 2002, CEO Parker said: "We are grateful the company's financial position has been stabilized. Our liquidity remains strong, and our revenue trends improved in the fourth quarter. As a conse-

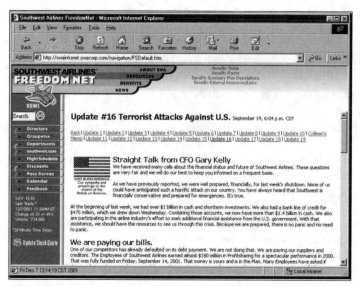

In the days after terrorists brought U.S. aviation to a temporary stand-still, Southwest Airlines emphasized frequent communication with employees, using its Intranet and publications. (Illustration courtesy of Southwest Airlines.)

quence, our board is pleased to be able to pay substantial profit-sharing to reward our magnificent 33,000-plus employees for their devoted and extraordinary efforts, particularly during such a threatening time for our nation and industry."

QUESTIONS FOR REFLECTION

1. The operations of all major U.S. air carriers were disrupted by the terrorist attacks of September 11. Why was Southwest alone able to recover so quickly?
2. How has Southwest profited from its no-layoffs policy?
3. What did Southwest do to control costs when it was back in the air?
4. In a message to employees, Southwest President Colleen Barrett said, "We have no competitors because we are all focused on one thing—restoring America's commerce." What do you think she meant?

Information for this case was drawn from the following: the Southwest Airlines Web site at http://www.iflyswa.com/about_swa/; Adams, M. (20 July 2002), "Major airlines take staggering blow to bottom line," *USA Today*, p. B1; Brooker, K. (28 May 2001), "The chairman of the board looks back," *Fortune*, p. 62; (October 2001) *LUVLines*, employee newsletter for Southwest Airlines; Mount, I. (February 2002), "Five ways to reduce labor without layoffs," *Business 2.0*, p. 29; Overholt, A. (May 2002), "Best of the best 2002," *Fast Company*, p. 50; and Trottman, M. (21 September 2001), "Aftermath of terror: Southwest Airlines considers cutbacks, halts delivery of planes from Boeing," *The Wall Street Journal*, p. A6.

CASE 4.   TEAMSTERS DELIVER PUBLIC SUPPORT DURING THE UPS STRIKE

Many businesses and homes that receive or send packages are familiar with the brown vans and brown uniforms of the United Parcel Service (UPS), and many customers have formed friendly ties with their UPS carriers. The power of these ties was demonstrated during the 1997 Teamsters' strike when public-opinion polls showed that two of three Americans sided with the union, rather than with UPS management, during the UPS work stoppage. A *CNN/USA Today* Gallup poll conducted in the second week of the strike found that 55% of Americans backed the Teamsters, whereas only 27% backed UPS. *Business Week* writers concluded on September 1, 1997: "For the first time in nearly two decades, the public sided with a union, even though its walkout caused major inconveniences."

UPS employs some 370,000 workers and handles 3 billion packages each year, an average of 12.2 million per day delivered by drivers. Some 185,000 UPS employees belonged to the Teamsters union. In its 90-year history, UPS had never before faced a national strike by its employees.

"How Could This Happen?"

Before the 1997 strike, relations between the Teamsters and UPS had traditionally been positive, according to *HRMagazine*. Quoting Lea Soupata, the senior vice president for human resources at UPS headquarters in Atlanta, the magazine

UPS drivers use a fleet of nearly 90,000 vans, tractors and other vehicles to serve every address in the United States and more than 200 countries and territories.

reported of the strike: "It was two weeks that felt like two years. Whether you were management or union, you were wondering, 'How could this happen to the UPS family?' "

UPS had adopted what it believed to be an effective labor-dispute plan, including creating a strike crisis manual. Media lists were updated, and spokespersons were trained. Yet Kate Miller argued in *Public Relations Quarterly* in summer 1999 that UPS failed to conduct adequate environmental scanning and issues management so it was not fully aware of the changes in labor trends and growing cynicism among the U.S. workforce.

The strike focused on several issues. The Teamsters argued that UPS relied too much on part-time workers. The union asked that more full-time employees be hired and that the wage gap between experienced full-time workers and newly hired part-time workers be reduced. Management had offered a pay raise of $1.50 per hour over 5 years to full-time employees and a $2.50 per hour increase over 5 years to part-timers with seniority. Controlling subcontracting, the practice of allowing UPS to use nonemployee truckers when a company driver was not available, was also a key issue. Pension benefits were also on the table.

Teamsters Communicate Their Views

Ron Carey, then head of the Teamsters Union, used skillful tactics in communicating labor's views. The union had given $2.7 million in political contributions during the 1995–1996 election campaign, 96% to Democratic candidates and another $209,000 in soft money to the Democratic National Committee. In contrast, UPS had given $1.3 million during the campaign season, and 64% of it went to Republican candidates. Carey was confident that President Clinton would not invoke the Taft–Hartley Act to intervene to prevent the strike.

Second, Carey prepared the Teamsters membership for the experience of the strike and for interactions with others about strike issues. He used videos and held rallies to inform members, and members were allowed to take other part-time jobs during the strike. The union also used a media blitz to inform the public about the Teamsters' causes. The *Boston Globe* reported on August 19 that before the strike began, the union had released a "flurry of news releases" and a "report on part-time work at UPS" to major news outlets. The union successfully played upon the familiarity many customers had with their local carrier, whom many saw during daily deliveries. They were skillful in exploiting fears among many Americans about their potential loss of full-time jobs. They were able to establish sentiment of support for these employees against a relatively faceless, large "management" force. Bill Schneider, a political analyst with the American Enterprise Institute in Washington, was quoted in the August 19 *San Francisco Chronicle:* "The union very skillfully undertook a PR offensive, exploiting the feelings of insecurity many Americans have about corporate downsizing. I don't think it was that people suddenly became champions of unions, but people were sympathetic with the

workers. Everyone knows and likes their UPS worker, who does hard, often unpleasant work, and brings people's goodies."

The support of other key U.S. and European labor unions was obtained;
Miller's *Public Relations Quarterly* article reports that in May, the Teamsters held
a global day of action with the theme "Part-Time America Doesn't Work," and
UPS facilities were picketed. The AFL-CIO endorsed the strike action, as did numerous other unions across the country.

UPS Responds Slowly

For its part, UPS did not begin external communications until after the contract ex-
pired. Its first press release was issued on July 31, and it did not address the issues
of the strike directly. Subsequently, UPS management did not allow its spokespeople to criticize Carey of the Teamsters directly, but instead were to focus on the
issue UPS believed had prompted the strike—its threat to pull out of the union's
multiemployer pension plan. Though much of the focus of the strike was on the
part-time workers used by UPS, UPS did not counter union complaints with information about the pay scale for part-timers and the like.

There was no designated spokesperson for UPS; CEO James P. Kelly was
deemed too new to the position, having served for only 7 months. Instead of one
speaker, responses to the 20,000 media inquiries a day came from a variety of
headquarters' sources, including those from human resources as well as public
relations.

Recovering From the Strike

To end the strike, UPS agreed to increase hourly wages for full-time workers by
$3.10 an hour and for part-time workers by $4.10 an hour. The company also
agreed to combine part-time positions to create 10,000 new full-time jobs.

After the 15-day strike was settled, UPS worked to regain the confidence of its
customers. Representatives of UPS called or visited many customers in the month
following the strike. Nevertheless, the company reportedly lost more than $750
million in revenue during the strike, and UPS continued to see a drop in its land-
based delivery customers. The strike led UPS to adopt some cost-saving measures
including washing the brown vans less frequently and allowing packages to stay
on trucks for one additional day if necessary.

UPS also worked to restore communication with employees. A video presentation featuring CEO Kelly was used to communicate the message: "Let's get back
to work and do what we know best—deliver packages." Managers also held town
meetings with workers and supervisors in the 60 UPS districts. Some workers reported feeling as though some managers were retaliating against strikers, but an
anonymous toll-free telephone line was established for employees to use in reporting any retaliation.

Averting a Second Strike

When contract negotiations came due in 2002, UPS wanted to avoid a repeat of the 1997 strike. Discussions began much earlier than in 1997. Negotiations again centered on job security, but this time the two sides were able to agree to terms without a strike being called. The union and UPS agreed upon a series of cost-of-living wage guarantees, banning of supervisors' working to handle packages, and so on.

QUESTIONS FOR REFLECTION

1. Identify the key stakeholders for UPS in this labor situation. What principles should characterize relationships with each?
2. Evaluate the communication strategy of the Teamsters. What public relations principles does the strategy illustrate?
3. How might UPS exploit the strength of the relationships between its carriers and customers?

Information for this case came from the following: Clayborn, Sam, "UPS vs. Teamsters Union: Why UPS lost and lessons learned for other negotiators," CMN #37, www.inionline.com; DeBare, I., & Hoover, K. (19 August 1997), "UPS, Teamsters reach a deal," *The San Francisco Chronicle*, p. A1; Gluckman, A. (21 November 1997), "A contract worth fighting for," *Dollars & Sense*, p. 10; Grossman, R. J. (September 1998). "Trying to heal the wounds," *HRMagazine, 43*(10), 85–92; Harrington, L. H. (March 2002), "High-stakes poker: UPS–Teamsters master contract negotiations are under way," *Transportation & Distribution, 43*(3), 37; Hirschman, D. (30 August 2002), "Teamsters approve UPS contract," *The Atlanta Journal-Constitution*; Lewis, D. E. (19 August 1997), "UPS strike: Massive preparation appears to have aided efforts by Teamsters," *The Boston Globe*, p. D1; Magnusson, P., Harris, N., Himelstein, L., Vlasic, B., & Zellner, W. (1 September 1997), "A wake-up call for business," *Business Week*, p. 28; Miller, K. (Summer 1999), "Issues management: The link between organization reality and public perception," *Public Relations Quarterly, 44*(2), 5–11; Schulz, J. D. (3 March 1997). "'Problem solving' labor talks," *Traffic World, 249*(9), 10ff; (1 February 2002), "UPS and Teamsters in early start," *Fleet Owner*; and (31 July 1998), "UPS has regained most of its customers lost during the strike," *Orange County (CA) Register*, www.Ocregister.com.

CASE 5. HANDLING A CRISIS: THE U.S. POSTAL SERVICE RESPONDS TO ANTHRAX ATTACKS

The U.S. Postal Service (USPS) may have faced its greatest modern challenge in the fall of 2001 when letters carrying anthrax spores were mailed, processed, and delivered to NBC News and to the U.S. Senate offices of Tom Daschle. Mail-processing centers in the Brentwood Road N.E. neighborhood in the District of Columbia and in Hamilton Township, New Jersey, became involved in the crisis when the dangerous letters passed through the facilities and were handled by USPS employees.

In the unfolding crisis, 5 people died and 13 others became ill. Many postal employees felt endangered by their ordinary work activities of gathering, sorting, and delivering mail. The letters prompted a post–September 11 wave of concern about terrorism risks to postal patrons, postal employees, and others dependent on the mail for their livelihoods.

The USPS has 38,000 post office retail outlets and delivers to 136 million addresses daily on an annual operating budget of about $70 billion. Nearly 800,000 employees delivered about 208 billion pieces of mail in 2000, processing almost half the world's mail volume.

The Threat Is Discovered

At first it appeared the anthrax crisis would be confined to the areas where the letters were delivered and opened. But that soon changed. On November 2, 2001, the *Wall Street Journal* detailed the discovery of the threat. According to the reports, when the contaminated letters were first discovered on October 15, the Centers for Disease Control (CDC) and Prevention told the USPS that there was no reason to worry about health of mail workers who might have come into contact with the letter to the Senate or to NBC. On Tuesday, October 16, after investigating the letters themselves, the CDC found that they contained a very potent form of anthrax able to float in the air for a long time. Postmaster General John "Jack" Potter directed questions to the CDC: What should be done about mail handlers working at Washington's main postal station? The Brentwood Road senior vice president for government relations and public policy told the *Wall Street Journal:* "They said there was virtually no risk of any anthrax contamination in the facility, that without the letter being opened at Brentwood, there was no risk of any anthrax escaping, so neither the facility nor the employees need to be tested."

However, postal workers Leroy Richmond, 56; Joseph Curseen, 47; and Thomas Morris, 55, reported that they were not feeling well.

On October 17, Postmaster Potter decided to have Brentwood tested, at USPS expense, even though the CDC said it was unnecessary. Testing of the machines began after 8 p.m. while employees were still working in the facility. Field-test results of the four machines that had processed the Daschle letter were negative.

Employees Infected by the Anthrax

However, as this was going on in the District of Columbia, acting New Jersey Gov. Donald T. DiFrancesco was announcing the first confirmed case of anthrax in a postal worker. The acting commissioner of the New Jersey state health department decided on October 19 to recommend 7 days of the antibiotic Cipro for all workers at the two Trenton-area postal facilities where the NBC letter had been processed.

That same day, Brentwood employee Leroy Richmond went to the Kaiser Permanente Woodbridge medical facility and reported that he was an employee worried about anthrax. He was sent to the emergency room at Inova Fairfax Hospital, where he was found to have some preliminary signs of inhalation anthrax. He was put on intravenous Cipro. The CDC continued to say it doubted that anthrax was the cause of the illness. However, on October 21, Mr. Richmond was confirmed as positive for anthrax, and the Washington, DC, Department of Health was notified. The CDC then recommended that all Brentwood employees be tested.

Early on October 21, Thomas Morris, one of the three Brentwood employees who had said they felt ill on October 16, came to the emergency room of the Greater Southeast Community Hospital. He died at 8:45 p.m., according to the newspaper account.

On October 22, the Brentwood postal workers were taken to DC General Hospital for anthrax testing. The hospital had been closed months earlier for financial reasons, but it provided a venue for the testing. Workers were given nasal swabs to test for exposure and put on a preventive 10-day round of Cipro.

Mr. Curseen collapsed at home on that morning. He was taken to the hospital where he was admitted with antibiotic therapy and put on a ventilator. He died 6 hours after arriving.

The Service Responds in Washington, DC

The USPS then responded by first shutting down the facilities from where the letters had been delivered. They were to remain shut for months. The Brentwood facility was then purged by pumping chlorine dioxide gas into the building, which had been completely sealed. After 24 hours, the gas was purged and the building again cleaned.

The USPS took a two-pronged approach to quieting concern about the safety of the mail. Consumers were urged to pay attention to the mail they were opening and to alert authorities promptly if they noticed an unsecured package or any mail that contained a white powder. Employees were also given additional training in awareness and reaction procedures. Throughout the system, workers were given gloves and masks to wear while processing mail.

The November 28, 2001, *Washington Times* reported that when announcing the new security measures for new technology to sanitize mail, Postmaster Potter said: "We're not going to be defeated.... It's clear to us, like other symbols of American freedom and power, that mail and our employees have become a target of terrorists. It is equally clear that we must take extraordinary steps to protect them both."

Communication Responses

Public relations experts were consulted. Burson-Marsteller and the USPS were later awarded the crisis/issues management Campaign of the Year 2003 award from *PR Week* for managing communication during the anthrax crisis. According to *PR Week*, Burson-Marsteller advised the USPS to focus on its business, which was the safety of the mail and its stakeholders. They advised, "Be the mailman, not the doctor." The firm sought to ensure that the USPS had four consistent elements to its messages: control of information, control of the message, control of the clock, and illustration of the unfamiliar. Controlling information meant knowing how to find and deliver the best information to each key group. Controlling the message meant consistency and clarity. Controlling the clock meant countering rumors with timely updates throughout the news cycles. Illustrating the unfamiliar meant teaching stakeholders about how the mail system works and how anthrax might be passed through the mail.

On March 21, 2003, *PR Week* reported that a November 2001 poll of postal employees revealed that 71% said they agreed with the statement, "I am proud to work for the Postal Service," a result up 3% from the same survey conducted in 2000.

Other Employees Worry About Safety

However, USPS employees' concerns were not confined to the Washington, DC, area. According to the October 27, 2001, *Palm Beach (FL) Post*, the American Postal Workers Union's Miami chapter went to court in late October to attempt to force the USPS to provide immediate medical testing for workers requesting it and to install safety equipment to detect and kill anthrax germs. United Press International (UPI) reported on January 4, 2002, that some postal workers in New York City, Washington, DC, and New Jersey were wearing pins that said, "I have a tendency not to believe these people," the last words of Washington postal worker Thomas Morris, Jr., to 911 operators before he died of anthrax in October. In January 2002, the Metro New York Area Postal Union went to court to sue to have the city mail-sorting facility tested thoroughly and decontaminated because some anthrax spores had lingered after the initial cleanup operations. An earlier lawsuit filed by the union had resulted in a judge's order to test contaminated machines at the Morgan Center.

Gerry Kreienkamp, spokesperson for the USPS in Washington, told UPI that the service was depending on the advice of experts at the CDC and the Occupational Safety and Health Administration. The service had sealed the floor where the anthrax-contaminated sorting machines were located. Susan Brennan, another

USPS spokesperson in Washington, DC, told UPI that postal workers had three options: Take a three-dose anthrax vaccine, take another 40 days of Cipro, or watch for symptoms. By January 4, UPI reported that 44 employees had enrolled in the vaccine program and 919 had opted for more antibiotics.

In February 2002, New York union leaders requested cleaning of the "high bay" area of their facility. The USPS worked with various federal agencies to establish protocols for the work. Researchers confirmed the presence of the anthrax spores, and then unions, management associations, and all employees were notified. Experts determined that no medical intervention was necessary. The USPS reassigned workers to other areas until containment structures could be built.

QUESTIONS FOR REFLECTION

1. There are multiple layers of stakeholders here: Identify the primary concerns of each group.
2. What happens when the advice you receive from an official expert source is inaccurate?
3. The relationship between the USPS and its employees was tested in this crisis. What steps should be taken by the USPS to restore full trust between management and employees?
4. The case illustrates the importance of public leadership. Assess the role and actions of the Postmaster General during the crisis.

Information for this case was drawn from the following: the PRSA Web site at www.prsa.org/_Awards/silver/html/6bw0211c03.html; Chen, K., Hitt, G., McGinley, L., & Petersen, A. (2 November 2001), "Trial and error: Seven days in October spotlights weakness of bioterror response," *The Wall Street Journal,* p. A1; (10 March 2003), "Crisis/issues management: Campaign of the year 2003," *PRWeek,* p. S1; Davis, M., Pillets, J., & Parello, N. (41 October 2001), "Anthrax found at White House mail center," *The Record* (NJ), p. A1; Day, T. G. (19 May 2003), Testimony before the National Security, Emerging Threats, and International Relations Subcommittee of the House Government Reform Committee; Ramstack, T. (28 October 2001), "Postal puzzles; anthrax scare means system faces major changes," *The Washington Times,* p. A1; Thompson, M. W. (3 December 2002), "For Postal Service, another level of anthrax damages," *The Washington Post,* p. A23; Twomey, S. (30 January 2002), "A recipe for safe mail," *The Washington Post,* p. A1; Pacenti, J., & Bierman, N. (27 October 2001), "Postal union's suit will seek anthrax tests, safety equipment," *The Palm Beach Post,* p. A1; and (5 January 2002), "Postal workers in court again on anthrax," *United Press International* Online.

The Management Champion of Social Responsibility

James E. Grunig, professor of public relations, University of Maryland

Organizational theorists tell us that different types of expertise become important in management when people with that expertise are able to solve problems that are crucial to that organization at a particular time. Public relations professionals are becoming empowered today because of their ability to solve problems of relationships, trust, and responsibility that threaten the survival of many organizations and result in poor performance by most others.

The public relations function provides a voice for publics when management makes critical, strategic decisions. Too often, management makes decisions without considering the consequences of those decisions on publics who have no say in the decisions. When management makes such decisions, many publics develop into activist groups who actively oppose the organization. Opposition typically results in litigation, legislation, regulation, and negative publicity that cost the organization a great deal of money.

Even if publics do not organize to oppose decisions, management has a responsibility to alleviate negative consequences of its actions—such as pollution, risky products, discrimination, economic hardship, or a dangerous workplace. Recognizing and alleviating these consequences is the essence of social responsibility, and the public relations function is the management champion of social responsibility.

Public relations managers are the voice of management to explain its decisions; but, more important, they also are the voice of publics. I have described this relationship between public relations, other managers, and publics as two-way symmetrical public relations. Others have called it collaborative advocacy. Still others have called the public relations professional an in-house activist. All of these terms suggest that the public relations professional has a duty to the organization that employs him or her, a duty to the publics that make up society, and to himself or herself. Increasingly, public relations professionals are the chief ethics officers of their organizations. This role is a challenging one, but it makes public relations one of the most relevant and interesting professions today.

James E. Grunig is a professor of public relations in the Department of Communications at the University of Maryland. He holds a PhD in Mass Communication from the University of Wisconsin. He has written or edited 5 books and more than 225 articles and chapters about public relations.

3

Stakeholders: Community

What characterizes a good neighbor? In your neighborhood, it may be someone who maintains a tidy lawn, or someone who has friendly children. It may be the homeowner at the end of the street with the beautiful garden or backyard pool. Yet what constitutes good neighborliness may also be conditional or contextual. The homeowner with the tidy lawn may also have a dog in the backyard that barks ferociously whenever anyone approaches its fence, or she may drive you to distraction during the holidays with an unapproachable standard of decorating. You may wish the friendly children were occasionally less so when you find their toys and playthings scattered across your yard or when their teenage son's car stereo wakes you up each Friday night when he comes home from a date. The level of familiarity you have with your neighbors may be based as much on your willingness to engage in a relationship, however give-and-take it may be, as on their willingness to accept the responsibility of your friendship, and your satisfaction with the relationship may fluctuate depending on time and context.

COMMUNITY RELATIONSHIPS MAY FLUCTUATE

Although community relationships for an organization or business may not exactly parallel your neighborhood example, there are some similarities. Effective relationship building and maintenance with community stakeholders may also be variable and contextual. Many communities welcome the financial investment and opportunities a new manufacturing plant brings with it, but they may also decry the increased traffic, noise, and waste produced at the plant. A corporation may seek locations that are quiet and relatively inexpensive, and then find transportation limitations and zoning restrictions a nuisance. As economic situations change, communities may find themselves faced with closing plant sites or empty "big-box" stores, even as businesses and corporations seek to adjust to the costs of modernization or environmental adaptation.

Frequently, the basic premises for community relationships are somewhat contradictory in that they mix altruism and self-interest in many interwoven layers. Practicing good community citizenship through environmental consciousness, cultural support and civic engagement helps develop and support a higher quality of life for an organization's employees and members, thereby making it easier to attract and retain quality employees. However, such behavior may also generate goodwill that makes it possible for tax incentives, abatements, and zoning decisions that may support the most bottom line of all business motives. Clearly, community relations may also overlap other key areas of practitioner behavior, including management of employee relations, public affairs, consumer relations, and activist groups.

CHANGING DEFINITIONS OF COMMUNITY

Another challenge and opportunity for practitioners and executives may come in defining their organization's community. For one-site locations, this is simple. But consider the questions facing regional, national, or international organizations. The *community* may be the area around headquarters, or it may include all the sites where there are major facilities. *Community* might also include all the market areas from which employees, donors, or consumers are drawn. In a global economy, businesses and corporations may even be held publicly accountable for the community-based behaviors of their subcontractors or suppliers, as well as for their own. Practitioners and executives must work together to define their communities and then to prioritize the publics within them.

RESULTS OF COMMUNITY RELATIONS

Why engage in community-relationship building? Organizations and businesses that seek to be known as good neighbors may have different objectives. Some of those may include:

- *Enhanced quality of life for employees and residents:* Contributing to the cultural, recreational, and artistic life of a community may enhance an organization's ability to attract and retain high-quality employees. It may also foster positive relationships between all those who benefit from programming as well as mitigate future complaints about liabilities of having certain organizations located in an area, such as traffic, noise, and so on.
- *Equipped labor force:* Supporting local educational systems, from PreK–12 through higher education, may further contribute to the employees' satisfactions as well as to the availability within the community of future em-

ployees equipped for the work force. Technical colleges and schools, for example, often work closely with industries and businesses to ensure that their curricula match the needs of the potential employers.

- *Regulatory intervention:* From the extensive tax breaks and incentives offered for building new facilities in a community to more commonplace requests for easing zoning or noise restrictions, businesses often need help from communities if they are to carry out their primary functions. These interventions may well reflect the need for a mutually beneficial relationship. For example, plant sites may need traffic signals to be placed strategically or better highways built to accommodate shipping; governments may need cooperation from plant sites about shift changes to better regulate traffic flow around peak hours. Businesses that receive tax exemptions during a specific time period may need to offer public infrastructure support in other ways, such as using local vendors whenever possible so that funding is circulated throughout the community.

What benefits may communities receive from these public relations practices? Some of these may include:

- *Increased resources for community activities:* Community-based national organizations such as the United Way are dependent on the cooperation of area businesses to help secure donations and volunteer leadership to support their network of social services. Employees who are encouraged by their businesses or organizations to volunteer also provide staffing and service help to agencies, schools, and cause organizations. Arts and cultural organizations may also find that businesses and corporations are primary means of grant support, whether locally or through their foundations. Facilities may be made available for civic meetings and celebrations or for public tours.
- *Increased fiscal support:* The financial contributions through taxes, payrolls, and purchases may be enormously important to local, or indeed regional, national, or international, economies. Small businesses within a community may succeed or fail based on the "turnover" of such dollars in local commerce.
- *Growth of related industries:* Having a major manufacturer locate in one's community may sharply increase the likelihood of attracting other similar large industries or even more industry-related small businesses, thereby increasing the economic health of the community. Chambers of commerce within communities often demonstrate this interlocking impact of industrial and businesses growth as they participate in recruitment efforts for individual and business relocation.
- *Enhanced sense of local pride:* Being known as the headquarters of a major company or organization or being known as a plant site for a national or international brand may offer communities "bragging rights" that instill pride

and raise morale throughout a community. The combination of factors that contribute to an overall improvement in the quality of life for area residents manifests itself in this contagious enthusiasm, which in turn may lead to more growth and development.

COMMUNICATING WITH COMMUNITY PUBLICS

Practitioners may use a variety of tools to send and receive messages from community publics. Local media may be important tools. Face-to-face contacts, meetings, and special events may also be utilized in building relationships with key opinion leaders. It is important for organizations to publicly explain their views and positions and to create opportunities for members of publics to react and respond to them.

However, effective community relations practices demand more than just communication through word or image. Practicing social responsibility—using the resources of an organization to promote ethically positive results for key stakeholder groups—may be the most effective public relations tool of all. Volunteering and donating are potent methods that demonstrate real commitment to enhancing and maintaining relationships.

There is also the practice of what some have called "strategic giving" whereby the good works of an organization or business directly tie into the branding of its products, goods, or services. Consider the book dealer who provides a free book voucher for every child who reaches the reading goal of his or her elementary grade level. Promoting reading? Yes. Stimulating traffic and building loyalty among families and potential customers at the same time? Yes.

Can businesses and organizations be good neighbors? Yes—when their behavior and communication supports the general well-being of their neighborhood, however that is defined by the organization in its dynamic 21st-century environment.

ADDITIONAL READINGS

Burke, Edmund M. (1999). *Corporate community relations: The principle of the neighbor of choice*. New York: Quorum.

Sagawa, Shirley, Eli Segal, & Rosabeth Moss Kanter. (2000). *Common interest, common good: Creating value through business and social sector partnerships*. Boston: Harvard Business School Press.

CASE 6. THE COMPANY FOR WOMEN PLEDGES SUPPORT

Avon Co., in business for more than 115 years offering beauty and health products in 143 countries, has long been associated with the sound of a doorbell ringing to welcome a representative into homes to sell products directly to women. However, in recent years, Avon has achieved fame for more than its line of beauty and clothing products. In 2003, the National Association for Female Executives rated it as the top company for executive women, and it has become known as the largest corporate partner in the fight against breast cancer.

Since 1993, Avon has been influential in raising more than $250 million in funds for cancer research, education and early-detection programs, clinical care, and support programs for breast cancer patients. Many of the funds raised locally are then spent locally. Avon especially targets use of its funds for those who are medically underserved, including low-income, elderly, and minority women, and women without adequate health insurance. Its efforts, working with Patrice Tanaka & Company (PT&Co.), won it a 1997 Silver Anvil award for Public Service. In announcing the 2000 awards of $14 million to breast cancer causes, Avon president and chief executive Andrea Jung told *Women's Wear Daily* on March 10 that this was "the best part of the job."

Take the Avon Pledge

Avon teamed with the National Alliance of Breast Cancer Organizations (NABCO), the Centers for Disease Control and Prevention (CDC), the National Cancer Institute, and the YWCA to communicate the need for early detection and to provide access to services for underserved women. Research conducted in 1996 showed that although the National Cancer Institute announced that the breast cancer death rate had dropped by 5%, Black women still had a higher mortality rate and a lower median age of death than White women. Fewer than half of the respondents to the American Cancer Society's (ACS) 1995 Mammography Attitudes and Usage Study reported mammography that complied with ACS guidelines.

The objectives of the 1995 Breast Cancer Awareness Crusade and the Crusade Online were to enhance awareness of Avon Products as a corporate leader in the fight against breast cancer and the crusade itself as a model of corporate/governmental/nonprofit partnership; to motivate women to respond to the message that early detection of breast cancer saves lives; to support sales of Avon's Pink Ribbon Pin and Pen as fund-raising products; and to raise money to fund grassroots breast cancer programs across the United States. The crusade won 15 awards and citations from the White House, the federal government, and health and philanthropic communities.

The awareness crusade employed a variety of strategies. Using the theme, "Take the Avon Pledge for Better Breast Health," sales of a pen adorned with a pink ribbon were promoted. Women were asked to use the pen to sign a pledge to follow the three-step recommendation to early detection of breast cancer. To support this strategy, a "Take the Avon Pledge" flier and brochure were distributed by more than 440,000 Avon sales representatives. Women were given a pledge card they could sign and keep, and a direct-mail campaign sought to have key opinion leaders sign the pledge. A shopping mall program invited women to sign giant pledge walls and to purchase the Avon fund-raising products. Advertising supported the October National Breast Cancer Awareness Month.

The pledge theme helped support Pink Ribbon pen sales. In the fourth quarter of 1995, $6.5 million was raised. More than 700 media placements generated more than 150 million media impressions. Influential women offering support included Rosalynn Carter, Olympia Snowe, Barbara Mikulski, and Dianne Feinstein. More than 16 million Pledge fliers were distributed. First Lady Hillary Rodham Clinton taped a message played at the shopping-mall events.

New media were important tools. In 1995 PT& Co. helped Avon establish a Web site devoted to the issue of breast cancer. Online events, conferences, chats, and "virtual support groups" were promoted through the site. An online initiative invited women to e-mail pledges.

Building Partnerships for Outreach

In 1996, Avon continued its emphasis, expanding its fund-raising product line to include Pink Ribbon Earrings and a Pink Ribbon Phone Card. The Avon Breast Cancer Leadership Initiative was created to highlight the leadership of educators, patient advocates, doctors, volunteers, and Avon representatives in offering under-reached women messages and services. A national teleconference and satellite media tour with the theme, "Building Partnerships for Breast Health Outreach," were created with the CDC and funded by Avon to promote the exchange of ideas about how to increase the number of women who receive screening. The Avon Breast Cancer Leadership Awards were created to award an unrestricted grant of $100,000 to 10 individuals who had made major contributions to breast cancer prevention and treatment. The director of the Office of Research on Women's Health from the National Institutes of Health chaired the awards committee. Avon worked with NABCO on a national survey to investigate the factors that motivated women to have mammograms and clinical examinations.

More than 350,000 women were reached with the early-detection message, and more than 60,000 of the women said they sought mammograms as a result. More than 300 million media impressions were achieved, including a cover story on breast cancer awareness in the *New York Times* magazine that quoted the crusade director. The campaign again won numerous awards.

Kiss Goodbye to Cancer

Avon continues to develop Pink Ribbon fund-raising products, including mugs, candles, and bears. All crusade products are priced at $4 or under; they come gift-boxed with an enclosed "Guide to Better Breast Health." The "Kiss Goodbye to Breast Cancer" campaign used a special fund-raising lipstick collection and an awards event to raise money and awareness. In October 2001, Avon partnered with "The Rosie O'Donnell Show" to give away a "Thanks for the Mammaries" T-shirt to the first 200,000 women who sent in a receipt for a mammogram. Avon held an e-Bay auction of dresses worn by celebrities such as Elizabeth Taylor and Sharon Stone; the "Little Black Dress Against Breast Cancer" campaign coordinated with a new Avon fragrance, Little Black Dress.

An "Avon Kiss Goodbye to Breast Cancer" concert was planned for September 2002. The concert, held in Avery Fisher Hall in New York's Lincoln Center, featured an awards ceremony to honor companies and persons who had contributed to the breast cancer fight. A portion of the proceeds from ticket sales went to the Avon Breast Cancer Crusade.

Avon Walks for Breast Cancer

One of its best-known means of partnering in the fight involved partners walking long distances as they raised money. Avon has sponsored "Avon Walks for Breast Cancer" in communities across the country, including walks in Washington, California, Colorado, Texas, Florida, Georgia, Illinois, and Massachusetts. The walks occur during a 3-day period where walkers are challenged to conquer 26.2 miles over a 2-day walk cycle or 26.2 miles the first day of walking with 13.1 miles the second day—the equivalent of one and a half marathons. Walkers are provided with tents and hot food during the overnight event.

When approaching its 2002 season of 3-day walks, however, Avon learned the event producer contracted to stage the events was experiencing financial difficulties. The producer, Pallotta TeamWorks, said it would be unable to help with walks scheduled in Atlanta, New York, and Los Angeles during October 2002, although 3-day events had already been completed in 10 other cities that year. The walk survived, but in May 2002, Avon decided the format should be altered. The 60-mile, 3-day walk was shortened to a 26.2-mile distance that could be walked in 1 or 2 days, depending on the walker's choice. The Avon Walk for Breast Cancer events were held in eight cities in 2003.

Other Initiatives

The AVONCares Program for Medically Underserved Women provides funds directly to the patient or her health care provider for diagnosis and then funding for such necessary expenses as transportation and child care during treatment. Through a variety of programs, fellowships and grants are given to individuals and centers across the country to support research, screening and imaging, educational seminars, and advocacy training.

Through the Avon Breast Care Fund, grants are given to local community programs that will identify women who need help, and offer education and assistance to them in obtaining screening and needed care. Avon also provides an expert Co-ordinating Center to work with the community-based programs to ensure that personnel understand the latest in education and care techniques. Since its inception, women in almost 50 countries have received help. More than 600 nonprofit community programs have been awarded grants totaling more than $37 million; in 2002, 114 programs were funded.

The Avon-National Cancer Institute Progress for Patients Program was created with a $20 million gift in 2001 to offer grants to cancer researchers and others seeking to identify new ways to detect and treat breast cancer. Since 2001, more than 200 investigators have received funds. Recipients include cancer research centers at the University of Colorado, Harvard, Johns Hopkins, Northwestern, University of Alabama at Birmingham, University of California at Irvine, Emory University and the Fred Hutchinson Cancer Research Center in Seattle.

QUESTIONS FOR REFLECTION

1. What is the public relations problem or opportunity that drives Avon's involvement in the crusade? What are the implications of this problem for its key stakeholders? Evaluate its development and use of partner stakeholders.
2. What are some of the extrinsic and intrinsic outcomes of this ongoing campaign? What are some of the potential liabilities?
3. Breast cancer research, prevention, and treatment is a cause that evokes strong empathetic responses from consumers and donors. What are the advantages and disadvantages when a corporation aligns its cause-related sponsorships with such an emotion-laden topic?

Information for this case was drawn from a variety of public sources, including the Avon corporate Web site at www.avoncompany.com, Patrice Tanaka & Co. Web site at www.ptanaka.com, and Crusade support sites at www.avonwalk.org. Additional information came from the following: (November 2001), "Avon's breast cancer crusade," *Happi-Household & Personal Products Industry, 38*(11); (November 1997), "Choose causes that resonate with women when considering sponsorship opportunities," *About Women & Marketing, 10*(11), 12; Finn, K. (9 August 2002), "Avon sets fall breast cancer events," *Women's Wear Daily, 184*(29), 7; L. K. (10 March 2000), "Avon donates $14M," *Women's Wear Daily, 179*(48), 7; Jacobson, T. (26 August 2002), "Avon vows to continue 2002 3-day walks," Release, avoncrusade@avon.com; Nugent, K. (20 April 2003), "3-day cancer walk revived" (Worcester, MA), *Telegram & Gazette*, p. B1; and Yoon, L. (6 February 2003), "Survey shows women making gains in corporate world; Avon rated the best employer for female executives," CFO.com.

CASE 7.   CHARITABULLS HELP OTHERS WIN AT LIFE

Mention the Chicago Bulls, and fans across the world think of superstars, NBA championships, and exciting competition. But the team is using its celebrity status to win more than championship rings. The nonprofit organization, CharitaBulls, was formed in 1987 with the motto, "Helping Others Win. At Life." The charitable foundation has contributed to local and regional causes, and its Bulls Scholars program that funds supplemental enrichment education for middle schoolers won a Golden Trumpet for Community Relations from the Publicity Club of Chicago in 2002.

Bulls Scholars Program Supports Student Retention and Enrichment

The Chicago Bulls Scholars Program was born in January 1999 with a $3.5 million grant from the Bulls to the Children First Fund: The Chicago Public Schools Foundation. The program was developed after the 1997–1998 season when Jerry Reinsdorf and the Bulls community relations staff asked the Chicago Public Schools (CPS) to identify academic needs. The Bulls Scholars program was designed to help students make a successful transition between middle school and high school.

In the program, some 40 students at each Chicago public middle school are chosen by their teachers to participate in after-school classes in English or algebra, which are taught by certified middle and high school teachers. By attending the course, completing assignments, and scoring well on the Chicago Academic Standards Examinations (CASE) at the end of the year, students may receive a high school credit in the subject area. The program is based on enrichment, rather than remediation.

The funding from the Bulls, which is managed by the School Partners Program, supports the costs of the teachers, texts, and technology. All of the participating middle schools have received wireless technology for use in the program, including IBM ThinkPads, two printers, and Internet connections; 10 Casio graphing calculators, one digital camera; and a multimedia cart.

Bulls players and office staff visit the participating schools regularly, and each school is invited to a game during the season. Rallies are held at the United Center to encourage and reward the students who are involved in the program. At the May 29, 2002, end-of-the-year rally, Bulls head coach Bill Cartwright, players Eddy Curry and Marcus Fizer, and former Bulls John Paxson and Bob Love appeared, along with the CEO of the Chicago Public Schools. The rally was emceed by Tom Dore, the Bulls TV announcer. A Chicago-based brother quintet, STRONG, performed. The Bulls fan interactive team, the IncrediBulls, also entertained the student group.

On Thursday, May 22, more than 530 seventh- and eighth-grade CPS students who completed the 2002–2003 program attended the Bulls Scholars Jam. The event, held in the arena, featured addresses from former Bull Bob Love, current Bulls guard Roger Mason, Jr., and broadcaster Dore, along with entertainment by the Bucket Boys, the IncrediBulls, Benny the Bull, and live music.

Bulls Scholars Score Well on Exams

Results of the program have been impressive. In 1998–1999, the average Scholar scored higher than 49% of their high school counterparts in English and 79% of their counterparts in algebra on the CASE exam. On the national Test of Achievement and Proficiency, 53% of the Scholars scored at or above grade level in reading, compared to 35% of other ninth-grade students. In math, 69% of the Bulls Scholars scored at or above their grade level, compared to the 44% of other ninth graders who did so.

In 1999–2000, 62.5% (366 of 586) of the students earned the credit. In the first year, 90.3% of the 390 students earned the credit. The Scholars in the program scored higher on achievement tests than other students in their schools, and nearly 75% earned high school credits before they were out of middle school.

Other Community-Support Projects

The Bulls also cooperate in other educational-relations programs, such as the NBA's "Read to Achieve" program where books are given to children, and players and family members assist with reading initiatives through the year. Scholarships are awarded to area seniors to attend college. Through an Adopt-A-School program, incentives are offered to encourage students to attend school and improve their grades. Financial assistance helps fund equipment for area schools. The Bulls also sponsor an annual art contest for elementary schools in area counties, and winning art appears in Bulls publications. The Bulls also support the Newspaper in Education program of the *Wall Street Journal.*

The Bulls' primary objective is to create positive educational and recreational opportunities for children and young people. Other CharitaBulls beneficiaries have included Special Olympics Illinois, City Year Chicago, James Jordan Boys & Girls Club, Chicago Park District, and the Chicago Public Library. During the holidays, the Bulls sponsor food drives, a party for underprivileged children, and participate in MLK and Black History Month activities.

The organization has given more than $1 million over 5 years to repair and restore 140 damaged city basketball courts and has donated more than $700,000 to fund the Men's and Women's Chicago Bulls/Chicago Park District Nite Basketball Leagues that are operated at parks throughout the city. More than 1,000 players age 18 to 26 participate. Working with the Chicago Police Department, the group sponsors the Chicago Bulls/Chicago Park District Inner City Hoops Program, a basketball league for at-risk students ages 9 to12.

CharitaBulls donated $4.5 million in 1994 to build a 40,000-square-foot building containing a computer center, art studio, science lab, clinic, gym, day-care center, dance and game rooms, classrooms, and more two blocks from the United Center. The building was named in memory of James Jordan, Michael Jordan's father. The Boys & Girls Clubs of Chicago operates the center as one of its units and serves about 1,500 neighborhood children and families annually. The foundation also supports other efforts to help renovate the neighborhood around the United Center.

Perhaps not surprisingly, focus is also given to basketball programs. The Bulls work with corporate sponsors to donate more than 200 tickets for each home game to local groups to provide a way for underprivileged children and adults to attend a game. Official instructional youth summer camps were begun in 1999. Children ages 6 to14 attend camps in more than 150 community locations, working through local park districts. The camp runs more than 3 hours a day for an entire week. The Bulls and the White Sox worked together in 2001 to establish a player development facility that offers private instructions, traveling teams, leagues, and tournaments for young players.

Local park districts throughout Illinois cooperate with the Bulls to offer "2ball," a youth skills competition played on a half-court. The 1-minute competition puts two players at different locations on the half-court in a shooting competition. Some 9,000 young people participate each year.

Sports-Related Events and Activities Support the Foundation

Funds for the CharitaBulls Foundation come through contributions to the Bulls and from special events and programs including a Tip-Off Luncheon, held each October 1, and FestaBulls, a sports memorabilia auction held every spring. Nearly $200,000 is raised annually through this event. Weekly online memorabilia auctions are held through the Bulls Web site, and in-game auctions are held during regular-season home games. A 50/50 Raffle offers an opportunity for one fan to take home 50% of the net earnings from a game's ticket sales, while the other half goes to the foundation.

Sponsors also donate to the foundation in response to a variety of game-based achievements, including the number of wins, dunks, free throws, points, steals, rebounds, and so on. Fees for personal scoreboard messages are donated to the foundation.

QUESTIONS FOR REFLECTION

1. Why would a successful sports franchise invest time and fund-raising efforts to support education or other local community projects?
2. How do the fund-raising efforts such as those previously described support relationships with key stakeholders? Why would sponsors be motivated to cooperate?
3. Why would children be among a key stakeholder group for a professional sports franchise or other entertainment company?
4. Evaluate the importance of local community-improvement projects as part of ongoing community relations for a for-profit enterprise.

Material for this case was drawn from information and news releases available at the Chicago Bulls' Web site at www.nba.com/bulls/community/communities.html, the Publicity Club of Chicago's Web site at www.publicity.oprg/trumpets2000.htm, and the Web site of Public Communications Inc. at www.pcipr.com/newsroom_archive/Chicago Bulls/. Other background was provided through fact sheets and releases by Public Communications Inc. of Chicago.

CASE 8.   WHEN IT COMES TO YOUR LAWN, DO IT NATURALLY

The dream of a verdant lawn covered with thick, green grass worthy of Easter baskets is shared by homeowners across America, but the dream is often made possible with the aid of pesticides, fertilizers, and heavy water use. In the mid-1990s, Puget Sound households, businesses, and parks had relied on nearly 1.1 million pounds of pesticides each year to help achieve that dream, pesticides that through run-off had affected local waterways. The region's composting facilities were pressured by the nearly 1,000 pounds of grass clippings produced by the average household, and homeowners used nearly twice as much water during the summer as during the winter season, which also strained available resources. A consortium of Puget Sound–area agencies worked together to create a 2001 Silver-Anvil award-winning campaign to persuade area homeowners to find a more natural way to achieve their dreams of attractive lawns.

The Roots of the Campaign

The communication team was composed of Pacific Rim Resources, The Frause Group, and Brumley Communications. The team used survey and focus-group methodology to conduct the research for the campaign. Through a telephone survey of 400 Seattle-area residents, they found that male heads of households were primarily in charge of lawn care, although women in the household had a strong influence on how the lawn was cared for. Follow-up focus groups indicated that information about changes in lawn care practices would need to be upbeat and simple if it were to be persuasive. The primary target public for the campaign would be male homeowners with household incomes of more than $30,000.

The team adopted one simple goal for the campaign: to promote public adoption of natural lawn care by changing lawn care behaviors. The slogan for the campaign was direct: "When it comes to your lawn, do it naturally." Objectives included increasing the number of people who practiced grasscycling and decreasing the number of residents who used weed-n-feed products on their lawns and those who relied on watering their lawns.

Campaign Blossoms Through Events and Exposure

Working with a budget of $350,000, the communication team developed strategies that included media relations and events, sports radio and TV advertising, special events, a video, an education kit, and the development of a humorous spokes-character, Bert the Salmon. Bert, a humorous baseball-cap-and-jacket-wearing fish, was designed to appeal to the target male audience. A brochure that featured Bert the Salmon and listed steps to overcoming barriers to natural lawn care was distributed before the public campaign was launched.

To focus media attention to the campaign, residents of the Renton neighborhood were recruited to participate in natural lawn care practices for 6 months. A neighborhood "Spring Cleaning" media event kicked off the period; residents cleared their homes of their gas mowers, pesticides, and fertilizers. The 19 participating residents were given free electric mulching mowers and were asked to weed by hand and to water their lawns infrequently rather than daily. At the end of the summer period, the media were invited back to interview the participants. Only two indicated they would not continue their natural lawn care practices. Media coverage of both events was strong and prompted inquiries from other neighborhoods.

Radio spots were aired during broadcasts of the Seattle Mariners baseball games in 1997 and 1999. Nineteen different 15-second spots featured a Mariner player interacting with Bert the Salmon to offer a natural lawn care tip. The radio spots cost $210,000 in 1997 and $128,000 in 1999. The cornerstone of the campaign was television advertising aired during Seattle Mariners baseball games. Because the target audience was men, the communications team reasoned that baseball was an excellent venue for getting its message across. A 30-second ad, which cost $25,000 to produce, was aired in 1998 and 2000. The group spent $260,000 in 1998 and $230,000 in 2000 on TV spots.

A toll-free information hotline (1-888-860-LAWN) was established. Callers could receive a "Habit Change Kit" with information about natural lawn care practices and a Bert the Salmon yard sign. Kits were also distributed at special events such as the Home Show and the Garden Show. Inserts in Seattle Public Utilities bills focused on water conservation and the impact of excessive water use on area waterways and salmon.

A 9-minute, 20-second video was also produced at a cost of $24,000. It was used during speaker presentations, as a promotional vehicle, and was streamed on the King County Department of Natural Resources web page.

Campaign Yields "Natural" Results

Media coverage of the campaign was strong, resulting in 162 articles and an estimated 15.8 million gross impressions.

Results of the campaign were encouraging. Periodic polling showed that the number of households reporting that grass clippings are left on their lawns "most of the time" rose from 27.7% to 41%. The percentage of households that reported they did not use a weed-n-feed product on their lawn increased from 46.8% to 60%, and the percentage of households reporting they did not water their lawns increased from 18.4% to 34%.

Promotion of natural lawn care practices continued after the formal end of the campaign, as this press release indicates:

Feb. 13, 2003

News Release

King County garden to "show" environmentally friendly gardening practices

King County, partnering with In Harmony Landscape Services, will give new meaning to the term "show garden" when it presents live theater to communicate the many benefits of natural gardening practices. The garden will be featured at the Northwest Flower and Garden Show, Feb. 19–23, in Seattle.

Local actors will play Ron and Karen, neighbors with contrasting gardening practices. Ron relies on chemicals and control techniques to make his garden grow, while Karen uses natural alternatives, such as choosing easy-care plants, building healthy soil, and attracting beneficial birds and insects.

The gardens will also visually depict these different gardening practices. Ron's garden will have a toxic green lawn and poorly chosen plants, pruned improperly. Oversized pesticide containers will represent the garden's dependence on chemicals.

Sharply contrasting Ron's garden, Karen's will feature lush, pest and disease resistant plants, birds and beneficial insects, a beautiful natural lawn, and clean flowing water.

In a five-minute skit, to run every 15 minutes throughout the show, Karen points out the problems with Ron's approach. She helps Ron to see how he can reduce dependence on pesticides by building good soil and planting the right plant in the right place.

A new Natural Yard Care brochure will also be available, providing tips and resources for gardening practices that are easy on the environment and the gardener.

Following the shows, viewers will be encouraged to seek additional information at King County's and WSU Master Gardeners' educational booths on the Sixth floor. Both County and Master Gardener volunteers will be available to answer garden and lawn care questions, as well as to provide more information on environmentally sound gardening and lawn care practices.

In Harmony Organic Based Landscape Services designs, installs and maintains natural lawns, trees and shrubs.

The King County Hazardous Waste Management Program works to reduce the risk to public health and environment from the use, storage and disposal of hazardous products, such as pesticides. To learn more about natural gardening practices, visit <u>Yard and Garden Topics</u> on the King County Web site at <u>http://dnr.metrokc.gov/topics/yard-and-garden/index.htm</u>

QUESTIONS FOR REFLECTION

1. What mutual benefits were served by this cooperation between public relations firms and the King County Department of Natural Resources and other area conservation groups?
2. What are the advantages and disadvantages of using an animal character as the "voice" of a public campaign?
3. Evaluate the use of the neighborhood natural lawn care experiment as part of the communication strategy.
4. What other evaluation techniques might have been used in this campaign to determine if objectives had been reached?

The information for this case was drawn from Silver Anvil Awards—01—Category 01C, Community Relations at www.prsa.org/_Awards/silver/html; Tina Reilly, "Bert the Salmon: Promoting natural lawn care in the Seattle area," available at www.toolsofchange.com/, and the King County Web site cited earlier.

CASE 9.   HABITAT FOR HUMANITY: BUILDING CORPORATE BRIDGES AND AFFORDABLE HOUSES

Habitat, a nonprofit ecumenical Christian ministry based in Americus, Georgia, has worked for almost 30 years to engage diverse volunteers in the effort to build affordable decent housing for low-income residents across the globe. According to its Web site, the organization "invites people of all backgrounds, races and religions" to volunteer on its projects. Founded by Millard and Linda Fuller in 1976, Habitat for Humanity International and its affiliates in more than 3,000 communities in 89 nations report that they have built and sold more than 150,000 homes to "partner" families with no-profit, zero-interest mortgages. Habitat has more than 2,100 active affiliates in 92 countries, all 50 states, the District of Columbia, Puerto Rico, and Guam.

The Foundation Is Laid

According to the Web site, the Fullers developed the idea for "partnership housing" after participating in the Koinonia community outside Americus, a group that had modeled the idea of no-profit, no-interest home building. From Americus, the Fullers moved to Zaire where they spent 3 years developing a similar housing program. After returning to the United States, they created the Habitat organization to extend the reach of the housing program.

Habitat saw a dramatic increase in growth after former U.S. President and Nobel Laureate Jimmy Carter and his wife, Rosalynn, took their first Habitat work trip, the Jimmy Carter Work Project, to New York City in 1984. The Carter's personal involvement in Habitat's ministry continues to bring the organization media coverage and national visibility, particularly through the annual Jimmy Carter Work Projects. Mr. Carter explains their work with the organization in a quote featured on the Habitat Web site, saying: "We have become small players in an exciting global effort to alleviate the curse of homelessness. With our many new friends, we have worked to raise funds, to publicize the good work of Habitat, to recruit other volunteers, to visit overseas projects and even build a few houses."

The Structure Is Developed

The organization's Web site explains how the Habitat process works. The organization can provide affordable options for low-income families because the houses built through Habitat are sold for no profit, with no interest charged on the mortgage. The homeowner invests his or her "Sweat Equity" in the home by working many hours on house projects, alongside volunteers who use donated materials or materials purchased through donations to construct the home. Prices of the homes range from $800 in some developing nations to an average of $46,600 in the

United States. Mortgages may run 7 to 30 years, and the monthly mortgage payments are used to build other houses.

The international headquarters provides information and training and other support services to Habitat affiliates worldwide, but the affiliates actually coordinate the local building projects from specific fund raising through construction and mortgage servicing. According to the Web site, "The affiliate's family selection committee chooses homeowners based on their level of need, their willingness to become partners in the program and their ability to repay the no-interest loan. ... Neither race nor religion is a factor in choosing the families who receive Habitat houses." The affiliates are also asked to "tithe," to give 10% of their contributions to fund house-building work in other nations.

Corporate Partners Donate, Blitz, and Build

Habitat for Humanity International's Corporate Sponsorship program invites corporations to join in the housing efforts. The involvement, according to the Habitat Web site, may offer "a wealth of benefits to corporations, including tax deductions, high-voltage public relations and a permanent positive effect on company morale." Companies may directly donate products or money, and they may also encourage employees to serve as Habitat volunteers. The corporate and foundation partners noted on Habitat's Web site range from *Ability* Magazine to United Airlines. To examine just a few of the partners' contributions:

> The "Do It Yourself Network," (DIY) a how-to cable network, has partnered with Habitat to produce and air a five-part workshop titled "Lending a Hand: Habitat for Humanity," that will focus on building a Habitat house. DIY will produce a training video for use in offering instruction for volunteers; copies are made available to the 17,000 U.S. affiliates. DIY also airs PSAs supporting Habitat.

> LaFarge North America, a diversified construction-materials company, provided more than $1 million in cash sponsorships, concrete, cement, gypsum, and other building supplies in 2001.

> First Energy Corp., which holds seven electric-utility operating companies, donated $3.3 million to Habitat to build energy-efficient homes in their business areas.

> Square D/Schneider Electric is a Cornerstone Society member. The corporation has a 3-year commitment to donate Square D brand load centers and circuit breakers for each of the Habitat homes built in the United States and Canada, a donation of products valued at more than $6 million. Its Web site reports: "We share in Habitat's commitment to safety and to ending sub-standard housing. Sharing this commitment allows us to help provide affordable housing for those in need and ensure that every home is equipped with safe, dependable electric products, the best electrical protection available."

Honeywell, a diversified technology and manufacturing corporation, funded the construction of five homes in a blitz-build in Albuquerque, New Mexico, September 25 to October 6, 2000. The Honeywell CEO Blitz Build 2000 involved more than 400 Honeywell volunteers from locations worldwide. Honeywell contributed more than $1 million to Habitat between 1995 and 2000 and donated 6,000 home security systems and 8,600 home thermostats. More than 3,400 Honeywell employees and retirees have built more than 50 Habitat homes in the United States and in Australia, Canada, and Hungary.

The Vinyl Institute, a trade association composed of manufactures of vinyl resin, additives and stabilizers, vinyl compound, and finished vinyl products, co-operated with Habitat to form the Vinyl Partners for Humanity. The partners participated in the 2001 Bayou Gator Blitz Build in Sulphur, Louisiana, and helped build four houses. One house was sponsored by the Partners, which also led the efforts to obtain donations of vinyl building products for all four homes. Certainteed and PPG donated significant building materials to the blitz.

Citibank, through its Citigroup Foundation, announced a $1 million grant to Habitat in October 2002 to support the company's nationwide employee volunteer program, which offers teams of employees from various units—Salomon Smith Barney, Travelers, Primerica, Citibank, CitiFinancial, and Citimortgage—the opportunity to partner with local volunteers in builds. Citigroup has given a total of more than $3 million to Habitat, and more than 6,000 employees in 20 states have helped build 63 homes. Support goes even further; Citigroup's Center for Community Development Enterprise has also invested $7.8 million in Habitat mortgages.

Robert Willumstad, president of Citigroup, also serves on the Habitat board of directors. In an October 4, 2002, company release, he said, "The combination of philanthropic giving, employee volunteerism and geographic breadth that Habitat offers aptly reflects our commitment help make every community where we operate a better place because we are there."

Sponsorships during the Jimmy Carter Work Projects are reserved for corporations who have made considerable contributions to Habitat. For example, during the Jimmy Carter Work Project in rural areas of Georgia and Alabama in June 2003, 102 houses were constructed by some 3,500 volunteers and prospective homeowners. Lowe's and Whirlpool were among the Premier Sponsors of the 2003 JCWP. Robert Tillman, Lowe's CEO, said in a Habitat release: "The partnership between Whirlpool and Lowe's is a fantastic opportunity for our two companies to contribute our combined strength to building adequate, safe housing with communities in need. Our two companies are united in the goal of inspiring hope and building lives—one home at a time—through this dynamic partnership with Habitat for Humanity International."

Andersen Corp., the world's largest manufacturer of wood windows, patio doors, and storm doors, has partnered with Habitat since 1995 when it first donated $300,000 of windows. Since then, Andersen has given more than $2 million in funding, and employee volunteers have invested more than 14,000 hours building Habitat homes. In 1998, Andersen funded construction of one complete home and gave more than 1,000 window units to the Jimmy Carter Work Project in

Houston; two dozen employees volunteered in the build. To celebrate its 100-year anniversary as a business in 2003, Andersen announced it would build 100 homes across North America; funds for the houses will come from five Andersen-related foundations.

Dow Chemical has been named a Lifetime Cornerstone Society Member of Habitat. It provided a 4-year $1 million donation to Habitat in 1997 and extended its partnership in 2001 with another 4-year $2 million pledge. In September 2000, at the Jimmy Carter Work Project in Plains, Georgia, Dow pledged a $5 million donation of its Styrofoam brand insulation for the next 25,000 homes to be built in North America through 2005. The corporation also sponsored one Habitat home at the Ed Schreyer Work Project in Ottawa, Canada; the Jimmy Carter Work Project in Durban, South Africa, and nine additional homes in Africa; and in Indianapolis, Indiana, and Plaquemine, Louisiana. Several crews of Dow employees have volunteered on builds around the world, including more than 60 employees and customers who participated in the JCWP 2002 in Durban.

Dow President and CEO Michael D. Parker, quoted in a company news release, said, "From both a business and a human perspective, Habitat's philosophy of giving a hand up, not a handout, is simply one of the best acts of humanity I can imagine."

QUESTIONS FOR REFLECTIONS

1. Habitat partnerships offer corporations and businesses a variety of philanthropic options. What objectives might be addressed through different types of involvement?
2. What are the strategic motivations for corporations and foundations to become involved with an international religious social service agency? What are the potential liabilities of such involvement?
3. Habitat celebrates the involvement of Jimmy and Rosalyn Carter. What are some opportunities and threats presented by celebrity involvement or identification with a charitable or social service organization?
4. How do group service opportunities improve employee morale?

Information for this case was drawn from the Habitat Web site at www.habitat.org; news releases including Roeder, S. (22 Jan. 2003). "Andersen Corporation to donate $5 million in cash and windows and thousands of employee volunteer hours to construct 100 Habitat for Humanity homes nationwide." PR Newswire; Vallentine, R. (6 June 2002). "Dow employees and customers lend a hand to former president Jimmy Carter in Durban," PR Newswire; Vincent, C. (3 Nov. 2002), "America's community bankers helps build tallest Habitat for Humanity house during annual convention," PR Newswire; Webber, B. (14 Nov. 2002). "Habitat for Humanity announces PSA campaign Ladies' Home Journal partnership," PR Newswire; Webber, B. (12 Feb. 2003). "Lowe's and Whirlpool join forces as 'premier sponsors' of the Jimmy Carter Work Project 2003," PR Newswire; Webber, B. (15 May 2003). "Nobel Peace Prize winner joins thousands of volunteers for Habitat for Humanity's Jimmy Carter Work Project," PR Newswire; and corporate Web sites at www.asia.citibank.com; http://content.honeywell.com/das/releases/6_9_00.htm; www.diynet.com/DIY/pressRelease/0,1031,325,FF.html;   *(continued)*

CASE 10:   COMMUNITY SERVICE CONSTITUTES CORE COMPETENCY OF TIMBERLAND

The message on the volunteers' gray T-shirts captured the spirit of the day. In black block lettering, it said: "Pull on your Boots and Make a Difference." The Timberland Company's offices around the world closed May 30, 2002, so that more than 2,000 employees and local partners could earn their regular pay by working on civic projects.

Near Timberland's headquarters in Stratham, New Hampshire, volunteers tackled improvements to park and playground equipment. About 60 Timberland employees in Lawrence, Massachusetts, focused on cleanup and landscaping around an elementary school attended by 375 inner-city children. On the slopes of Maine's Mount Agamenticus, more than 50 employees and Timberland business partners cleared brush from trails used by hikers and cross-country skiers.

By the time the New England projects got under way, the day of activities was half over. It had started shortly after sunrise in Japan when 25 Timberland employees showed up at the Chiyoda Volunteer Center to clean and repair wheelchairs for the elderly. Later, Timberland volunteers in Singapore did fix-up/paint-up work at the Yishun Family Service Centre for disadvantaged families. Still later, some 30 Timberland employees in Milan worked to raise funds for materials that would give disabled children a chance to participate in individual and team sports.

A Record of Serving

Timberland closed its headquarters offices for the first Serv-A-Palooza, the company's name for the daylong community service event, in 1998. All international offices were shuttered to join the annual Serv-A-Palooza for the first time in 2002.

Although the global Serv-A-Palooza is a major commitment to community service, it is simply a new entry in the company's long record of paying wages—rather than lip service—to employees whose civic efforts demonstrate corporate social responsibility.

(*continued*)   www.dow.com/styrofoam/na/habitati/20011219a.htm; www.squared.com/us/ squared/corporate_infor.nsf; www.vinylinfo.org/humanity/whatispartnership.html; http:// www.whirlpoolcorp.com/social_responsibility/habitatforhumanity/default.asp. Other sources include Attrino, T. (13 July 1998), "SAFECO helps build low-income homes," *National Underwriter Property & Casualty, 102*(28), p. 9; Buchoiz, B. B. (September 1996). "Building morale off-site," *Crain's Small Business-Chicago, 4*(7), p. 18; and Gunsauley, C. (1 Sept. 2001). "Charity projects improve employee motivation, morale," *EBN, 15*(10), pp. 63–64.

The company that became Timberland, under the ownership of the Swartz family, began as the Abington Shoe Company in Boston. In 1973, the name Timberland was first applied to the company's innovative waterproof leather boot, and the boot became so popular so fast that the name Abington was dropped in 1978 in favor of Timberland. Soon, casual shoes and boat shoes were added to the product line, and the company entered the international market, starting in Italy.

By the time Timberland sponsored its first global Serv-A-Palooza in 2002, the company employed 5,400 people in 20 countries around the world and was operating its own retail and factory stores, including 77 stores in the United States, 35 in Europe, and 93 in Asia. In addition, Timberland products—expanding beyond footwear to include apparel and accessories—were sold through independent retailers, department stores, and athletic specialty shops.

Shares in the company were originally offered to the investing public in 1987 and have been listed on the New York Stock Exchange (symbol: TBL) since 1991. Revenues in 2002 were $1.2 billion. In 2003, the Swartz family controlled about 82% of ownership voting power.

The Service Spirit Sinks In

For years, the company supported community causes and cultural life, as corporations customarily do, through financial contributions. In 1989, the Timberland custom was altered—in a small way at first. Writing in *The Brookings Review*, Timberland's chief executive officer, Jeffrey Swartz, described what happened:

> I received a letter one day, the standard, well-intended plea for charity from yet another worthy nonprofit. This one, City Year, was an urban peace corps of sorts, starting up in Boston, near where I live. The letter described 50 young people, out to save the world, lacking only boots for their feet. Would I send along the boots?
>
> Who knows why I did or why the cofounder of City Year decided to come to my office and challenge me to spend four hours doing community service with him and a small group of young leaders near our headquarters in New Hampshire. But I sent the boots, Alan Khazei paid the visit, and I accepted the challenge to serve. And I found myself, not a mile from our headquarters, face to face with the stories you read in the newspaper, face to face with a vision for America not unlike the one that drew my grandfather to leave Russia in steerage so many years ago. I spent four hours with the corps members from City Year and some young recovering drug addicts in a group home. I painted some walls and felt the world shaking under my feet.

City Year Partnership

Moved and inspired by the experience, Mr. Swartz looked for ways to make community service an integral element of the corporate culture at Timberland. Initially, the company strengthened its involvement with City Year, a nonprofit program that enlists college-age young adults in a yearlong commitment to civic improvement efforts. The nonprofit calls itself an "action tank."

Alan Khazei, the City Year CEO who first hooked Timberland on community service, explained that "An 'action tank' is both a program and a think tank—constantly combining theory and practice to advance new policy ideas, make programmatic breakthroughs, and bring about major changes in society. City Year is an action tank for national service, working to advance and improve the concept and delivery of voluntary national service so that, one day, giving a year of service will become a common expectation and a real opportunity for millions of young Americans."

In 1992, Timberland launched a program giving all of its employees the opportunity to roll up their sleeves and spend the day working on community improvement without losing a dollar of pay. Under this new Path of Service program, employees could use up to 16 hours of paid time annually for civic service. Three years later, the number of hours was raised to 32 and, not long after, was increased to a total of 40 hours annually.

In the early years of Path of Service, participation was far from universal. Employees shrugged off the opportunity because they were too busy to miss a day on the job, and some supervisors discouraged any excused absence, suspecting that volunteers simply lacked enough work.

Stay the Course

When Timberland posted its first annual loss in 1995, some creditors, investors, and employees suggested that the Path of Service was an expendable distraction, diverting attention from the demands of running the business. Layoffs of some U.S. workers underscored the concerns.

Yet, Path of Service was not simply protected but promoted even more energetically, and a loss of 53 cents a share in 1995 became a profit of 91 cents in 1996, which grew to $2.02 in 1997 and $2.52 in 1998. That year, the *Christian Science Monitor* published a flattering feature on the company's volunteerism and included Jeffrey Swartz's comments on a question often raised about costs of civic service and motivations for pursuing it.

"We think that doing well and doing good are inextricably linked in our business," the newspaper quoted him as saying. "There's a skeptical notion out there—is this about business or philanthropy? My answer is that this is how we earn our right to do business."

Employee participation in volunteer efforts has climbed along with the company's success, and Timberland estimated that almost all have been involved in community efforts at some time.

More Opportunities for Service

Path of Service and the global Serv-A-Palooza demonstrate Timberland's commitment to community relations in big ways. Another program, Service Sabbatical, is smaller but just as remarkable. Each year, up to four employees, who must have 3 years on the company's payroll, receive 3-month to 6-month paid leaves to work full-time at nonprofit organizations that are dealing with civic issues.

Timberland lures its customers into community service as well. For Earth Day each year, the company sponsors projects where Timberland employees, customers, and business partners gather for a day of outdoor work to repair some of the damage that the planet's population inflicts on Mother Earth.

On Earth Day in April 2003, about 4,000 customers, community leaders, and members of the Timberland community from 258 participating stores pitched in to serve and preserve the planet at more than 100 conservation sites worldwide. For example, a task force of 100 in the New York borough of Queens developed green space and a learning garden through a partnership with Public School 19. Along the Thames River in London, a team of 80 restored a stripped stretch of shoreline.

Best Companies to Work For

Acknowledging Timberland's knack for combining community service and employee relations, *Fortune* magazine put the organization on its very first list of "100 Best Companies to Work For" in 1998 and has kept it there since then. The ranking uses results of a random survey of employees as well as information supplied by the company on culture, philosophy, and benefits. The employee survey, accounting for two thirds of the score, measures trust in leadership, pride in work and in the company, and employee fellowship.

For Timberland and all other companies committed to community service, measuring the direct effect of civic programs on relationships with important publics is complex, and results are not uniform or consistent.

Consumers and other publics may not learn about community programs unless corporate sponsors talk about them in some way—speakers bureaus, news releases, editor's advisories, advertisements, Web sites, brochures, and so on. Yet, these public pronouncements appear smarmy and self-congratulatory to many people and may do as much harm as good.

Sharing Information on Good Works

In a report on the Harris Interactive/Reputation Institute survey of corporate reputations, the *Wall Street Journal* said:

Almost unanimously, the public says it wants information about a company's record on social and environmental responsibility to help decide which companies to buy from, invest in and work for. But philanthropy is a tricky facet of corporate public relations. Good deeds can redound to a company's credit .... But they can be overlooked if untrumpeted, making the company a target for unfair criticism, and they can backfire if consumers view the purported philanthropy as profiteering or if the company fails to live up to the good-neighbor image it projects. In short, promoting philanthropy is perilous, and companies can find they're damned if they do and damned if they don't.

Because public relations professionals often hesitate to talk up good works, the number of people aware of them remains low. The annual Harris Interactive/Reputation Institute survey measures 20 attributes of corporate reputation, and the one that elicits the largest percentage of "not sure" responses concerns a company's support for good causes.

QUESTIONS FOR REFLECTION

1. Are some kinds of business operations more likely to engage in community relations programs than others? Why would Timberland be a prime candidate for community activities?
2. Initially, most employees passed up the chance for a paid day off to work on community projects. Why would they do that?
3. Some critics say "doing well by doing good" is a tired platitude, and for-profit businesses should allocate funds for community activities only if they provide some tangible payoff for the business. Does this view make sense?
4. The *Wall Street Journal* warns that corporate philanthropy can be risky. How can it backfire?

Information for this case was drawn from the following: the Timberland Company Web site at http://www.timberland.com/cgi-bin/timberland/timberland/corporate/tim_press.jsp; DeConto, J. (23 April 2002), "Helping Earth Day on Mount A," *Portsmouth Herald*, p. 8; DiMassa, C. (10 November 2002), "Good turns: Being a CEO 'in the tradition of Abraham,' " *The Los Angeles Times,* p. B2; Irwin, N. (20 July 1998), "Giving 'a boot' to community service," *The Christian Science Monitor*, p. B6; Marquis, C. (13 July 2003), "Doing well and doing good," *The New York Times*, p. C2; and Swartz, J. (Fall 2002), "Doing well and doing good," *The Brookings Review*, p. 23.

4

Stakeholders: Consumers

Think about your last trip to a shopping mall. You may have visited stores such as Abercrombie & Fitch, the Gap, or Victoria's Secret that have established brand strength for themselves. Inside other stores you may have sought certain brands of clothing or accessories—Nike, Levi's, Russell, Sony, Timex, or Fossil—and avoided others you don't like or don't recognize. You may have completed some purchases after extensive research and others on an impulse. Similar stories may be told of your latest car purchase or trip to a grocery store or pharmacy. When you visit your mailbox, you may find it crammed full of catalogs, and when you visit your electronic mailbox, it, too, may be filled with promotional messages from retailers whom you've visited or purchased from online.

THE CONTEMPORARY CONSUMER

Consumers—those who buy the products and goods or use the services businesses provide—are likely the most voluntary of all stakeholders. In the U.S. marketplace, consumers may be the most jaded of all stakeholders as well, constantly provided with a variety of options, constantly bombarded with messages and reminders of the merits, real or hyped, of the goods available. Conversely, sometimes they comprise the most loyal group of stakeholders—bound to certain brands by memories of in-home use from decades ago or allied because of features and benefits derived from brands they enjoy. They are the ones who remember slogans and jingles better than their multiplication tables, and they are the ones who willingly become walking billboards for the logos and brands emblazoned on hats, T-shirts, jackets, and bags they carry.

Consumer groups also reflect the rapid changes within national demography. Practitioners should remain knowledgeable about the growing racial and ethnic diversity of their key consumer publics and be able to strategize with management personnel about the most effective ways to reach these consumers. Similarly, changes in the age patterns or social-role patterns of consumer groups should be noted and researched. Stereotypes about the needs of varying groups among consumers should be replaced with sound research into needs, desires, and capabilities of key publics.

Contemporary consumers are also protected by a variety of national, state, and local regulations promoting their safety, as well as a growing slate of civil torts that enable them to sue when they assert that a product, good, or service was delivered in a deceptive or injurious manner. Maintaining a "1-800 help line" or a product-information e-mail and Web site may become the full or partial responsibility of the public relations department, perhaps working in concert with customer service representatives. Well-publicized consumer-related crises of the past 20 years should remind practitioners of the need for extreme care during initial or reactive product-related communication. Practitioners must be aware of the need for clarity when communicating with various consumer groups and particularly conscious of the varied abilities of groups to understand technical or product-related communication.

KEY OBJECTIVES

Maintaining a relationship with a satisfied consumer is far easier than trying to rebuild a relationship that has been hurt by poor service, pricing disagreements, or product failure. Building and maintaining brand loyalty may be a central objective for the practice of consumer relations. Other key objectives may include:

- Providing clear and timely information about products, goods, or services so that consumers may make good decisions.
- Providing avenues for feedback so that consumer questions and complaints are handled in an efficient and cordial manner.
- Supporting the introduction of new products, goods, or services through coordinating media relations, advertising, and product publicity efforts.
- Celebrating successes of branded products or services through special events and other publicity efforts.
- Developing relationships with emerging consumer groups, such as those found in new cultural or ethnic communities, new age or gender demographic groups, and so on.

INTEGRATED COMMUNICATION

Developing relationships with consumers is a multidimensional affair that often requires cooperation across departments or personnel within a business or corporation. The practice of integrated marketing communication may better describe how organizations can reach and hear from these stakeholders. For example, consider an American automaker that is introducing a new high-performance model to its line. Certainly, the product should be introduced at the annual car shows for automotive-beat journalists and critics to assess and comment on. Vehicles should be made available for test drives by these same media opinion leaders. Releases about the new line and its features and benefits should be disseminated. An advertising campaign geared to begin with the actual release of the line would be essential. Yet even that may not be enough. What about brokering use of the car as the central vehicle in a major motion picture due for a Labor Day release, or using it as the grand prize in a national contest geared at high school and college students, or working with local distributors to link sales of the unit to a sales competition? The manufacturer may also use its national clout to offer buyers a zero-percentage car loan for purchases within its first month on the market. The public relations, advertising, and marketing efforts would all work together to target key consumers—and to establish the new brand as one with a distinct image and personality attractive to those consumers.

This multiplicity of messages is even more necessary in a crowded media marketplace, where consumers receive messages about products, goods, and services from all forms of mass media, including the Internet, where persuasive messages may be found in obvious places, such as a constant stream of pop-up ads, and more subtle venues, such as chat rooms where browsers find open, frank, and sometimes staged discussions of the merits and drawbacks of particular brands and suppliers. Canny consumers have at their fingertips the ability to search for reviews of products, multiple price comparisons, and deep background on corporations and businesses. No longer are shoppers merely comparing prices between competing grocery ads in the Thursday newspaper. Among the plethora of tools available to practitioners seeking to disseminate information about products, goods, and services are direct mail, broadcast advertisements, print ads, Internet ads, movie theater ads, product inserts, packaging, catalogs, brochures, trade shows and exhibits, displays, outdoor ads, specialty products, product placements, spokespersons, logos, personal appearances, and media placements—and the list changes with each new technology. Certainly, the need for veracity and constancy in messages grows in this environment.

BUSINESS-TO-BUSINESS COMMUNICATION

Similarly, public relations may form the conduit for communication between businesses and industries as well. Vendor-to-vendor relationships, supplier-to-supplier relationships, and wholesaler-to-retailer relationships may all depend on the ability of public relations practitioners to identify needs or motivations and to supply the type of information and opportunity in a trustworthy manner that would establish a mutual ground for business exchange. From the production of clear catalogs and brochures to engaging exhibits and demonstrations at trade shows, the practitioner may need to facilitate communication between businesses hungry for profitable advantages.

ADDITIONAL READINGS

Argenti, Paul A., & Janis Forman. (2002). *The power of corporate communication: Crafting the voice and image of your business.* Boston: McGraw-Hill.

Dilenschneider, Robert L. (2000). *The corporate communications bible.* New York: New Millennium Press.

Ries, Al, & Laura Ries. (2002). *The fall of advertising and the rise of PR.* New York: HarperBusiness.

Thorson, Esther, & Jeri Moore. (Eds.). (1996). *Integrated communication: Synergy of persuasive voices.* Mahwah, NJ: Lawrence Erlbaum Associates.

CASE 11. "WOULD YOU LIKE YOUR TACO
WITH OR WITHOUT PESTICIDE TODAY?"

Genetically modified foods—called *frankenfoods* by critics—became a hotly debated subject in Europe during the 1990s, but they barely raised a stir in the United States.

Advocates for consumers and environmental causes warned about risks to human health that might result from genetically modified crops, and they tried to get U.S. food processors to disclose the use of these ingredients on product labels. Yet, their pleas were politely rebuffed by some food companies and simply ignored by others.

Corporate giants in agriculture and food set up their own advocacy alliances to counter the skeptics. They trumpeted the promise of biotechnology's genetic engineering, pointing to higher levels of nutrition, lower levels of pesticides, and greater crop yields for the world's undernourished.

Apparently indifferent to the debate, most American consumers paid little attention. Half did not even know, as the decade ended, that supermarkets already were stocking foods made with biotech crops, including baby formula, muffin mix, tortilla chips, and meatless burgers.

"There's no evidence that genetically engineered foods on the market are unsafe to eat," said *Consumer Reports* magazine in September 1999. "But, continued vigilance is crucial."

Traces of Biotech Corn

One year later, Friends of the Earth, an international environmental organization, announced that independent laboratory tests of a leading brand of taco shells had found traces of a biotech corn that was not approved for human consumption. The taco shells were being sold by Kraft Foods under the Taco Bell label.

The corn, named StarLink by its inventors at Aventis SA, had been engineered to offer built-in protection against the European corn borer insect. To create this feature, the scientists transplanted a gene from the bacillus *Thuringiensis bacterium,* a common soil organism, into the corn. The extra gene enabled the corn to produce a protein (Cry9C) that is toxic to the corn borer. In essence, the corn contains its own insecticide, saving farmers time and money.

Biotech corn itself was not the taco shells' problem. In fact, there were eight varieties of similar corn available at the time, and only StarLink had failed to get approval for use in consumer foods. In tests performed for the Environmental Protection Agency (EPA), StarLink had shown properties that are found in human allergens, and allergens can provoke reactions in vulnerable people ranging from skin rash to anaphylactic shock and death. As a result, the EPA told Aventis that StarLink could be used only to make livestock feed and ethanol fuel, but the agency did not determine conclusively that the corn was or was not allergenic.

Friends of the Earth, in its September 18 news release announcing the lab results, called on Kraft Foods to remove the Taco Bell taco shells from supermarkets immediately. The same day, the Union of Concerned Scientists (UCS) issued a statement urging the Food and Drug Administration (FDA) and the EPA to investigate the situation.

The UCS said: "If substantiated, this development would be another indication that the current regulatory scheme for genetically engineered foods is inadequate to protect public and environmental health and would heighten the need for better procedures to identify potential allergens and enforce legal restrictions and prohibitions."

Biotech Advocates Voice Skepticism

However, representatives of the biotechnology industry initially expressed skepticism about Friends of the Earth report, challenging the reliability of tests used by the independent lab to detect the StarLink corn.

From the outset, Kraft faced an urgent need to respond quickly to the news, address consumers' anxieties, demonstrate leadership, and plan a course of action that would lead the company though a thicket of complications.

Consumers are very impatient when questions involving family health remain unanswered. They would want to know, as soon as possible, if the lab results were correct and—if they were—would want information on any harm that might come to people who had eaten the taco shells. They also would want to know if the corn was in other consumer products, what Kraft was doing to get the products out of supermarkets and homes, how livestock corn got into consumer foodstuffs, what precautions Kraft would take to prevent any recurrence, and so on.

Anticipating those concerns, Kraft issued a statement 1 day after the Friends of the Earth's announcement. In it, the company explained that new independent lab tests were planned to confirm or discredit the earlier results. Kraft said: "It is clear that StarLink corn should not be used in the production of human food. If the presence of the Cry9C protein is confirmed, we will recall the product."

Kraft Issues Q&A

The same day, Kraft issued additional information in question-and-answer (Q&A) format. It included nine Q&A pairs, including these:

Q. How did this Cry9C protein find its way into your product?
A. We don't know if it is indeed in the corn, and if so, how it may have happened. We are working closely with the FDA to investigate this matter further.
Q. Have you had any complaints of illness or adverse reactions to eating this product?

A. No, we have had no confirmed reports of illness or food sensitivities linked to eating Taco Bell Home Originals taco shells.

Q. Are you going to recall the product?

A. No, not at this time. We are continuing to work with the FDA and will take the appropriate actions in consultation with them. Any decision to recall the product must be based on confirmation that the Cry9C protein from StarLink corn is present in the product. If it is found to be present, we will re-call the product.

Q. Is it safe to eat this product?

A. Yes, we have no reason to believe it is not safe to eat it. We have seen no evidence that indicates that the Cry9C protein is unsafe, but we are doing everything possible to learn if there are any safety concerns. If the presence of the Cry9C protein is confirmed in our Taco Bell Home Originals Taco Shells, we will recall the product.

In terms of risk communication, the company could provide consumers with few answers to overcome the situation's major unknowns, which were the validity of the lab tests, the source of the unapproved corn, and the potential for allergic reactions. Most consumers would simply avoid the product until the doubts were resolved.

Kraft Recalls Product

Four days after Friends of the Earth first reported the lab results, Kraft announced a voluntary recall of all Taco Bell Home Originals taco shells—2.5 million packages or more—after new tests corroborated the earlier results.

The September 22 announcement quoted the Kraft Foods chief executive as saying: "As soon as we learned that there might be an issue in the supply chain we purchased from, we have been guided by one priority—the safety of our products and their compliance with all regulatory requirements. Testing has now indicated the presence of StarLink, and we are immediately withdrawing all affected products."

The company also said it was suspending production of taco shells, which generated revenues of about $50 million a year for Kraft, until the quality of the finished product could be assured. The shells represented less than 3% of Kraft Foods' North American revenues for 2000.

Again, the company offered details for consumers in Q&A format, simultaneous with its recall announcement, including these examples:

Q. Is there a health concern if I've eaten one of these products?

A. Some of these products have been found to contain a variety of corn that is in the process of being reviewed for approval for use in food. This corn, known as StarLink, has been approved for animal use, but not for use in food. On that basis alone, these products should not be eaten. However, at this point there appears to be no evidence of adverse health effects.

Q. What should I do with the Taco Bell products I've purchased?

A. You should not eat any products containing Taco Bell taco shells, and you can return them to the store where you purchased them for a full refund.

Kraft Offers Recommendations

Kraft also presented recommendations for biotechnology. The company suggested that advances in plant biotechnology should be approved only when:

- They are safe for consumer foods as well as livestock feed.
- Valid tests are available to detect them in both crops and finished products.
- Government agencies review them before they enter the market.
- Biotech crop stewardship requirements are stiffened to safeguard the food supply from farm to finished product.

Commenting on the taco shell recall, *Business Week* magazine offered a recommendation of its own:

"None of this has led the biotech-food industry to soften its opposition to labeling or to any special regulations for biotech products. But it's time for a change," the magazine said. "Biotech foods are new, they are different, and they deserve special regulations. The industry should drop its opposition to tougher regulations. That could boost consumer confidence and disarm the critics."

QUESTIONS FOR REFLECTION

1. In what ways would Kraft's initial response, provided the day after release of the first lab results, have relieved consumer anxieties?
2. In what ways might you have altered the first response, using only the information that was available at the time?
3. Are there any inconsistencies between Kraft's initial response and the information that it released with the recall announcement?
4. What intermediaries or organizations could help Kraft manage its relationships with consumers who were troubled by the StarLink corn incident?
5. If Kraft wanted to push for adoption of its recommendations on biotech crops, what alliances or coalitions might it try to establish? What could coalition partners do?

6. *Business Week* seems to suggest that the food industry should give further consideration to labeling that would disclose biotech ingredients. What would be the upside to biotech labeling? The downside? Are there other alternatives?

Information for this case was drawn from the following: the Kraft Foods Web site at http://www.kraft.com/newsroom/; a Kraft Special Report recall Web site at http://www.kraftfoods.com/special_report/special_news.html (no longer available); Brasher, P. (22 September 2000), "Kraft Foods recalls taco shells," The GE Food Alert Campaign Center, http://www.gefoodalert.org/News/; Carey, J., Licking, E., & Barrett, A. (20 December 1999), "Are bio-foods safe?" *Business Week*, p. 70; (18 September 2000), "Contaminant found in Taco Bell taco shells," Friends of the Earth news release; Ingersoll, B. (2 October 2000), "Aventis to pay for U.S. to buy modified corn," *The Wall Street Journal*, p. B28; Kilman, S., & Lueck, S. (25 September 2000), "Kraft recall focuses on biotech oversight," *The Wall Street Journal*, p. B2; Kilman, S. (27 September 2000), "Aventis halts seed sales of genetically engineered corn," *The Wall Street Journal*, p. B4; Lueck, S., & Kilman, S. (2 November 2000), "Biotech-corn problems lead to recall of 300 products, disrupt farm belt," *The Wall Street Journal*, p. A2; Pollack, A. (23 September 2000), "Kraft recalls taco shells with bioengineered corn," *The New York Times*, p. C1; Raeburn, P., Forster, J., & Magnusson, P. (6 November 2000), "After Taco Bell: Can biotech learn its lesson?" *Business Week*, p. 107; Rissler, J. (18 September 2000), "Illegal, potentially allergenic altered corn found in taco shells," Union of Concerned Scientists news release; (September 1999), "Seeds of change," *Consumer Reports*, p. 10.

CASE 12.   A CHANGE IN NAME—A CHANGE IN IMAGE? FROM PRUNES TO DRIED PLUMS

Shakespeare's Romeo posed the question years ago, and it still poses a problem for some product representatives: Does a name really matter? Members of the California Prune Board (CPB) believed that names do carry image implications, and with counsel from Ketchum Public Relations, waged a successful campaign to obtain FDA approval to change the name of their fruit from "prune" to "dried plum." In May 1999 the CPB requested the name change after research showed that the name "dried plum" offered a more positive connotation than "prune" and would encourage more people to try the fruit.

Changing the Name to Protect the Image

The CPB hoped the name change would attract its target audience, women 35 to 50, a group believed to make the majority of household purchasing decisions. The nutritional value of prunes—or dried plums—was well known, but they were not seen as a trendy or youth-oriented product. Instead, they were often the target of jokes about regularity or aging.

"People have told us that dried plums evoke a more positive 'fresh fruit goodness' image. They've said they're more likely to eat dried plums than prunes," said CPB Executive Director Richard L. Peterson in a June 2000 news release.

Changing a commodity's name, although unusual, wasn't an entirely new idea. California prunes aren't the only commodity product to have gained approval to change their name. The kiwifruit was previously called a Chinese gooseberry, chickpeas were known as garbanzos, and the Chilean sea bass was once known as the Patagonian toothfish.

How do you go about changing the name of a very familiar food product? First, you obtain federal approval for the change. The CPB enlisted the help of its senators in the lobbying effort. California Senators Barbara Boxer and Dianne Feinstein supported the name change and wrote a letter to the FDA to encourage the transition. "It's important, I think, for our economy that we sell our produce here and abroad and that we give our people every chance that we can to sell the most that they can," Boxer said. "And clearly, if you call a dried plum a dried plum instead of calling it a prune, it sells better. So I'm all for that. I think we're talking about jobs, we're talking about all kinds of good things that can happen once we can sell this product as a dried plum."

The petition worked. In June 2000, the FDA granted the CPB permission to use "dried plums" as an alternative name to "prunes." However, prune juice will retain its name; the FDA said calling a product "dried" fruit juice would be contradictory.

Then, after gaining the legal approval for the name change, you must change the packaging and begin educating the buying public about what they'll be seeing in grocery stores and cookbooks. Under the FDA's ruling, prune packers were required to change the product's name in two phases. In the first phase, both names (dried plums and prunes) appeared on packaging for 2 years. In addition, an industry-wide consumer education program was conducted to minimize confusion among consumers. The second phase completed the transition to dried plums as the only name on packaging in the United States. The fruit will still be called "prunes" when they are exported, however.

Witnessing About the Change

Ketchum Public Relations worked with the board to gain media attention for the name change. The creative campaign, called "The Federal Witness Reidentification Program," relied on consumer-and-trade radio, print, television, and Internet sources to announce what Ketchum called the "top secret news" that "a fruit had been discovered living under an assumed name" and that prunes had been "masquerading as a 'regular' old fruit."

More than 563 million media impressions were generated by the campaign, Ketchum reports. The campaign got mentions on "The Tonight Show With Jay Leno" and the "NBC Nightly News With Tom Brokaw."

Following the name change, sales of "dried plums" increased by 5.5%, the first increase in 6 years.

The CPB also changed its name to the California Dried Plum Board to more accurately reflect its "new" mission to expand the worldwide demand for California dried plums. California produces 99% of all the dried plums grown in the United States and 70% of the world's supply. The board represents the industry's 1,250 growers and 22 packers of California dried plums. Its primary function is to promote consumption of dried plums worldwide through advertising, public relations, sales promotion, and education programs to encourage increased consumption of the fruit. The $10 million-plus program is totally funded by the growers and handlers through crop assessments.

Ketchum is a full-service communications company that was named the 2002 Agency of the Year by *PRWeek* magazine. It has won a number of PRSA Silver Anvil awards for work in public relations for corporate, food and nutrition, health care, technology, and brand-marketing clients.

QUESTIONS FOR REFLECTION

1. What is the problem identified in this case? What are the advantages and disadvantages associated with changing a well-known name for a commodity or brand? What would have been the advantages and disadvantages of implementing other strategies to change the image of the product?
2. What are the implications of this case for maintaining mutually beneficial relationships with consumers, or with association members? In what ways would the name change affect growers and packers? What are the motivations for members to affiliate and maintain a relationship with the CPB?

Information for this case came from the California Dried Plum Board Web site at www.californiadriedplumbs.org and from Ketchum Web site at 222.ketchum.com. Other information was drawn from the following: Brasher, P. (1 February 2001), "Prunes are now 'dried plums,' " AP Online; Castaldi, P. (4 September 2001), "Dried plums take flight: Reinvention works!"; (11 December 2000), "Introducing the California Dried Plum Board," California Dried Plum Board Release, *Business Wire*; Hinckley, D. (28 April 2002), "Prunes' newest wrinkle," *New York Daily News*, p. 23; Jones, P. (14 August 2002), "Dressing up prunes," *The Seattle Times*, p. C1; (April 2003), "What's in a name?," *Incentive, 4*, 24; and Reuters (13 September 2000), "Prune gets $10 million makeover—as dried plum," www.cnn.com.

CASE 13.   TIRE TREAD TROUBLES DRIVE FIRESTONE INTO CRISIS OF CONFIDENCE

Viewers who watched KHOU-TV's Monday night news on February 7, 2000, saw the first public report on a possible relationship between Firestone tire failures and rollovers of Ford Explorer sport utility vehicles (SUVs).

Anna Werner, reporting for the CBS affiliate in Houston, said she had identified more than two dozen accidents involving Fords with Firestone tires that resulted in 30 deaths. Investigators' records said the tread had peeled off Firestone Radial ATX tires on the Explorers.

In her news report, Ms. Werner said that Firestone had expressed full confidence in its tires and that Ford had suggested driver error, perhaps in the form of underinflation, as a possible cause.

Before that first February report aired, correspondent Werner had visited the National Highway Traffic Safety Administration (NHTSA) in Washington, DC, the federal agency responsible for reducing deaths, injuries, and economic loss resulting from traffic accidents. NHTSA officials told her they had no evidence Firestones were implicated in a disproportionate number of Explorer rollovers.

Despite the absence of confirming NHTSA data, the KHOU news team decided its figures were strong enough to go ahead with the report.

Letter Condemns False Messages

Three days later, Firestone's vice president of public affairs, Christine Karbowiak, sent a letter of complaint to the station and its owner, pointing out items in the report she claimed were misrepresentations or falsehoods. Subsequently, KHOU posted a copy of the letter on its Web site.

"This series," wrote Firestone's Ms. Karbowiak, "has unmistakably delivered the false messages that Radial ATX tires are dangerous, that they threaten the safety of anyone using them, and that they should be removed from every vehicle on which they are installed. Each of these messages is simply untrue."

The letter noted that tread separation might result from a number of external causes, such as puncture, and would not by itself indicate a defect. The Firestone executive said the company had given the station details that could have balanced the report.

Ms. Karbowiak continued: "In fact, I am advised that the failure to report such balancing information when it is in your reporter's hands prior to the broadcast may be grounds for finding of actual malice."

Some people thought they saw the thinly veiled threat of a lawsuit in the Firestone letter, but KHOU continued to follow up on the original report and advised worried Explorer drivers who contacted the station to call NHTSA's toll-free number.

In succeeding months, the federal agency received 90 complaints of tread separation and on May 2, 2000, opened a defect investigation into some 47 million Firestone tires with the ATX, ATXII, and Wilderness AT model designations. NHTSA issued no news release concerning the investigation nor did it make a public announcement.

USA Today Brings National Attention

Not until *USA Today* published a story on August 1, 2000, did most Americans learn about the questions raised by KHOU. *USA Today* said NHTSA had received reports of 30 crashes and four deaths potentially related to tread separation.

Once the *USA Today* story was repeated on television networks and cable news channels, it stayed in the headlines for weeks—not just in the United States but also in South America, the Middle East, and Asia, where problems with Fords and Firestones also had been reported. Some news reports noted that Ford had voluntarily replaced Firestone tires for owners of many Ford pickups and SUVs in Venezuela and elsewhere even before the KHOU-TV report.

As the news media swarmed around the story, no one seemed able to explain what was causing the tread separations and rollovers. Most occurred in the summer months in locales with high year-round temperatures. Maybe heat, a natural enemy of tire life, was involved. Some observers said the Explorer's high center of gravity caused instability, and others suggested tire quality might have suffered during chronic labor strife at Firestone's plant in Decatur, Illinois, which produced

There are nearly 1,500 Firestone Tire & Service Centers in the United States. Following Firestone's recall in 2000, the federal government toughened tire performance rules for all manufacturers.

many of the suspect tires. Others speculated that the combination of Firestone tires and Explorer engineering created the problem. No one knew for sure, and the mystery remained unsolved for months.

Before the investigation reached a conclusion, the news media's interest warmed and cooled and warmed again as new developments periodically sparked headlines. Before year-end:

- Firestone and Ford would abandon their mutual defense posture and end up accusing each other.
- Hearings on Capitol Hill would shed more light on the conflict and tempt some members of Congress to make themselves look good by making the manufacturers and regulators look bad.
- NHTSA would confirm that an insurance company researcher had told the federal agency in 1998 about possible tread separation problems on some Firestones.

Firestone began producing Radial ATX tires in 1990 to serve as original equipment on the Ford Explorer, which was introduced in March for the 1991 model year. The tire was redesigned in 1995 and 1996 and given two new model designations, Radial ATXII (pronounced a-t-x-2) and Wilderness AT. Through the 1990s, the tires were installed on millions of new Explorers, Mercury Mountaineers, Ford Ranger and F-Series pickups, Mazda Navajos, and Mazda light trucks. By summer of 2000, Firestone made about 14.4 million tires in the three models, and an estimated 6.5 million were still in use.

After the first *USA Today* article, Firestone insisted that its tire performance data reinforced the company's contention that the tires were safe and reliable, and Ford did not contradict the tire company. But when Sears Roebuck, the nation's largest tire retailer, announced it would stop selling the Firestone Radial ATX, ATXII, and Wilderness tires on Friday, August 4, the situation began shifting.

On the same day, Ford's chief executive, Jacques Nasser, said "We're clearly very, very concerned about the situation.... We have teams that are working around the clock. Once we know exactly what the issues are, we will act, because we feel a responsibility to our customers, for their safety and for the safety of their families."

The following Monday, NHTSA said it had received 270 complaints about the tires, including allegations that they may have been involved in 46 deaths and 80 injuries since their introduction in 1990.

Déjà Vu All Over Again

For many middle-aged drivers, the Firestone story was déjà vu. The company had barely survived a crisis in 1978 when the federal government forced it to recall 13 million Firestone 500 steel-belted radials. Though reports in 1978 linked the tires to 41 deaths, the company resisted recalling them for 18 months. Weakened by its drawn-out battle with the government and shunned by many motorists, Firestone—one of the oldest and proudest names in American motoring—was acquired in 1988 by Japan's largest tire company, Bridgestone, which began operating as Bridgestone/Firestone Inc. In 1992, the combined operation closed its headquarters in Akron, Ohio, and moved to Nashville, Tennessee.

After Bridgestone took control, Firestone's fortunes eventually turned around, and the company began gaining on its larger rivals—Goodyear and Michelin. Preparing to observe its 100th anniversary in 2000, Firestone planned a big celebration and created a special Web site tracing company history back to its earliest days and founder Harvey Firestone's close friendship with Ford founder Henry Ford. Throughout most of the 20th century, Ford Motor Company was, in fact, Firestone's most important customer.

The Firestone celebration was quickly overshadowed by the escalating tread separation issue. Eight days after *USA Today* put the problem on the nation's news agenda, Firestone announced a voluntary recall of 6.5 million tires in a single size (P235/75R15) with the Radial ATX, ATXII, and Wilderness AT designations.

Unpopular Recall Plan Compounds Problems

While some public relations experts were criticizing Firestone for waiting too long to address the issue, the recall plan itself created further problems. Like shoes, tires are produced in a big variety of sizes, widths, and styles. All of the tire warehouses of all of the tire makers around the world did not contain 6.5 million tires in the size needed. To achieve an orderly replacement process, Firestone planned to complete it in phases, taking 9 months or more.

"Because the preponderance of incidents is in the four southern states and given the limited supply of replacement tires at this time, the company will be undertaking a three-phase recall starting in Arizona, California, Florida and Texas," Firestone announced. "The second phase for the recall will be implemented in Alabama, Georgia, Louisiana, Mississippi, Nevada, Oklahoma and Tennessee. The final phase will include the remainder of the states."

The three-phase plan provoked an outcry from Ford owners in all 50 states, who wanted their tires replaced immediately. In response to the howls, Firestone doubled production at its U.S. plants, airlifted replacement tires from Bridgestone in Japan, and purchased tires from competitors. By the end of August, it had replaced more than a million tires.

On August 31, NHTSA recommended that Firestone recall another million or so tires in a variety of sizes sold mainly as replacements on pickups and SUVs, but the tire company said it was not necessary.

Hearings in Congress

Committees of the U.S. House of Representatives began hearings in September to learn more about the tread separation problem and examine the role of NHTSA in fixing it. As the hearings started, NHTSA said that it had received reports of 88 fatalities related to the tires and 250 injuries.

Appearing before a congressional panel, Ford chief executive officer Jacques Nasser and Firestone CEO Masatoshi Ono testified about product safety and their role in protecting the public. The hearings also produced testimony from a researcher at State Farm Mutual Automobile Insurance Company who had alerted NHTSA in July 1998 to an unusual pattern of tread separation cases involving the Firestones. The early warning apparently got little agency attention at the time it was received.

In December, Firestone announced the results of its 4-month investigation into the tread separation problem, and they contained no surprises. John Lampe, who succeeded Masatoshi Ono as CEO, said analysis of 2,500 recalled tires pointed to a combination of factors, acting in concert, as the cause of the elevated failure rate.

"Our team's findings confirm what the initial statistical claims information demonstrated from the outset—that a small number of tires generated higher rates of tread separation claims when used on Ford Explorers and that our recall initiated in August was more than adequate to protect the public," Lampe said.

Ford and Firestone Quarrel

By the time Firestone reported its findings, the company had replaced more than 5.5 million tires in the recall of 6.3 million. The issue of a wider recall, first raised by NHTSA on August 31, continued to simmer, but Firestone rebuffed new agency requests on the matter.

Eventually, Ford took the initiative in May 2001 to replace 13 million Firestone tires on its vehicles at a cost of $3 billion. The automaker said the tires had higher failure rates. Stung, Firestone announced a few days later that it would no longer supply tires to Ford's operations in the Americas and accused the company of clouding the issue.

"We have always said that in order to insure the safety of the driving public, it is crucial that there be a true sharing of information concerning the vehicle as well as the tires. Ford simply is not willing to do that," Firestone CEO John Lampe said in a statement. "We believe they are attempting to divert scrutiny of their vehicle by casting doubt on the quality of Firestone tires."

Brave words but subject to amendment. Firestone yielded 5 months later and recalled an additional 3.5 million Wilderness AT tires made before May 1998. NHTSA closed the defect investigation it had begun in May 2000, saying that it had received reports of 271 fatalities related to the tires under study.

Of the expanded recall, Firestone's Lampe said, "We recognize that a lengthy confrontation with NHTSA would continue to bring into question the quality of our products and delay our ongoing work of rebuilding the company."

In 2003, Firestone promised to spend $15 million on a 3-year consumer education campaign, including the use of national media, with the goal of persuading motorists to take better care of their tires. The campaign addressed tire inflation, tire use, tire maintenance, driving safety, and car maintenance.

Firestone's promise was a major provision in its settlement of a nationwide class-action lawsuit stemming from the recall. The company denied wrongdoing or liability and said it entered the settlement to avoid the burden of protracted litigation. The settlement did not affect hundreds of unresolved personal-injury lawsuits involving allegations about the recalled tires.

QUESTIONS FOR REFLECTION

1. How should Firestone have handled its hundredth-anniversary celebration after *USA Today* published its first story on the Ford/Firestone rollover accidents?

2. Firestone and Ford attempted to cooperate in the early stages of the crisis. Why did the cooperation deteriorate?

3. Considering the high demand for replacement tires and the impossibility of meeting the demand immediately, what alternative strategies might Firestone have considered?

4. Do you think that Firestone has succeeded in restoring its reputation?

Information for this case was drawn from the following: the Firestone Web site at http://mirror.bridgestone-firestone.com/news/media_center_fr.html; the National Highways Transportation Administration Web site at http://www.nhtsa.gov/cars/problems/Equipment/Tires/index.html; Aeppel, T., Ansberry, C., Geyelin, M., & Simison, R. (6 September 2000), "Road signs: How Ford, Firestone let the warnings slide by as debacle developed," *The Wall Street Journal*, p. A1; Bradsher, K. (1 September 2000), "Local TV uncovered national scandal," *The New York Times*, p. 1; Crock, S., & St. Pierre, N. (16 October 2000), "The tire flap: Behind the feeding frenzy," *Business Week*, p. 114; Eldridge, E. (11 August 2000), "Ford owners demand new tires," *USA Today*, p. 1 (accessed 25 January 2001); "Firestone letter to Belo & KHOU executives," khou.com, http://www.khou,com/news/stories/1290.html; Grant, L., & Healey, J. (4 August 2000), "Sears stops selling tires involved in probe," *USA Today*, p. 1; Rutenberg, J. (11 September 2000), "Local TV uncovered national scandal," *The New York Times*, p. C17; St. Pierre, N. (8 September 2000), "The Firestone fiasco: Was the NHTSA 'asleep at the wheel'?" *Business Week*, p. 98; Zimmerman, A. (12 September 2000), "News media get in line to take credit for bring about Firestone tire recall," *The Wall Street Journal*, p. A4.

CASE 14.   A NEW LOOK FOR WORK? DOCKERS PROMOTES BUSINESS CASUAL

Casual Fridays—a concept that was embraced by many businesses and organizations—brought relief to some employees who had tired of wearing suits, heels, ties, and starched shirts to work every day. The concept also prompted new sales and renewed prominence for an American corporation long known for producing clothes meant for work. Levi Strauss proudly says it has been producing work clothes for more than a century, and it has been busily promoting a new style of work clothes in recent years that has contributed to this major shift in corporate culture in the United States.

The style? Business casual. The cause? Levi Strauss might argue that it was its line of trousers known as Dockers that made it all possible. Its Web site (http://www.levistrauss.com) proudly reports that within a year after the introduction of the Dockers® brand in 1986, the Dockers® khakis had become the fastest-growing apparel brand in history. A poll commissioned by the company in 2001 found that 66% of those surveyed in a nationwide poll of U.S. office workers said they dress casually for work every day, up from 53% in 1997, and more than 80% said they wear casual businesswear at least 1 day a week. They also believed it was paying off for their employers. Sixty percent of those polled in The National Businesswear Survey in February 2001 said wearing casual clothes made them more productive, and 58% said it improved employee morale.

A "Guided" Tour

The company sought to promote its new line in a manner that allowed workers to learn about the fashion of business casual while also contributing to a socially responsible cause.

Paine PR of Los Angeles won a PRSA LA Prism award for "The Style Tour" promotion for its combination of product-promotion savvy and social responsibility. Using a 53-foot truck to house its stage, Levi's sponsored fashion tours in 10 cities in 2000 and 15 cities in 2001, staying a couple of days in each city. Levi Strauss also created a *Casual Businesswear Resource Guide*, which it distributed to businesses across the company. The guide offered tips on what clothing might be available and what policies might be appropriate for companies to adopt. Visitors who wore Dockers as they visited the mobile fashion tour were given a $25 gift card toward additional purchases.

At each of its tour stops, Levi's would choose from among 200 candidates for office-wardrobe makeovers by stylists provided by tour partners *Vogue* and *InStyle*. The 10 local men and women who were chosen would get new wardrobes, from shoes and socks to sometimes even leather jackets. At a special San Francisco stop on the tour, Levi Strauss CEO Phil Marineau received a makeover.

Stylish Giving

In addition to promoting its business-casual clothing lines, however, Levi Strauss also offered workers a chance to participate in a charitable cause by giving away clothing no longer needed. Levi Strauss partnered with two national clothing charities—The Women's Alliance and Career Gear—to sponsor clothing drives as a part of The Style Tour. Dockers® and Slates® brands invited those attending the style tour stops to donate "their softly worn, formal business attire" to the charities' outreach efforts.

A news release from Levi Strauss described the launch efforts in this way:

"DOCKERS® KICKS OFF 10-CITY STYLE@WORK™ TOUR TO HELP PROFESSIONALS BE STYLISHLY CASUAL FOR BUSINESS"

Tour Will Also Include Used Clothing Drive to Benefit Local Charities

SAN FRANCISCO (September 21, 2000) — Dockers®, the nation's leading brand in casual businesswear, will kick off a 10-city tour this Friday to provide consumers with advice on how to project personal and professional style for today's evolving "business-casual" environment. Dockers® is taking its Fall 2000 collections on the road, providing professionals (men and women) with casual businesswear tips and recommendations, as well as complimentary head-to-toe wardrobe makeovers by guest stylists from *Vogue* and *InStyle* magazines. "According to recent surveys, 85 percent of U.S. companies have gone business-casual at least one day a week and more than 50 percent allow casual dress five days a week," said Maureen Griffin, Marketing Director for the Dockers® brand. "Yet, many employees admit they are still confused about what 'business-casual' means."

Kicking off Friday, September 22 in Indianapolis and concluding in Portland, Oregon, on November 25, the 53-foot custom-made mobile "style" truck, complete with mirrors, dressing rooms and a runway, will spend two days in each market. On Fridays it will go to high-traffic business sites and on Saturdays it will be at May Co. retail locations, including L.S. Ayres, Kaufman's, Filene's, Strawbridge's, Hecht's, Foley's, Famous Barr, Robinson's-May and Meier & Frank. In addition to Indianapolis and Portland, the Dockers® Style@WORK™ Tour will make stops in Cleveland; Boston; Philadelphia; Washington, D.C.; Pittsburgh; Houston; St. Louis; and Los Angeles.

As consumers make the transition to casual businesswear, Dockers® will collect their used clothing to be donated to local charities. Collection bins will be available at each event.

"As more companies offer casual businesswear dress policies, we hear an increased number of people asking questions about what to wear to the office," Griffin said. "Casual businesswear to many people means a polo shirt and a pair of khakis, and while this is a great option, we want to help people build on these essentials. Today there are so many more options for maintaining personal and appropriate style at work. Our goal with the Dockers® Style@WORK™ Tour is to offer consumers more solutions for their business-casual wardrobes." In support of the brand's newest twist to its NICE PANTS™ advertising campaign, which premiered nationally on primetime television earlier this year, the tour will showcase Dockers® as a complete business-casual resource — offering professionals appropriate, versatile, stylish and comfortable casual businesswear solutions from head to toe.

Dockers® was first introduced in 1986 to fill the void between rugged jeans and dress pants. Dockers® has expanded from a line of men's casual pants to an ensemble brand featuring complete collections of casual businesswear tops, pants, shoes, belts, outerwear and hosiery for men and women, as well as lines within those categories (including new Dockers® Recode™ for men and women—available exclusively at better department stores—and a boys' collection). Dockers® Fall 2000 product offerings are available in better department stores nationwide. For more information, please call (800) DOCKERS or visit the Dockers® Web site at www.dockers.com.

QUESTIONS FOR REFLECTION

1. Why would such a promotion work so well at increasing sales and goodwill?
2. What research would be necessary to help develop such a plan?
3. What does the success say about Levi Strauss' understanding of the consumers who buy their products as well as its own corporate mission and position within the marketplace? What does the willingness of the Levi Strauss CEO to undergo a public "makeover" illustrate?
4. What are the potential pitfalls of linking a product promotion with charitable efforts?

Information for this case was also drawn from Sandra Dolbow (4 September 2000), "Dockers redefines casual wear @ Work," *Brandweek,* p. 18; Marcia Pledger (25 September 2000), "Dockers taking it to the street," *Cleveland* (OH) *Plain Dealer;* and the Levi Strauss Web site.

CASE 15.   WARNER BROS. (AND OTHERS)
ARE WILD ABOUT *HARRY*

The Harry Potter series of books and films has produced magic, not only for its characters, a brown-haired, glasses-wearing young boy and his pals at Hogwarts School of Witchcraft and Wizardry, but for those companies involved in promoting the sales of the books, films, and related Potter merchandise. For example, Warner Bros. and its parent company, Time Warner Inc., have grossed an estimated $1.5 billion in revenue from worldwide box office receipts and DVD, television, and merchandising sales of *Harry Potter and the Sorcerer's Stone.*

On November 15, 2002, the film release of *Harry Potter and the Chamber of Secrets* continued the magic, setting box office records everywhere it opened, and surpassing $100 million at both the domestic and international box offices in just 10 days after its initial release. With international box office receipts in excess of $800 million, *Harry Potter and the Chamber of Secrets* soon joined the lists of the highest-grossing films of all time.

Promoting the Films

The film studio got involved early and inexpensively. Just before the first book, *Harry Potter and the Sorcerer's Stone*, became an international sensation, Warner Bros. reportedly paid Rowling $50,000 for film rights to the book. The following year, the studio paid an additional $500,000, this time to exercise its option to make a movie.

AOL Time Warner/Warner Bros. offered a variety of ways to promote the films and merchandise. AOL Moviefone offered advance ticket sales for the *Harry Potter and the Chamber of Secrets* 3 weeks before its U.S. premiere. Moviegoers in most major markets were able to buy tickets either by visiting Moviefone.com, AOL Keyword: Harry Potter, or by calling the AOL Moviefone telephone service, known by familiar local numbers such as 777-FILM. In addition, AOL 8.0's Sneak Peek Sweeps of Harry Potter and the Chamber of Secrets offered chances to win passes to one of 20 exclusive sneak preview screenings taking place across the country on November 14, 1 day before the film's U.S. release. Entrants were also given the chance to win *Harry Potter and the Chamber of Secrets* gift packs, a $1,000 holiday shopping spree, or a year of AOL membership. More than 1 million advance tickets were sold.

A 2-minute promotion for *Harry Potter and the Chamber of Secrets* was aired on the WB network in September 2002, the first time such a long clip was used to promote the movie. The clip aired during a premiere of a new WB program, "Family Affair." *Entertainment Weekly* featured a cover story on the release of *Sorcerer's Stone,* and an advance review ran in *TIME*. The June 23, 2003, *TIME* contained a seven-page article with sidebars titled "The Real Magic of Harry Potter."

Warner Bros. developed a Web site (http://harrypotter.warnerbros.com) that features information on the characters, cast, and crew of the films; Hogwart's-inspired games, merchandise, activities, music from the soundtrack, deleted scenes from the films, and a chat room. Visitors may order DVDs or videos of the films online at the site. Reuters reported that in the weeks prior to the November 2001 release of *Harry Potter and the Sorcerer's Stone,* the Web site drew some 573,000 unique visitors, and more than 3.8 million unique visitors visited the site when the film opened. In November 2002, when the second movie was released, more than 3 million visitors again came to the site.

Magical Merchandising

EastWest Creative designed a 4-week promotion to support the release of *The Sorcerer's Stone* video and DVD that involved a Web-based trivia competition. As players answered questions correctly, they were sent to one of 90 worldwide partner sites to search for the messenger owls. Those who found them earned rewards such as a screensaver or bookmark, and some 17,000 "instant pop-up" winners received posters, coloring books, postcard books, and T-shirts. Ten grand-prize winners were flown to London for the release of the *Harry Potter and the Chamber of Secrets* film, and one bonus winner got a walk-on role in the film. The game, launched in 12 countries and in seven languages, was promoted in the United States by print ads in AOL Time Warner's *People*, AOL banners, and on-air live "owl sightings" during national broadcast of the Atlanta Braves games.

Coca-Cola invested an estimated $150 million to participate in the Potter film promotion in 43 countries. The investment included usage rights to advertising campaigns to contests. In October and November, Coca-Cola offered a "Catch the Golden Snitch and Win" promotion in which game cards were enclosed in multi-packs of Coca-Cola Classic and caffeine-free Coca-Cola. Those who found the Golden Snitch card were then eligible to win a trip to London and receive $5 movie certificates. The 925 game winners were rewarded with visits to castles such as Herstmonceaux Castle, Great Fosters, and Windsor Castle in which Potter themes were developed through costuming and special events. The closing banquet in the Natural History Museum featured appetizers and drinks named after Potter characters or objects.

Special codes on the eight cards also allowed consumers to find behind-the-scenes images of the film when they visit Livethemagic.com. Similar prizes were available through Coca-Cola's Minute Maid juices. The soft-drink corporation also used its Potter promotion to tie in with a national literacy-promotion program in which it donated 1 million books to schoolchildren.

To avoid oversaturation, Warner Bros. offered licenses to fewer than 90 U.S. licensing partners, and only a few hundred products were released. But that left room for the development of Harry Potter party napkins, figurines, snow-domes, stuffed animals, candy, bookends, lamps, candy, tattoos, wrapping paper, lunchboxes, picture frames, calendars, ornaments, sweatshirts, backpacks, key chains, CD wallets, stationery, and rubber stamps. Retailers such as Toys R Us and Kmart featured merchandise tied to the *Sorcerer's Stone* film, and sales were strong. Mattel Inc. was the master licensee for the games, puzzles, trading cards, and other items. Lego Systems Inc. has developed Hogwart's Express train and Hogwart's Castle kits. Electronic Arts offered video games and computer-based ancillaries. The release of the fifth book, *Harry Potter and the Order of the Phoenix,* brought with it new merchandise, such as a robe with fiber-optic lights, a magic wand, and fake forehead scars.

The promotions were apparently effective. The NPD Group, a firm that provided marketing information online, began offering a "Harry Potter Prophet" in March 2001, a series of seven reports to track popularity of the Harry Potter products and attitudes and behaviors of children and adults relating to the books and films. According to their first report based on a March 2001 survey of 1,511 adults and children, 95% of children and 90% of adults surveyed had heard of Harry Potter, more than half of the children had read at least one of the books, and of those who have read at least one book, almost two thirds of children planned to see the movies. The Prophet also reported that 40% of children and adults who had read at least one of the books had already purchased a Harry Potter-related product.

Celebrating the Books

Scholastic, Inc., the U.S. publisher of the series, spent more than $3 million to promote the June 2003 release of *Harry Potter and the Order of the Phoenix*. Readers could reserve copies of the book during the 5 months prior to its release. More than 1.3 million copies of the book were ordered through Amazon's Web sites, Barnes & Noble.com reported it sold 896,000 copies the first day, and the Barnes & Noble bookstores sold 286,000 copies in just 60 minutes. The book's release at 12:01 a.m. June 21 was touted through parties, advertising, and promotions. A countdown in New York's Times Square and a billboard on Sunset Strip announced the release. Wal-Mart supercenters held special midnight events featuring cupcakes with Harry Potter themes. Many bookstores across the globe featured theme parties with employees dressed as characters.

A national billboard campaign supported the book's release. The Seattle Mariners, Baltimore Orioles, Oakland Athletics, and Houston Astros held "Harry Potter" days with costume contests and scoreboard promotions. Scholastic distributed more than 15,000 "event kits" to bookstores and other retailers, which planned release parties. The kits included stickers, buttons, a trivia quiz, and suggestions for handling long lines of prospective buyers. Scholastic distributed 3 million bumper stickers, 50,000 window displays, 9,500 countertop cutouts, 24,000 stand-up posters with countdown clocks, and 400,000 buttons to promote the "Phoenix" release. Scholastic also held an essay contest with the top prize of a trip to London to hear J.K. Rowling read from the book and participate in an interview at the Royal Albert Hall.

Rowling donated the only signed edition of the *Order of the Phoenix* to the New York Public Library, with an inscription that read "To the People of New York with Love and Admiration from J.K. Rowling."

Scholastic Inc. planned a first printing of 6.8 million copies, an all-time U.S. publishing record. When Scholastic released *Harry Potter and the Goblet of Fire* in July 2000, it became the fastest-selling book in history. Within 48 hours, 3 million copies were sold and Scholastic went back to press for an additional 3 million immediately. All four Harry Potter books published by Scholastic in the United States in hardcover and paperback have sold a total of nearly 80 million copies since September 1998, when the company first released *Harry Potter and the Sorcerer's Stone*.

Scholastic also used its Web site to promote the Potter books. At www.scholastic.com/harrypotter.books, readers can use a pronunciation guide and find discussion guides for the five books. There is also a chat room for comments from student readers and a screensaver that can be downloaded. The page also contains recommendations for other "great" children's books.

QUESTIONS FOR REFLECTION

1. How may public relations practice augment product promotion? What aspects of this case illustrate traditional public relations practice and which illustrate more integrated-communication efforts?
2. Should the techniques of product promotion be the same for products marketed to children as those marketed to adults?
3. What are the benefits gained by generating such widespread publicity for a product's release? Are there cautions as well?
4. Evaluate the strengths and weaknesses of the cross-merchandising efforts highlighted in this case.

Information for this case was drawn from the Web sites cited earlier and "www.aoltw.com/companies/warner_bros_index.adp and www.scholastica.com. Other sources included Blais, J. (5 June 2003), "Creating magic with marketing," *USA Today*, p. D2; Brady, D. (30 June 2003), "Harry Potter and— what else?" *BusinessWeek*, pp. 79–80; Capell, K. et al. (9 August 1999), "Just wild about Harry Potter," *BusinessWeek*, p. 54; D'Innocenzio, A. (29 October 2001), "Harry Potter merchandise is magical," *AP Online*; Gibbs, N. (23 June 2003), "The real magic of Harry Potter," *TIME*, pp. 61–67; (19 June 2003), "Harry Potter fever heats up as 'Phoenix' readies to rise," *Agency France Presse*; Hein, K. (7 October 2002), "Coke puts players in the game to help unveil Potter's secrets," *Brandweek*, p. 6; Hobbs, L. (4 July 2000), "Greet Harry at a Potter party: Stores get mystical for latest book in series," *Palm Beach Post*, p. A1; Italie, H. (5 June 2003), "Publisher revs up promotion for new Harry Potter Book," *AP Worldstream*; Katz, R. (9 December 2002), "Harry Potter fans get thrills at Coke incentive," *MeetingNews*, p. 11; Kirkpatrick, D. D. (16 June 2003), "Merchandisers try to harness Harry Potter's magic," *International Herald Tribune*; Leith, S. (1 February 2002), "Coke confident of 'Potter' benefits," (*continued*)

(continued)   *The Atlanta Journal-Constitution*, p. C1,8; Lyman, R. (30 December 2002), "A big fat increase at the box office," *The New York Times*, p. E1; Murphy, D. E. (21 June 2003), "Harry fans count down, raise a butterbeer," *Portland (ME) Press Herald*, p. A1; Mnyandu, E. (11 June 2003), "Harry Potter not magic enough for U.S. bookstores," *Reuters Entertainment*; Odell, P. (1 May 2003), "Bird watching," *Promo, 16*(6); Palmeri, C. et al. (3 December 2001), "Boffo at the box office, scarce on the shelves," *BusinessWeek*, p. 53; Reuters (11 September 2002), "'Harry' synergy/The WB plugs 'Potter' movie," *Newsday*, p. A18; (28 March 2001), "NPD introduces new report to track Harry Potter phenomenon," Release, *Business Wire*; Sanger, E. (10 July 2000), "Potter and the toymakers' tale," *Newsday*, p. 18; Thorn, P. (11 February 2001), "Potter, Potter everywhere," *Denver Rocky Mountain News*, p. 1E; Thorn, P. (20 June 2003), "Get caught up on all things 'potter': The future," *Denver Rocky Mountain News*, p. D27; and (1 November 2001), "Traffic skyrockets at studio's Harry Potter Web site," *The Toronto Star*.

Forming Effective Relationships With Journalists

Lee Duffey, president and founder, Duffey Communications

The love–hate relationship between public relations professionals and journalists is notorious. On one hand, we provide journalists with the information and access they need. On the other hand, some PR professionals provide "junk" information without targeting their pitches, leading to animosity from journalists. Think of yourself as an information broker to avoid falling into the "junk dealer" trap.

Despite this conflict, it is possible to forge successful relationships with journalists by understanding and respecting their job. First, consider the motivations of both sides. Journalists need to produce interesting, unbiased coverage. Your motivation is to publicize an organization's key messages.

At times, these motivations clash. When and if they do, a successful PR practitioner maneuvers through the situation professionally, doesn't take rejection personally, and lives to pitch another day.

Strengthen the relationship by always being professional. Respect the journalist's time; don't call without providing value-added information. Hint: "Did you get my press release?" is not a good reason to call back. Trust your instincts in every situation—if it smells bad, it's spoiled. Your reputation is on the line with every contact you make, so don't compromise your standards.

Over time, journalists will recognize that you send focused pitches and will reward you with attention and respect. That doesn't mean they'll cover everything you send, but they will listen to your ideas once they respect your work. Journalists are usually on deadline and are inundated with irrelevant information daily. It's your job to break through the clutter with engaging information and get your organization's story told.

In following this advice, it's understood that PR professionals should maintain honesty and integrity in media relations. Once you set the expectation for quality work, your relationships with journalists will build results for your organization and for your career.

Lee Duffey is the president and founder of Duffey Communications, the Southeast's largest independent public relations, marketing, and public affairs agency and one of the nation's top-ranked firms.

5

Stakeholders: Media

MEDIA STAKEHOLDERS SERVE INTERVENING PUBLICS

Media relations is a busy highway with traffic traveling in both directions between journalists and public relations practitioners, and the rules of the road are observed as courtesies rather than enforceable regulations. In one direction, journalists ask practitioners for help in gathering information for news stories or verifying details. In the other, practitioners distribute news announcements to the media or ask journalists to consider story ideas for publication.

The traffic generally moves smoothly at high speed, though collisions occur when drivers don't know the rules or don't care to follow them. For practitioners, the rules include conventions like the use of Associated Press style in news releases, courtesies like returning phone calls promptly, and an absolute rejection of falsehoods and deception.

Reporters and editors are seldom the ultimate target of public relations programming. Instead, gatekeepers who work in broadcasting and publishing represent an intervening public, controlling the flow and presentation of information to readers, listeners, and viewers. Ultimately, public relations programs aim to reach consumers, regulators, government officials, activists, and others whose opinions and actions will affect the practitioner's organization.

PURPOSES OF MEDIA RELATIONS

Reaching target publics through news media exposure is a common practice in public relations for at least six reasons:

- *Efficiency:* Mass media, such as Web sites, daily newspapers, and television, reach individuals by the hundreds of thousands or even millions with unsurpassed speed.
- *Credibility:* Individuals often believe that information in reputable media, such as the *New York Times* or CBS-TV's "60 Minutes," is more trustworthy than the same information presented by an organization.
- *Targeting:* Individuals who read or watch certain kinds of media or programming may have predictable interests or habits, enabling the practitioner to tailor messages with greater precision and mutual benefit.
- *Agenda setting:* Media attention often determines which topics come up in general conversation, and a practitioner may want to get people talking about a specific subject.
- *Economy:* Messages that appear in the news media involve comparatively low costs for the practitioner's organization.
- *Time shifting:* Print media, in particular, allow individuals to pick their own best time and place to digest information. The same is true, to a lesser extent, for Web sites, CDs, and DVDs.

THE SELF-INTERESTS OF THE MEDIA

Reporters and editors care little about the reasons that lead practitioners to favor news media for distributing information. Instead, journalists focus on satisfying their audiences' need for news and preferences in entertainment. If public relations materials help a news organization do its job well, journalists are happy to use them. Materials that contain no news or useful information are tossed.

In developing strategies and key messages to reach the ultimate target public, practitioners usually give painstaking thought to the target's self-interest and to circumstances that will make it easy for a target public to follow through with whatever action is desired. Yet, practitioners often neglect the self-interests of the intervening public—the editors and reporters—as well as the mission of a news organization.

At a personal level, journalists want many of the same things practitioners want—good income, increasing responsibility, stability with a respected employer. In journalism, these rewards depend on gaining the respect of peers, career advancement, challenging assignments, and recognition.

Reporters rate themselves and others according to the importance of assignments they handle, number and quality of the stories they get published or broadcast, and prominence given their stories in the news product (front page, above the fold, top of the newscast, and so on).

TIME PRESSURES IN MEDIA RELATIONS

To do their jobs well on a daily basis, most reporters must focus on choosing a story idea or chasing one down, gathering information efficiently, finding a strong news peg, and writing a vivid and compelling account. They must do it quickly, never falling behind the competition and beating it if possible, and they must meet the deadline of their publication or newscast. Before handing in a news story, a reporter needs time to check it to make sure that it's fair, accurate, and reasonably complete.

Considering these time pressures, no one should be surprised that journalists prefer to deal with a practitioner who has earned their trust by providing information that's never misleading, earned their appreciation by providing it quickly, and earned their respect by packaging it in formats that are easy to digest and use. Accommodating the self-interests of intervening publics serves the self-interest of the practitioner's organization.

ELECTRONIC MEDIA RELATIONS

The Internet gives a media relations practitioner a number of tools to use in helping reporters do their jobs faster and better. Almost all organizations—big and small—maintain Web sites, and on the home page of these Web sites is a hypertext link to what is often called the press center or news bureau. A prominent and easy-to-find link will get more use.

Journalists often visit an organization's Web site, looking for information they need, before placing a phone call to a media relations manager. Because it's available around the clock and throughout the week, reporters can get details they need whenever they want them.

A Web site's news bureau usually contains recent news releases and archives of old ones. An elementary news bureau also should list the names, phone numbers, and e-mail addresses of the media relations staff.

Better Web sites contain much more. The news bureau page should offer links to:

- Fact sheets.
- Organizational history.
- Executive biographies.
- High-resolution photos of leaders, products, and operations.
- Reproducible charts and graphs.
- Annual and quarterly reports.
- Electronic news kits.
- Executive speeches.
- Significant dates in the organization's past.
- A calendar of major upcoming events.

Some Web sites include audio files for radio actualities, video clips of products in use, PowerPoint presentations, and spreadsheets for financial information.

UP TO DATE AND EASY TO USE

To protect reporters from using out-of-date information, media relations sites need regular attention from practitioners to keep facts, figures, and faces current. Items like biographies and fact sheets should indicate when their most recent update occurred, reassuring journalists that the information is fresh.

Because these pages for the news media should load quickly into an Internet browser, they should look spare, clean, and uncomplicated, placing a premium on ease of navigation. A search function can make a Web site easier to use, but it's not a substitute for careful planning in creating and positioning hypertext navigation links.

The news bureau pages should avoid files that load slowly or that are difficult or slow to print through office printers. Some portable-document-format (PDF) files, though preserving the appearance of the original paper document, often are slower in loading, reading, and printing.

The Internet also gives media relations practitioners the opportunity to maintain relationships with reporters through e-mail, but it's a mixed blessing. E-mail has been abused by marketing spammers and lazy public relations practitioners so that reporters may not bother to read your e-mail unless they know you, trust you, and sense news potential in the subject line of your message. The subject line's purpose is similar to that of a headline—to get attention and convey the essence of a message.

Reporters say that they're unlikely to open an e-mail with attachments because it carries the risk of a computer virus infection.

Research sponsored by the Institute for Public Relations (IPR) found that practitioners and reporters alike said in 2001 that the Internet has led to improvements in news reporting and the practice of media relations.

"Journalists believe the Internet has made their jobs easier and improved the quality of their work," according to IPR's *Magic Communication Machine* report. "Journalists now rate e-mail equal to the telephone as the preferred medium for interviewing news sources. And, journalists report they regularly use the Internet when gathering information for news stories."

NO SUBSTITUTE FOR HUMAN CONTACT

Despite the efficiency offered by the Internet, reporters and practitioners point out that it's no substitute for a trusting relationship. Web sites make facts and figures easily accessible, but tracking down nonroutine details still requires human contact. To make stories come alive, journalists need to quote what people—not documents—say, and media relations managers set up the interviews that add depth and humanity to news. Reporters and practitioners need each other.

Bobbie Battista, formerly host of CNN's *Talk Back* cable program and now a media relations consultant, offered this advice: "Establish a relationship with one reporter at each station or publication. Over time, if you always are honest and straight, rapport will become trust."

ADDITIONAL READINGS

Jones, Clarence. (2001). *Winning with the news media.* Tampa, FL: Video Consultants Inc.

Kent, Michael L., & Maureen Taylor. (Spring 2003). *Maximizing media relations: A Web site checklist.* Rhinebeck, NY: Public Relations Quarterly.

Wade, John. (1992). *Dealing effectively with the media.* Menlo Park, CA: Crisp Publications.

Wright, Donald K. (2001). *The magic communication machine: Examining the Internet's impact on public relations, journalism, and the public.* Gainesville, FL: Institute for Public Relations.

CASE 16.   MEDIA INTEREST IN TRANSPLANT DRAMA STOKES ANXIETY IN HEALTH CARE PROFESSIONALS

Jesica Santillan spent most of her childhood in Arroyo Hondo, a sun-baked Mexican village of 400 people surrounded by fields of sugarcane. Located halfway between the Jalisco state capital of Guadalajara and Puerto Vallarta on the Pacific Coast, the village has one paved road and little else in community resources. Arroyo Hondo families have a hard life. Many depend on work in cane fields or the local sugar mill, and individuals often earn less than $10 for a 12-hour day.

Jesica's parents, Melecio and Magdalena, learned early that their daughter suffered from restrictive cardiomyopathy, a condition involving heart muscle stiffness that also affects breathing. No cure for the disease exists, and about 70% of those who develop it die within 5 years of the onset of symptoms. In most cases, the only satisfactory solution is a heart transplant.

The Santillans could not arrange transplant surgery for Jesica in Mexico. Desperate and determined, the parents took their 13-year-old daughter to the United States illegally in 1999 and made their way to North Carolina, where relatives were living.

The family moved into a mobile home in a rural county northeast of Raleigh and began investigating what they would have to do to get Jesica's life-threatening condition corrected. Knowing medical care for Jesica would be far beyond their means (some estimates put the figure at a half-million dollars), the family solicited donations from friends and neighbors, while churches and civic groups put containers in local shops to collect contributions.

During the 2002 holidays, Jesica Santillan posed with her mother, younger sister and brother for a family photo. (Photo by Mack Mahoney.)

Now Near Duke

The Santillans' new Carolina home was only an hour's drive from the Durham campus of Duke University Medical Center, one of the preeminent health care organizations in the United States.

Year after year, *U.S. News & World Report* ranked Duke among the nation's top hospitals. Separately, Duke specialties such as heart, pulmonary, and pediatrics also earned high rankings on the *U.S. News* lists. The Discovery Channel ran a documentary series, called "Hospital," on the lives of patients and caregivers at Duke Hospital, and *TIME* magazine published a cover story on a day in the life of Duke. CBS-TV's "60 Minutes" program profiled a Duke oncologist in 2002. By most accounts, the institution's public relations efforts were highly successful.

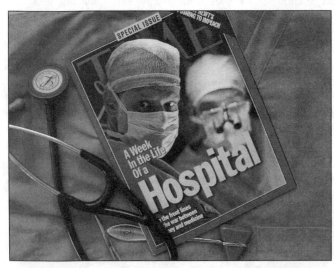

In 1998, *TIME* magazine focused on Duke University Hospital in a special edition on healthcare in America.

The medical center is proud of its reputation—justifiably so. Describing its approach to medicine, Duke says that "patients can count on receiving high-quality healthcare that is delivered with empathy and compassion. The medical leadership that has earned Duke such renown is the result of an innovative approach that stresses multidisciplinary collaboration and a close 'bench-to-bedside' relationship between clinical care and research that gives our patients access to the very latest treatments."

For Jesica, her parents, and friends in North Carolina and Arroyo Hondo, Duke Hospital represented her best chance at life. They were full of hope.

Mack Mahoney Aids Santillan Family

One of Jesica's new friends was Mack Mahoney, a Carolina homebuilder who'd seen her story in a local newspaper. Inspired by her struggle for survival, he organized efforts to raise funds for a transplant operation. Fluent in Spanish, Mr. Mahoney also assisted Jesica's parents, whose conversational English was limited, in their discussions with the health care professionals at Duke. Subsequently, he received medical power of attorney to participate in the Santillans' health care decisions.

As Jesica's case attracted the attention of major news outlets in Raleigh and Durham, Mr. Mahoney persuaded one of North Carolina's U.S. senators to help shield the family from deportation while they waited for organs that would be suitable for transplant. The operation, surgeons had decided, would require a set of lungs as well as a heart.

Finding compatible organs for a heart-lung transplant is a long shot. To match an organ donor and recipient, health agencies consider their physical size, blood type, the expected time in transit for the organs, and the recipient's position on the national waiting list. At any time, the national list of individuals awaiting this combination may include 200 names, but the number of heart-lung transplant operations performed in the United States in a single year might not exceed 30.

The United Network for Organ Sharing administers the nation's organ procurement and transplantation network, collecting and sharing information on organ need and availability. The network includes regional organizations that enlist donors and monitor availability.

The Discovery Channel ran a 13-part documentary series on the lives of the patients and caregivers at Duke University Hospital.

Transplant Surgery Scheduled

On Friday, February 7, 2003, a Duke surgeon learned from the network that a heart and lungs were available from the New England Organ Bank. He reserved them for Jesica, now 17, who was expected to live only 6 more months with her own heart. A Duke surgical team flew to Boston to remove the organs and hurry them back to Durham. (Heart and lungs ordinarily must be implanted no more than 8 hours after removal.)

Meanwhile, Jesica's surgeon timed his procedures so that he would complete the removal of her organs at about the same time that the donor's heart and lungs arrived at Duke. The coordination itself was successful, but routine tests performed near the end of the surgery disclosed a tragic error. Although the transplant network and Duke both had procedures to ensure blood group compatibility between donor and recipient even before surgery could be scheduled, the safeguards had failed somehow.

The donor's blood group was A, and Jesica's was O. People with blood group O, the most common group in the U.S. population, are universal donors; they can give blood to other groups. However, people in blood group O can safely receive blood or organs only from people in group O.

The operating team finished its work, and the surgeon went immediately to Jesica's parents to tell them of the mistake and its implications. Her body's immune response would attack the incompatible organs as it would an infection, and her only hope of survival would be a second heart-lung transplant using organs from a group O donor. Duke notified the United Network for Organ Sharing that Jesica urgently needed another set of organs.

Media Kept in the Dark

Meanwhile, the family, physicians, and hospital's public relations staff agreed privately that, until more was known about what went wrong, the media would be given only basic reports on her condition. The organ mismatch would remain confidential as the search for a new donor was pressed.

In the days immediately after the operation, the director of the medical center's news office told reporters: "She is rejecting the organs that were transplanted into her." Nothing was said about the error.

Hour by hour, the Santillans and Mr. Mahoney grew more fearful that the girl would die before the transplant network could find a donor in blood group O, and they apparently came to believe that a directed donation—where the family of a dying patient would choose Jesica to receive the organs—was the quickest and best solution. To reach as many potential donor families as possible, a broad public appeal in the media would be needed.

While impatience was agitating those closest to Jesica, Duke's reticence stirred suspicion in news reporters from Raleigh and Durham. Five days after the surgery, some reporters heard privately from Mack Mahoney that the transplanted organs came from a donor with a different blood type, but the media held back those details, apparently unable to verify them.

The director of the medical center's news office told the media: "It's far too early to have definitive answers regarding this case. Any comments now would be speculative. Nevertheless, this patient's sequence of care is under careful review."

News of Error Breaks

Then, Mr. Mahoney openly discussed the organ mismatch on Friday, February 14, after waiting a week for Duke to get results using the transplant network. The first media report of the error appeared the same day. A day later, Duke doggedly dodged the dark truth when reporters asked if the family's version of events was true.

The associate director of the medical center's news office told reporters: "Duke Hospital is continuing a careful review of the sequence of care that she received. That's the only information I have for you. This is all I can say. At this point, our priority is to help Jesica and her family through this difficult situation. We hope a suitable donor can be found."

While Duke remained tight-lipped, the family's account of the surgery gained the attention of national news organizations and received heavy coverage in North Carolina.

Late on Monday, February 17—10 days after the surgery—Duke acknowledged the mismatch in a public statement given to the media and posted on the medical center's Web site under the headline "Duke University Hospital Implements Additional Transplantation Safeguards." Quoting the hospital chief executive officer, the statement said, "This was a tragic error, and we accept responsibility for our part."

The New England Organ Bank said its records showed Duke was told the donor's blood group at several points in the procurement process, and the information also accompanied the organs on the trip to Durham. Duke did not dispute the statement.

On Tuesday, the organ mismatch story got coverage throughout the day on CNN Headline News and Fox News Channel, as well as on cable's news/talk programs. The *New York Times* was preparing a front-page article for the following day. The Associated Press, Reuters, BBC, and other worldwide news organizations carried reports.

A Second Donor Is Found

Despite the long odds against finding a compatible set of organs for a second operation, the transplant network told Duke near midnight Wednesday that a donor had been identified. Surgery began at 6 a.m. Thursday and finished at 10:15 a.m. At first, Jesica appeared to tolerate the second operation well, but the initial outlook dimmed quickly. She was pronounced dead on Saturday, February 22.

Seventeen days after Jesica's death, the chief executive officer of the Duke University Health System sent a memo to the health care staff offering his perspective on the tragic error and suggesting what the institution might learn from subsequent events and the attention they received in the media. The CEO, a physician named Ralph Snyderman who also served as Duke's chancellor for health affairs, said the case involved three central issues:

- Medical questions about mistakes and how to prevent them.
- Ethical questions about transplants and end-of-life decisions.
- Communications questions about a patient's privacy rights, needs of the patient's family, and the public's right to know.

"Some have asked, why didn't Duke announce the blood-typing mistake immediately after the first transplant and launch a public appeal for compatible organs?" he wrote on March 11. "One reason is that Jesica's family initially asked us not to. Another reason is that it would not have been appropriate for us to initiate publicity. The organ procurement system used by all hospitals was designed to allocate organs on a fair and equitable basis while considering the degree of need."

A "60 Minutes" Interview

As Duke employees were digesting the memo, Dr. Snyderman and Jesica's surgeon, Dr. James Jaggers, were sitting for videotaped interviews with CBS-TV's "60 Minutes." In a segment that aired March 16, the two physicians and others at Duke recounted the fateful steps that led to the failed transplant.

When journalists in Durham and Raleigh learned that "60 Minutes" was interviewing Duke's top medical officer, some suggested that the medical center was continuing to stiff-arm them. Durham's *Herald-Sun* noted that Dr. Snyderman "still hasn't responded to repeated requests by *The Herald-Sun* for an on-the-record interview about the tragedy," but the CEO and Jesica's surgeon "have granted interviews to CBS '60 Minutes' reporter Ed Bradley."

On the day after the "60 Minutes" broadcast, the medical center's Web site offered this explanation for Duke's decision to welcome the CBS crew: "Because of the widespread publicity regarding this patient, Duke University Hospital felt it important to address some of the complex issues in a nationwide forum. We agreed to participate in a '60 Minutes' story because they offered to address this event in a fair and comprehensive manner."

Acknowledging Mistakes

Dr. Snyderman wrote a reflective op-ed column, published under the headline "Owning Up to Mistakes in Medicine," that appeared April 26, 2003, in the *News & Observer* of Raleigh.

"In order to prevent mistakes, one needs a culture of safety and an openness to identify risks freely," he wrote. "If mistakes or near misses occur, healthcare workers must own up to them promptly and honestly so they can be addressed and corrected. But doing this is extremely difficult because the current environment for litigation encourages professionals to do otherwise."

He mentioned, approvingly, proposed federal legislation that would create a system for voluntary, confidential, nonpunitive error reporting to encourage analysis of mistakes and improvement of patient safety.

"We believe that disclosure of errors in an atmosphere that focuses on solutions, not blame, will make healthcare safer for everyone," he wrote.

QUESTIONS FOR REFLECTION

1. What's meant by a "bench-to-bedside" relationship?
2. What reasons might explain Duke University Hospital's initial decision to provide the news media with reports only on Jesica's condition?
3. The Santillan family and friends decided to pursue a broad public appeal for a second set of organs for transplant. What strategy and tactics would you have recommended?
4. Duke's chancellor for health affairs said the case involved questions concerning a patient's privacy rights, needs of the patient's family, and the public's right to know. How would you balance these three?

Information for this case was drawn from the following: the Duke University Medical Center Web sites at http://news.mc.duke.edu/mediakits/detail.php?id=6498 and http://www.dukehealth.org/news/default.asp; Avery, S., & Martinez, A. (25 February 2003), "Duke caught in PR quagmire," *The News & Observer*, p. A1; Cheng, V. (19 February 2003), "Duke's image takes a blow," *The News & Observer*, p. A9; Draper, M. (13 February 2003), "Girl's miracle fleeting," *The News & Observer*, p. A1; (30 May 2003), "Duke's amazing PR coup continues," *The Herald-Sun*, p. B1; Eisley, M. (16 February 2003), "Mistake alleged in blood match," *The News & Observer*, p. B1; Fass, A. (9 June 2003), "Duking it out," *Forbes*, p. 134; Grady, D. (19 February 2003), "Donor mix-up leaves girl, 17, fighting for life," *The New York Times*, p. A1; Kirkpatrick, C. (18 June 2003), "Duke Hospital admits to botching transplant," *The Herald-Sun*, p. A1; Snyderman, R. (26 April 2003), "Owning up to mistakes in medicine," *The News & Observer*, p. A19; and Weissert, W. (7 March 2003), "Mexican village was ready, but Jesica's funeral not to be," *The Herald-Sun*, p. A10.

CASE 17.   PHONY NEWS RELEASE LEADS TO LOSSES FOR INVESTORS AND A PRISON TERM FOR FORMER COLLEGE STUDENT

The evening shift at Internet Wire in Los Angeles gave routine handling to a request from Porter and Smith PR for distribution of an Emulex Corporation news release. The e-mail message from Ross Porter, with release attached, asked for distribution the following day, Friday, August 25, 2000, at 9:30 a.m. EDT.

Porter's e-mail message used jargon, such as "please bill me as the first release out of the 10 pack," that was familiar to Internet Wire staffers and led them to accept its authenticity. Accordingly, they prepared the release for transmission to the thousands of news organizations and financial analysts reached by Internet Wire.

Teed Up for Trouble

Although the distribution request itself appeared routine, the content of the news release was anything but. It announced that:

- Emulex was revising downward the earnings figures issued earlier in the month.
- The SEC was investigating the company's accounting practices.
- Paul Folino, the Emulex chief executive officer, was leaving.

As predetermined, Internet Wire dispatched the release as stock markets in New York City were opening Friday, and it was soon picked up and passed along by reputable financial news outlets such as Bloomberg News and the CNBC television channel. The price of Emulex common shares, which had closed the previous day at $113.06 on the Nasdaq Stock Market, began slipping, slowly at first and then with gathering speed after Bloomberg published its first headline at 10:13 a.m. EDT. Soon, the news was mentioned on CNBC, Dow Jones News Service, the CBS Marketwatch Web site, and others.

Back at Emulex headquarters in Costa Mesa, California, executives had begun arriving for work about 7 a.m. PDT and were stunned by the plunging share price. The company's recent financial results had been exceptional, and its outlook was promising.

Emulex described itself in 2000 as "the world's largest supplier of fibre channel host adapters," devices used by equipment makers such as Hewlett-Packard and IBM in networking applications. In an earnings news release issued August 3, Emulex had trumpeted record levels of revenues and earnings for the company's most recent quarter and reported revenues of $140 million and net income of $33 million for fiscal year 2000, which ended July 2. Emulex CEO Paul Folino indicated that Emulex was well-positioned to benefit from growth.

Trading Halted

Like others at the company, Mr. Folino was shocked to hear about the stock's nose-dive when he walked into his office shortly after 7 a.m. Friday and began trying to figure out what could account for it. He soon heard about the news release on Internet Wire and realized that the company was the victim of a cruel hoax. Promptly, he asked authorities at Nasdaq to halt trading in Emulex and protect investors from further effects of the fraud.

In the 16 minutes before Nasdaq suspended Emulex trades at 10:29 a.m. EDT, the price of a common share had plunged from $103.94 to a bottom of $43. Investors who sold shares that morning lost almost $110 million and had little hope of recovering it.

Once trading was suspended, Mr. Folino and others went to work on a news release explaining what had happened and refuting the claims contained in the false release. The rebuttal circulated widely across the Internet and financial news wires, and Nasdaq reopened trading at 1:30 p.m. EDT. By the end of the day, the stock had climbed to $105.75 a share.

Although the stock snapped back quickly, questions lingered about the performance of financial news organizations and their rush to publish without independent verification. At Bloomberg News, an editor said that standard practice calls for a reporter to check with a company before writing a story, but the protocol was skipped in this instance. A Dow Jones New Service editor said that his organization trusts the verification process of electronic-release distribution services, such as Business Wire and PR Newswire, and had received assurances that Internet Wire used a similar procedure.

From the moment the fraud was discovered, Emulex management had wondered who the culprit was and why he or she had done it. Authorities quickly determined that Ross Porter, author of the e-mail that conveyed the false release to Internet Wire, was fictitious, as was the Porter and Smith PR firm. They suspected that someone with inside knowledge of Internet Wire had concocted the hoax to drive down the price of Emulex shares. A drop in price could benefit an investor who had sold Emulex short.

Short Sellers Expect Bad News to Be Good

In investing, most people expect to benefit when good news causes a company's stock price to rise. However, some investors—short sellers—benefit when bad news causes a stock to drop in price. Here's how.

A short seller anticipates, presumably for good reasons, that the price of a certain stock is too high and will fall below current levels. Using a brokerage firm's services, he or she *borrows* shares from a stockowner and *sells* them to other investors at the current price. The short seller expects to *purchase* shares after the price has fallen, replace the borrowed shares, and pocket the difference between the current and future (presumably lower) price.

The practice involves the risk of losing money—potentially a lot of money—if the share price goes up instead of down and the short seller must purchase pricier shares to replace the ones that he or she borrowed and sold.

Investigators Get a Lead

To solve the Emulex mystery, law enforcement authorities began looking for someone who knew Internet Wire's operating procedures and also had been involved in trading Emulex shares. They asked if any employees had recently quit the public relations wire service and were told that Mark Simeon Jakob, a 23-year-old man from El Segundo, California, had left on good terms about a week earlier. From separate sources, they learned that Mr. Jakob had been involved in short selling 3,000 Emulex shares on August 17 and 18, expecting the price to drop below $81 a share.

Mr. Jakob had studied during the summer at El Camino College in Torrance, a 2-year institution not far from his home. Soon after classes ended, he quit his Internet Wire job and went on vacation, registering Wednesday, August 23, at the Luxor Resort & Casino in Las Vegas for a 3-day stay.

The Luxor is a gambling palace that envelops guests in opulence and fantasy. A 10-story sphinx, taller than Egypt's original, towers above the entrance. The hotel itself, a 350-foot-high pyramid encased in glass the color of onyx, shoots the brightest beam of light on the planet skyward from its pinnacle, and the casino floor below covers almost three acres.

While Mr. Jakob was enjoying what the hotel describes as "accommodations and amenities worthy of Queen Nefertiti herself," Emulex began trading above $100 per share, far more than the $81 price that prevailed when Mr. Jakob borrowed 3,000 shares. On Thursday, the young man's brokerage firm issued a $20,000 margin call, requiring him to place that amount of cash into his account to partially cover the increased value of the shares he had borrowed and sold but not yet replaced. With Emulex trading above $113 per share, Mr. Jakob faced a potential loss of $97,000 on his short sale if the stock did not come down.

After receiving the margin call, he flew back to Los Angeles and drove to the Library Media Technology Center at El Camino College, though he was no longer a student there. He used the library's computers to draft the fake Emulex news release and open a Yahoo! e-mail account under the name of the fictitious Porter and Smith PR agency. As Ross Porter, he sent the damaging release to Internet Wire, climbed into his car, and drove back to Las Vegas.

Timing Is Everything

At Internet Wire, the staff accepted "Porter's" apparent authority and assumed the release had been verified. Using normal procedures, they readied it for distribution. Internet Wire had been incorporated in 1999, evolving from a similar service started 5 years earlier. It has emphasized its pricing advantage in competing with the established giants of the electronic-release distribution business, PR Newswire and Business Wire. All three services offer publicly held companies a convenient and dependable mechanism for providing timely and fair disclosure of important news, as required by the SEC.

When a company plans to announce news that might affect an investor's decision on buying or selling its stock, it often provides the release to a service such as Internet Wire a few hours in advance, with instructions to distribute it when notified or, alternatively, at a specific time. Companies often prefer to issue major news outside regular trading hours of the major stock exchanges to give investors time to digest it before acting, sending it either after the market closes for the day or well before it opens in the morning. The Nasdaq Stock Market and New York Stock Exchange, for example, both are open from 9:30 a.m. to 4 p.m. on weekdays.

On Friday morning after the fake Emulex release went out, Mr. Jakob checked financial news sites on the Internet and saw that his plot was succeeding. His release had been used by major news services like CNBC, and the price of Emulex stock was slipping. Using his online brokerage account, he covered his short sales by purchasing 3,000 shares at about $62 per share to replace those he borrowed when the price was around $81. Far from facing a $97,000 loss, he made a profit of about $54,000.

When the price continued downward, Mr. Jakob purchased another 3,500 shares of Emulex for an average near $52, expecting the price would climb again when the hoax was discovered—as it did. He sold these additional shares on Monday at a profit exceeding $186,000.

An Arrest Is Made

An investigation by the FBI, SEC, and U.S. Attorney's office identified Mr. Jakob in a matter of days, and he was arrested on Thursday, August 31. He pleaded guilty 4 months later to two counts of securities fraud and one count of wire fraud and was sentenced in August 2001 to 44 months in federal prison.

The day before Mr. Jakob's arrest, the *New York Times* scolded Internet Wire, the financial news media, Emulex, and the Nasdaq in an editorial headlined "Caveat Investors."

"Internet Wire has called the perpetrator a 'very sophisticated criminal.' But in truth, the low-cost service and several reputable media organizations dropped the ball; this criminal could have been thwarted with a single phone call. Emulex and the Nasdaq can also be faulted for not reacting more quickly to events. Surely in this day and age investors should not lose billions to fraud simply because California is in a different time zone."

In 2003, Internet Wire changed its name to Market Wire.

QUESTIONS FOR REFLECTION

1. Internet Wire faced the challenge of restoring customer trust in its distribution services. What steps would you recommend to rebuild confidence?
2. Though Emulex was an innocent victim of this fraud, were there any precautions that the company might have adopted to prevent or minimize this situation?
3. The Dow Jones News Service said that it has relied on the verification procedures of distribution companies like PR Newswire and Internet Wire to confirm the authenticity of new releases. Do you agree that news organizations have no obligation to check further?
4. What changes would you make in Internet Wire's operations?

Information for this case was drawn from the following: the Emulex Web site at http://www.emulex.com/corp/index.html; Market Wire Web site at http://www.marketwire.com/mw/corp_co_overview; (30 August 2000), "Caveat investors," *The New York Times*, p. A22; (8 August 2001), "Defendant in Emulex hoax sentenced," U.S. Securities and Exchange Commission news release; (11 September 2000), "Emulex's swift IR limits bogus release damage," *Investor Relations Business*, p. 1; Ewing, T., Rose, M., Rundle, R., & Fields, G. (1 September 2000), "E-mail trail leads to Emulex hoax suspect," *The Wall Street Journal*, p. C1; Ewing, T., Waldman, P., & Rose, M. (28 August 2000), "Bogus report sends Emulex on a wild ride," *The Wall Street Journal*, p. C1; Gentile, G. (1 September 2000), "Portrait of a criminal," *The Associated Press*; Glassman, J. (30 August 2000), "Stock hoax should affirm faith in markets," *The Wall Street Journal*, p. A26; (1 August 2001), "Hoaxer is sentenced to 44 months in jail in Emulex Corp. case," *The Wall Street Journal*, p. A4; Mrozek, T. (6 August 2001), "Man who perpetrated $110 million fraud against Emulex stockholders sentenced to nearly four years in prison," U.S. Department of Justice news release; and (31 August 2000), "Stock hoax suspect had motive," *Wired News*, http://www.wired.com.

CASE 18.   SHEIK'S LEISURE RESORT PROJECT
GETS ROYAL TREATMENT

Sophie Rhys-Jones had been working in public relations for 14 years when she and
fellow practitioner, Murray Harkin, began talking seriously about combining resources to set up a new agency. The two were the same age, 32, possessed youthful
energy and good looks, and had a lot of professional experience in common. Both
had served broadcast clients and first met when Murray was promoting a program
for the British Broadcasting Corporation.

Early in her career, Sophie handled publicity for Capital Radio. Later, she joined
Macmillan Cancer Relief to work on fund-raising events and then went to
MacLaurin Group public relations soon after it was founded in 1993. At MacLaurin,
her clients included Britt Allcroft Group film productions, Chrysalis Group broadcast properties, Red Rooster Film, and radio entertainer Chris Tarrant.

Murray's career in public relations and marketing had begun at about the same
time. First, he worked on consumer and business-to-business accounts with Roger
Haywood, a reputation management expert and author of books on public relations. Subsequently, Murray joined Shandwick International's Rogers & Cowan
unit, which specialized in entertainment industry clients, and then served for 3
years as a group managing director at The Entertainment Partnership.

RJH Public Relations Formed

For Sophie and Murray, the appeal of running their own shop and capitalizing on
what they'd learned while producing profits for others was irresistible. In
early1997, the pair formed RJH Public Relations with Sophie as chairman and
Murray as managing director. They opened their first office in London's West
Kensington neighborhood.

In a short time, they had built up a respectable client list that included MG
Rover Group autos, Thomas Goode china and crystal, Boodle & Dunthorne jewel-
ers, Sotogrande's Almenara Golf-Hotel on Spain's Mediterranean coast, and the
Banyan Tree Seychelles resort. For RJH Public Relations, the barometer of success was rising, and business was good enough to move their London offices to a
tony Mayfair address.

Sophie earned the admiration of some Britons and the envy of others when, 2
years after opening the agency, she wed Prince Edward, third son of Britain's
reigning monarch, and was styled the Countess of Wessex. Her husband had established a career in film production before their marriage, and she continued her
daily work at RJH Public Relations as Sophie Wessex.

As the agency's profile rose, some new business simply dropped into its lap.
Out of the blue, Murray was invited to meet in March 2001 with a sheikh who was
planning a new international sports and leisure resort for Dubai in the United Arab

Emirates at the southern end of the Persian Gulf. The sheikh was interested in engaging RJH Public Relations and wanted more information on its capabilities.

Meetings at the Exclusive Dorchester

Murray first sat down with the Arab chief in early March but reached no agreement on formalizing a business relationship. Following up on Wednesday, March 14, Sophie—who had not yet met the potential new client—accompanied her partner to the Dorchester, a legendary London hotel where the sheikh was staying, for further discussions.

She and Murray were eager to outline the agency's capabilities and expressed strong interest in the project. If RJH Public Relations could win the assignment, the job promised to pay £20,000 (about $32,000) per month for 2 years.

During the idle chitchat that often accents business meetings as strangers warm up to each other, the conversation wandered to subjects closer to London than to Dubai. The incidental topics included British politics, public figures, and Sophie's in-laws. On the central matters of the talks, the discussions apparently ended on a positive note.

The tone turned sour almost immediately. Just days later, the countess discovered that the sheikh was a sham and the resort project was a scam. It was an undercover sting operation set up and surreptitiously taped by a reporter for the *News of the World*, a tabloid owned by Rupert Murdoch. One of the sting's goals was to obtain evidence that the countess was trading on her connections to the royal family for business purposes—a low practice for anyone near the monarchy.

The *News of the World* had begun its investigation in February 2001 after a resentful account manager at RJH Public Relations carried tales to the newspaper, alleging business indiscretions by Sophie and other misbehavior by Murray. Before the March 14 meeting with the countess, the tabloid's staff had taped earlier conversations with her partner in which they probed for damaging or embarrassing revelations.

Damage Control Attempted

Once Sophie learned the real purpose of the Dorchester meeting, RJH attorneys moved quickly to limit potential damage by pressing legal action against the tale-telling employee and the *News of the World*.

The countess also contacted Buckingham Palace and talked with the Queen's private secretary and the director of communications for the monarchy. At this point, nothing had yet appeared in the media. The two palace officials met on Wednesday, March 21, with leaders of the Press Complaints Council (PCC) to solicit advice and explore alternatives.

The PCC is an independent body that investigates complaints from the public concerning the editorial content of British newspapers and magazines. The PCC has no contemporary counterpart in the United States. The council examines complaints under the code of practice, a self-regulatory guide that applies to all national and regional newspapers and magazines. The publications' editors drafted the code. In a typical year, about 60% of complaints concern questions of accuracy, and most of the remainder allege intrusions on privacy.

In the confidential meeting at Buckingham Palace, the PCC executives apparently gave conventional advice: Wait for publication, and then submit a formal complaint if warranted; or, contact the newspaper promptly, and try to arrange some accommodation or compromise. The second alternative was chosen.

An Exchange Leads to an Interview

When the palace communications director talked with the tabloid's editor, the two agreed on a trade. In exchange for the tapes and a promise to keep material from the Dorchester meeting out of the newspaper, the tabloid could have an exclusive interview with the countess if it would permit palace officials to review the story and headline before publication.

On Thursday, March 22, a reporter for the *News of the World* sat down with the Countess of Wessex in Buckingham Palace for an unprecedented interview. With the palace communications director sitting nearby, Sophie Wessex answered questions about some of the most private details of her life. She talked about her fertility, the couple's desire for children, and rumors concerning her husband's sexual orientation.

Before the exclusive interview was published, information on the fake sheikh's transcripts—which the *News of the World* had agreed to suppress—somehow got into the hands of editors at competing tabloids. When the *News of the World* ran its interview under the headline "Sophie: My Edward is NOT gay" on Sunday, April 1, a competing tabloid on the same newsstands carried an account of the conversations secretly recorded at the Dorchester.

Tape Transcripts Published

One week later, the *News of the World* broke its promise and devoted its cover and nine more pages to the taped conversations. The verbatims included comments from Murray Harkin acknowledging a familiarity with cocaine and suggesting he knew young men who might be interested in dinner parties.

On the tapes, Sophie's comments were less surprising though certainly indiscreet. London's *Sunday Telegraph* quoted her as hinting that clients might possibly get "some kind of additional profile or benefit from being involved with us because of my situation...."

Her incidental remarks included references to Prime Minister Tony Blair and his wife that were at times flattering and at other times critical. Similarly, she commented both favorably and unfavorably on other public figures, including her brother-in-law Charles, the Prince of Wales.

In Great Britain, the royal family is expected to remain completely detached from politics and partisanship. For this reason, her comments on the national budget and the parties' leaders represented the most notable neglect of protocol.

The Palace Goes Public

As many Britons were poring over the Sunday newspaper accounts of the tapes, Queen Elizabeth called the Earl and Countess of Wessex to meet with her at Windsor Castle, just outside London. Later in the day, the Buckingham Palace news office issued two statements—the first for the queen and the other for the countess.

The first said (using the original capitalization):

> The Queen has discussed issues arising from this week's media coverage with The Earl and Countess of Wessex.
>
> Her Majesty accepts that despite the difficulties of recent days, both the Earl and Countess understandably want to try to pursue working careers and they have her full support in doing so. It is not an easy option and they are breaking new ground, but it is right in this day and age that they should be allowed to do so.
>
> In following careers they are always open to accusations of exploiting their Royal status in pursuit of their own business interests. Both the Earl and the Countess vigorously deny that they have deliberately set out to do so. The Queen deplores the entrapment, subterfuge and innuendo and untruths to which The Earl and Countess have been subjected in recent days.
>
> The Queen recognizes that there are and always have been real issues around ensuring, and being seen to ensure, that Royal and business interests do not conflict where members of the Royal Family pursue their own careers. Ways to address and avoid such potential conflicts of interest need to be reconsidered in light of this episode and this will be done over the coming weeks.
>
> Whilst this is undertaken, The Countess of Wessex has suggested, and The Queen has agreed, that The Countess of Wessex should step aside as Chairman of RJH, as the issues facing the company are considered.

The statement from Sophie covered much of the same territory. She expressed both regret at causing embarrassment and appreciation for support she received from the monarch and from colleagues.

"I believe my overriding duty is to support The Queen and the Monarchy," her statement said (original capitalization retained). "I realize fully that I am in a privileged position, and I am conscious that my conduct must be above reproach. I am deeply distressed by the carrying out of an entrapment operation on me and my business but I also much regret my own misjudgement in succumbing to that subterfuge."

Resignation Precedes Expulsion

As Buckingham Palace issued its two statements, RJH Public Relations issued one of its own, announcing the departure of Murray Harkin and introducing his successor. It made no reference to the reason for the resignation or the turmoil of the preceding week.

Three days later, the Institute of Public Relations (IPR), a professional association whose 6,500 members included the countess and her partner, announced an inquiry into Murray's role in the mess. The IPR is similar to the Public Relations Society of America.

"The Institute of Public Relations confirms that it has launched a preliminary inquiry into the allegations made against Mr. Murray Harkin in a national newspaper," it said. "The IPR has asked Mr. Harkin for a statement of circumstances surrounding the matters reported in the *News of the World*. The institute has received a number of approaches from members concerned that he may have breached the institute's code of professional conduct and has brought the profession into disrepute."

Although the London tabloids and other British media provided generous coverage of Sophie's indiscretions, the widely respected *Economist* weekly newspaper offered barely a yawn in its edition of April 14, commenting:

"At most, the Sophie tapes bear on the moderately interesting but minor question of whether it is possible for a moderately interesting but minor royal to work in a sensitive career such as public relations without becoming entangled, by accident or design, in a conflict of interest."

The IPR was less charitable toward Murray. In October 2001, it expelled him after he failed to offer any answers in the institute's inquiry into the circumstances of the meetings with the fake sheikh.

QUESTIONS FOR REFLECTION

1. Sophie Wessex was a public relations professional with 16 years of experience when she fell for the tabloid newspaper's sting. What might she have done to prevent the embarrassment?

2. The communications director at Buckingham Palace struck a deal with the tabloid newspaper to trade an interview with the countess for the surreptitious tapes. What more favorable terms might he have proposed?

3. What advice would you have given the countess on preparing for the interview with the tabloid?

4. In editorial comment, the *Economist* asked whether a member of the royal family could "work in a sensitive career such a public relations without becoming entangled ... in a conflict of interest." What are the risks?

Information for this case was drawn from the following: the British Monarchy's Web site at http://www.royal.gov.uk/output/page231.asp; the RJH Public Relations Web site at http://www.rjhpr.co.uk/about.htm; Alderson, A. (8 July 2001), "Edward and Sophie glad to remain royal workers," *The Telegraph*, p. 1; (14 April 2001), "Bagehot: The royal appendix," *The Economist*, p. 56; Greenslade, R. (9 April 2001), "A sting in the tale," *The Guardian*, p. 1; (7 April 2001), "Inside Sophie's PR business," *BBC News*, http://www.bbc.co.uk/1/hi/uk/1265452.stm; McAllister, A. (23 April 2001), "Cinderella, career gal," *TIME*, p. 8; Reid, T. (3 April 2001), "Royals stung by Brit tabloid's fake sheik," *The Washington Post*, p. C1; Reid, T. (9 April 2001), "British tabloid prints Sophie's choice words," *The Washington Post*, p. C2; (11 April 2001), "Sophie Wessex and Mr. Murray Harkin," *Institute of Public Relations*, press release; Summerskill, B. (8 April 2001), "Fallout of a royal farce," *The Observer*, p. 1; and (accessed 14 August 2003), "What is the PCC?" *Press Complaints Commission*, http://www.pcc.org.uk/about/whatis.html.

CASE 19.   BISHOPS, PRIESTS, AND REPORTERS: THE CATHOLIC CHURCH AND MEDIA COVERAGE OF SEX-ABUSE SCANDALS

The scandals involving how the Catholic hierarchy dealt with priests accused or suspected of improper sexual behaviors became national news after the *Boston Globe*'s Pulitzer Prize-winning January 2002 series reported that Catholic priest John Geoghan, accused of molesting children in his parishes, had for more than three decades been shuffled from parish assignment to parish assignment rather than being turned over to authorities for prosecution. Although there had been some coverage of the issue in 1985 when the U.S. Conference of Catholic Bishops adopted policies that were to address how the Church would deal with such troubled priests, renewed media coverage of the issue captured the attention of other reporters, attorneys, Catholic laity, government officials, and self-reported victims across the nation and across the world.

After the *Globe* series began, similar revelations then came from across the country—bishops in Palm Beach, Lexington, Milwaukee, and New York resigned after it became known that priests in their dioceses had also been reassigned rather than turned over to civilian authorities for prosecution. Investigative articles appeared in Dallas and in other Boston newspapers, as well as on ABC and NBC News, and then appeared in newspapers and broadcast stations across the country as self-reported victims came forward, pressing suits and seeking to tell their stories. To help journalists understand developments across the country, The Poynter Institute for Media Studies hosted an Abuse Tracker on its Web site where published stories could be posted for referrals.

Since the scandal became public, more than 225 clergy (of the more than 46,000 U.S. priests) have been taken off duty or have resigned, according to the Associated Press. Six U.S. bishops have resigned in connection with the scandal, and priests and bishops from Australia, Hong Kong, South Africa, Ireland, Poland, and Canada were implicated in either the scandal or cover-ups of sex-abuse cases. *PR Week* reported in April 2002 that since 1985, the church had paid an estimated $1 billion to resolve molestation charges against its priests.

Church's Response to Stories Varies

The Catholic leadership responded to the media stories and lawsuits in numerous ways, ranging from negotiations to denials to acts of penance. Andrew Walsh, writing in the fall 2002 *Religion in the News*, said, "The American bishops are caught between a Vatican that resists structural change, and a laity and media that want more accountability." In an April 2002 article in *PRWeek*, James Burnett detailed some of the problems with the church's reaction to the crisis. The church did not use a single spokesperson, but used a variety of local leaders. Different parishes developed and instituted different plans for dealing with past and existing abuse crimes. Church leaders were often too slow to respond when the allegations became public, thereby allowing time for media coverage to set the public agenda.

Some dioceses did make some effort to counter media coverage. The Los Angeles Archdiocese hired crisis communication specialists Sitrick & Co. to help it communicate newly adopted policies dealing with sexual offenders. In the summer of 1997, the Diocese of Dallas, Texas, had hired a public relations counselor to help it respond when it was ordered to pay damages totaling nearly $120 million for harboring a priest who had molested children. The Diocese of Oakland established its Ministry for Victims of Clergy Sexual Abuse; the chancellor of the diocese, Sister Barbara Flannery, acted as spokesperson for the diocese during the crisis.

One example of the church's delayed reactions to intense media coverage: A 76-page report compiled by the Massachusetts attorney general released in July 2003 reported that at least 789 children and perhaps more than 1,000 were abused by 250 priests and other church workers since 1940; the report was based on a 16-month investigation that involved the review of 30,000 pages of church documents and 100 hours of grand-jury testimony. A church spokesperson issued a written statement the afternoon the report was released saying the archdiocese would review the findings over the next few days "before making any further public response."

Anvil Publishing reported that Donna Morrisey, spokesperson for the Archdiocese of Boston, told a March 20, 2003, meeting of the Boston PRSA that she believed she had not been kept fully informed about the clergy scandal in Boston. She said she was only able to admit there had been problems after thousands of documents became public following a court order to open them. The documents detailed the abuses and the church's knowledge of them. She and only one administrative assistant worked to field up to 300 media calls a day during the crisis.

Lay Catholics reported they felt the church had mishandled the crisis, according to results of a *New York Times*–CBS poll cited in the June 2002 edition of *Baptists Today*. Only 27% of the Catholics interviewed said the leaders had done a good job of handling the issue, although some 63% approved of their parish priest. The poll of 1,172 adults reported that 88% said church leaders should be held responsible for the way they deal with the problem. A group of laypersons within the Catholic Church formed an activist group, Voice of the Faithful, to seek reform within the church.

The Leadership Contemplates Changes

The U.S. Conference of Catholic Bishops did attempt to forge a response to the crisis. The conference assembled in Dallas in June 2002, but *PR Week* called what ensued nothing less than a "communications circus." More than 700 U.S. and international journalists and numerous activists arrived to cover the meeting. For the first time at such a meeting, laypersons were invited to address the bishops. The bishops released the Charter for the Protection of Children and Young People, which called for local dioceses to form oversight committees to be staffed by laity. Accused priests were to be treated with "zero tolerance." Kathleen McChesney, a former FBI official, was selected to run the office that would audit U.S. dioceses to determine if they were following the guidelines to prevent abuses.

However, the Vatican did not approve the U.S. plan for intervention. Pope John Paul II argued that the "zero tolerance" policy did not demonstrate a belief in repentance or forgiveness, and thus he told the U.S. cardinals to reconsider procedures for dealing with priests. Catholic bishops met in Washington in November 2002 to consider how they would adapt their plans to the Vatican's orders. This time the conference was more private; Bishop Wilton Gregory, president of the U.S. Conference of Catholic Bishops, would not agree to media interviews until after the discussion and vote. (The group did revise its guidelines to comply with the Vatican's orders.)

Following the U.S. crisis, the Catholic Church of England and Wales released a set of public relations guidelines. The approach called for openness and the creation of a new oversight group, the Church Office for the Protection of Children and Vulnerable Adults.

A U.S. oversight committee was also formed. It was initially headed by former Oklahoma Gov. Frank Keating, president of the American Council of Life Insurers. The committee of laypeople included businesspeople, attorneys, a psychiatrist and psychologist, and former White Chouse chief of staff Leon E. Panetta. The group was asked to issue an annual report. However, before such a report could be issued, the group became involved in its own public controversy. In May, Los Angeles Cardinal Roger M. Mahony had led the California bishops to pass a resolution saying they would not respond to the committee's surveys that had been designed to assess the extent of the abuse problem in the church. New York Cardinal Edward M. Egan told a council of priests that he would not reveal names of accused priests nor how the cases had been resolved. Keating then gave an interview to the *Los Angeles Times* in which he said the bishops were somewhat like "La Cosa Nostra" in their willingness to cover up wrongdoing. Following that interview, a majority of the 13-person board of laypeople said the comments were inappropriate and that Keating should resign. In June 2003, he did so, which prompted a renewed concentration of media attention on the Church. After resigning, Keating wrote a June 19 *New York Times* op-ed piece in which he outlined his views about the church's future. Acknowledging that he was resigning in order to resume working full time and from frustration over the lack of cooperation from what he called a "small minority of church leaders," he went on to say that he was optimistic that the board's work would be successful. He wrote a "few opponents of the board have said we went too far, engaging in what one resistant diocesan newspaper termed a 'witch hunt.' " Keating said a few leaders "turned to their lawyers when they should have looked in their hearts." However, he wrote, the responsibility of the board, church leaders, and laity is to restore "trust in our church. That work continues. With God's help, it will succeed in cleansing the church of a vast stain."

Coverage Continues

Public disclosures about the crisis continued throughout the summer of 2003, as bishops in New Hampshire and Arizona revealed they had signed government agreements indicating there had been some diocese involvement with reassigning accused priests. On a more positive note, in August 2003, following the resignation of Boston Archbishop Bernard Law, Sean O'Malley was appointed as archbishop to provide leadership in Boston where the media crisis had begun. According to the *New York Times*, one of his first actions was to dismiss the attorneys who had been negotiating settlements and to hire an attorney he had worked with earlier to reach settlements with abuse victims in his former parish. Within days, he announced the first concrete settlement of $55 million for 542 victims. The actions were greeted with positive media coverage across the country.

QUESTIONS FOR REFLECTION

1. The scandal offers an ongoing example of the powerful interaction of media, opinion leaders, government, and sources. Identify the priority publics for the U.S. Catholic Church within this crisis. What would have characterized effective communication interactions with each?
2. Journalists covering this story often reflected publicly about their struggles with the ethical and moral ways to report stories involving an organization to which they and/or many readers were deeply committed. What principles should guide such coverage?
3. This crisis involved privacy issues involving priests, victims, and settlements. What principles should guide public communications about such sensitive issues?
4. The Roman Catholic Church is a highly diverse, international organization. What does this crisis imply about the need for crisis planning for such organizations?

Information for this case was drawn from numerous press stories about the crisis, including Associated Press. (13 August 2003), "Files show archdiocese paid $21 million in abuse cases," *The New York Times*; Barnett, D. (18 October 2002), "Vatican rejects U.S. bishops' sex abuse guidelines," *Agence France Presse*; Burnett, J. (22 April 2002), "Crisis and the cross," *PRWeek*, p. 17; Butterfield, F. (24 July 2003), "789 children abused by priests since 1940, Massachusetts says," *The New York Times*; Chabria, A. (17 June 2002), "Comms circus ensues as Catholic bishops convene," *PRWeek*, p. 3; Chabria, A. (1 July 2002), "Church starts long journey to PR redemption in Dallas," *PRWeek*, p. 9; Chabria, A. (10 June 2002), "LA archdiocese accused of generating a 'PR snafu,' " *PRWeek*, p. 2; Chabria, A. (2 September 2002), "New cathedral helps rebuild LA archdiocese's reputation," *PRWeek*, p. 2; DePasquale, R. (23 July 2002), "Archdiocese rebuffs reform group," *AP Online*; Editorial. (12 August 2003), "Boston's exemplary friar," *The New York Times*; Goodstein, L. (13 June 2003), "Bishops uneasy on whom to protect," *The New York Times*; Goodstein, L. (16 June 2003),   *(continued)*

(*continued*)   "Chief of panel on priest abuse will step down," *The New York Times*; Goodstein, L. (11 June 2003), "Louisville archdiocese to pay $25 million abuse settlement," *The New York Times*; Griese, N., (Ed.) (April 2003), "Boston archdiocese spokeswoman: PR was kept in the dark on crisis," *Crisis Counselor*, www.anvilpub.com/cc_april_2003.htm; Hood, J. (13 May 2002), "Media drawn to church's abuse-prevention program," *PRWeek*, p. 4; Keating, F. (19 June 2003), "Finding hope in my faith," *The New York Times*; Lampman, J. (6 November 2002), "Bishops walk fine line on abuse policy," *The Christian Science Monitor*, p. 3; LeDuff, C. (3 June 2003), "Phoenix bishop admits moving accused priests," *The New York Times*; Lepper, J. (6 May 2002), "US scandal prompts UK church's PR drive," *PRWeek*, p. 4; Nolan, B. (10 November 2002), "U.S. bishops to vote on revised policy," (New Orleans, LA) *Times-Picayune*, p. 1; Patriot Ledger staff and news services (18 October 2002), "Lawyer: 'It's no surprise': Felt they were sacrificed, priests hail the decision," *The Patriot Ledger* (MA), p. 1; Paulson, M. (27 April 2002), "Law seeks to curb organizing by laity," *Boston Globe*, p. A1; Paulson, M. (17 December 2002), "Vatican: Final OK given to U.S. bishops; child-protection policy," *Boston Globe*, p. A39; Pfeiffer, S., & Carroll, M. (23 July 2002), "Law to reject donations from Voice of the Faithful," *Boston Globe*, p. A1; Religious News Service (June 2002), "Poll shows divide between lay Catholics, church leaders," *Baptists Today*, p. 16; Rezendes, M., & Robinson, W. V. (23 November 2002), "Church tries to block public access to files," *Boston Globe*, p. A1; Sims, C. (3 April 2003), "Boston archdiocese is sued by San Bernardino diocese," *The New York Times*; Walsh, A. (Summer 2002), "Bishops up against the wall," *Religion in the News*, 5(2), 8–11; Walsh, A. (Fall 2002), "Scandal without end," and "After the *Globe*," *Religion in the News*, 5(3), 4–7; White, G. (5 June 2002), "Church may ban future molesters," *The Atlanta Journal-Constitution*, p. A3; and Zezima, K. (21 July 2003), "Massachusetts won't charge church chiefs in sex scandal," *The New York Times*. The Poynter Institute for Media Studies maintained an "Abuse Tracker: A digest of links to media coverage of clergy abuse" on its Web site at www.poynter.org.

CASE 20.   *BOWLING FOR COLUMBINE* STRIKES AMMUNITION SALES AT KMART CORP.

Public relations practitioners may have become used to e-mailed questions or phone calls from reporters, and some have faced the glare of video cameras from "60 Minutes" or "Dateline" television reporters. Imagine, however, being called to the lobby of corporate headquarters to respond to a request from documentary filmmaker and social critic Michael Moore to accept the "return" of bullets purchased at a Kmart store that were used in the 1999 Columbine High School shootings in Littleton, Colorado, bullets that were now lodged in the bodies of students who survived the assaults.

Kmart public relations practitioners at the corporation's headquarters in Troy, Michigan, did indeed have to respond to such a request—and used it as an opportunity to announce a change in corporate marketing strategy that turned what could have been a dark and painful media image for the retail chain into a strong statement of corporate social responsibility captured in the documentary *Bowling for Columbine*.

Prize-Winning Documentary Investigates Gun Violence

Bowling for Columbine, which won the 55th Anniversary Prize at the 2002 Cannes Film Festival and the 2003 Oscar for documentaries, was directed by Michael Moore. Moore is well known for his first documentary, the 1989 *Roger & Me*, in which he attempted to question the CEO of General Motors, Roger Smith, about the closing of a GM plant in Flint, Michigan, and for other books and film projects that focus on American corporate and political policies Moore finds unacceptable.

The *Bowling* documentary focuses on gun violence and fear in America. It includes investigations into the shooting of a child by a child in Flint, Michigan, an interview with National Rifle Association (NRA) president Charlton Heston, and gun sales and use in Canada. The emotional climax of the documentary, however, may lie in the two visits Moore makes to Kmart corporate headquarters with the students. The ammunition used by the teenage killers at the high school had been purchased at Kmart.

Film critic Roger Ebert described the documentary's scene this way: "The moment comes at the conclusion of one of the public psychodramas he has become expert in staging, in which he dramatizes evildoing (as defined by Moore) in the way calculated to maximize the embarrassment of the evildoer."

The first visit to the headquarters was brief. A public relations official met with the three. Then, Moore and the young students are shown shopping in a Kmart store where the teens purchase many rounds of ammunition to remove them from the store.

The second visit to headquarters was quite different. That time, a corporate spokesperson announced that Kmart will phase out the sale of ammunition over the next 90 days. The cancellation of ammunition sales was to be completed within 3 months as stocks were depleted. Company officials made the announcement in June 2001 at a press conference following a 4-hour meeting of executives, Moore, and the students. Moore said, "I'm totally, totally stunned by the response from Kmart today."

Company spokesperson Julie Fracker told the Associated Press that the abolition of sale of guns and ammunition was based on marketing concerns and had been under review prior to the filmmaker's visit. "Obviously, we consider ourselves a socially conscious business, but this was a business decision made in the best interests of the company," she said.

Moore said he got the surprise of his life when Kmart officials announced they would quit selling handgun ammunition. Moore told the *Sacramento Bee*: "It stunned me. You can see it in the film. I'm so used to rejection."

The president and CEO of National Shooting Sports Foundation commented on the decision for the Associated Press, saying: "It is both unfortunate and inappropriate that Mr. Moore has used media scare tactics to strong arm Kmart into making this decision. All Americans are deeply concerned about the issue of school violence, but to blame a retailer who sells ammunition for causing these tragedies is intellectually lazy and dishonest."

(The documentary came at a time of economic crisis for the chain. Kmart Corp. became the largest U.S. retailer ever to seek bankruptcy protection in January 2002 when it filed for Chapter 11 reorganization. The reorganization strategy included closing more than 320 stores and one distribution center. The corporation emerged from bankruptcy in spring 2003.)

Previous Lawsuits Targeted Gun Sales at Kmart

Moore was not the first celebrity to focus attention on Kmart's gun and ammunition sales. Before the filming of the documentary, celebrity spokesperson Rosie O'Donnell had resigned from her representation of Kmart in protest of its gun and ammunition sales. Activist groups had protested sales at Kmart and other large retailers.

Kmart had faced increasing costs for insurance against liabilities for workers' compensation plans and for gun sales. In 2001, Kmart was ordered to pay $1.5 million in compensation and another $1.5 million in punitive damages to the parents of a Park City, Utah, man who had purchased a 12-gauge shotgun, which he used the next day to commit suicide. The gun was sold by a 17-year-old salesperson who the store's ex-security officer testified had never signed a gun-sales training manual indicating he had read it.

In 1993 Kmart had been ordered to pay $12.5 million in damages to a women left a quadriplegic after being shot by her former boyfriend with a .22-caliber rifle he bought at a Kmart in West Palm Beach, Florida. The ex-boyfriend was reportedly so intoxicated when he purchased the rifle that he could not legibly complete the federal firearms form required by law, and the Kmart clerk completed the form for him, *Business Week* reported. The corporation appealed the ruling.

QUESTIONS FOR REFLECTION

1. How may an organization or individual prepare for hostile media inquiries or "ambush" interviews? Conversely, how may an organization or individual benefit from speaking out on issues brought onto the public's agenda by news coverage?
2. Documentaries and film offer a depth of coverage unlike that found in most media. Are there special practices that should be used in this type of media relations?
3. How should corporations respond when faced with liability lawsuits? What responsibilities do organizations assume when they manufacture or sell products that require due care in use?

Information for this case was drawn from Associated Press (2 July 2001),"Kmart pulls handgun ammo from shelves," ESPN.com; Ebert, R. (7 September 2002), "Moore hits corporate target in 'Columbine,' " *Chicago Sun-Times*, p. 22; Hunt, S. (14 September 2001), "Federal jury tells Kmart to pay another $1.5 million," *The Salt Lake Tribune*, www.sltrib.com; Merrick, A. (22 January 2002), "Kmart lays out plans to trim its size, boost efficiency, in bankruptcy filing," *The Wall Street Journal*, WSJ.com; Kmart Corp.(14 January 2003), "Kmart received commitment for $2 billion in exit financing as company prepares to emerge from Chapter 11," *PR Newswire*; Reid, D. (25 October 2002), "'I'm trying to connect the dots between the local violence and the global violence,' says director Michael Moore of his new film, 'Bowling for Columbine.' " *Sacramento Bee*, accessed at www.bowlingforcolumbine.com/reviews/2002-10-25-sacra.php. More information about the documentary is also available at that Web site.

6

Stakeholders: Investors

One of the hottest business news stories of 2004 involved speculation about Google's plan for an initial public offering (IPO) of common stock. Created in 1998 by two Stanford University graduate students, Google quickly replaced Yahoo! as the world's leading Web search site and was handling more than 200 million queries daily when rumors about an IPO began circulating.

Web users knew that Google was technologically successful, but hard information about its performance as a company—its operating and financial results—was unavailable. As a privately held company, Google was not obligated to share the details with anyone. It did not publish an annual report and did not release quarterly earnings.

The *Wall Street Journal* said that people familiar with the numbers estimated 2003 revenues at $800 million and net income between $100 million and $200 million. Google generated revenues by selling advertising space on its web pages and by licensing its search technology to companies like Time Warner's America Online.

AN ATTRACTIVE INVESTMENT

If the estimates were correct, the company clearly represented an appealing investment opportunity: Its net profit margin exceeded 12% (at least a third higher than the margin of public technology companies at the time), and its usage growth rate was the best in its business segment.

The people who built Google into a valuable property had few avenues to access the wealth they had created. Venture capital firms had provided funds for Google's growth. The founders and other employees had devoted their human capital—ingenuity, talent, time, faith—to make the enterprise successful. People had risked cash and careers to start the company, manage it effectively, and earn its top ranking. Now, gaining a financial reward beyond a paycheck would require changing the company from a privately held organization into a public stock corporation with shares trading on an exchange.

The *Wall Street Journal* and other business media said that investment bankers estimated Google's value at $15 billion to $25 billion. The value, or market capitalization, would be the product of the number of Google shares sold multiplied by the price per share.

INVESTMENT BANKERS

Companies generally use investment bankers, such as Merrill Lynch or Goldman Sachs, for help in issuing new securities, such as an IPO of common stocks. The investment bankers offer expertise in:

- Setting the price at which stocks will start trading.
- Lining up likely investors in advance.
- Using broker networks to create a market for the securities once they are available.

Investment bankers also help companies prepare the documents they are required to file with the SEC in advance of an IPO. For weeks before a public offering of stock and for weeks afterward, companies face SEC restrictions on what they may say publicly about their operations, their outlook, or their results. This interval is called the quiet period, and its purpose is to restrain exuberant promotion of stocks. It applies to all newly registered securities—not just IPOs.

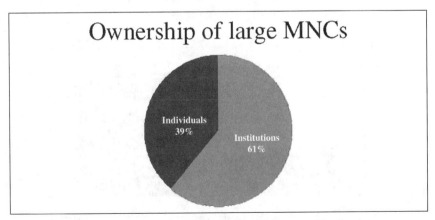

Institutional investors held 61 percent of total shares in large multinational corporations surveyed for PricewaterhouseCoopers in 2002. Individuals owned 39 percent. (Source: PricewaterhouseCoopers. Chart by L. Lamb.)

Companies generally avoid publicity during the quiet period and use their Web sites to fully disclose relevant information in dispassionate terms. In investor relations, the quiet period is a sensitive time. Fearful of risking SEC sanctions, practitioners often avoid the media altogether because the SEC has provided little guidance.

QUIET PERIOD NOT DEFINED

According to the SEC:

> The term "quiet period," also referred to as the "waiting period," is not defined under the federal securities laws. The quiet period extends from the time a company files a registration statement with the SEC until SEC staff declares the registration statement "effective." During this period, the federal securities laws limit what information a company and related parties may release to the public ....

> Despite the restrictions, the SEC has encouraged companies to continue making normal corporate announcements in the ordinary course of business during the quiet period.

When the quiet period has ended, companies are free to provide investors and potential investors with as much information as they might need to make a sound decision on whether to buy, sell, or hold securities. Additionally, the commission watches companies closely to ensure that investor information does not frame the facts to emphasize the good news and obscure the bad news. Regulations also govern the minimum amount of information that companies must disclose.

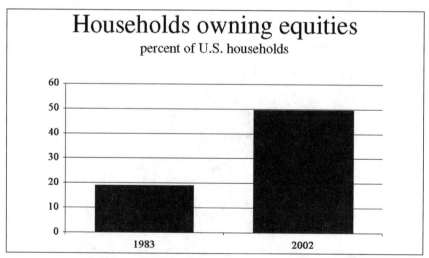

According to The New York Times, the proportion of U.S. households owning shares of stock or mutual funds rose to 49.5 percent in 2002 from 19 percent in 1983. (Source: New York Times. Chart by L. Lamb.)

SEC GOALS

The SEC describes its role like this:

> The laws and rules that govern the securities industry in the United States derive from a simple and straightforward concept: all investors, whether large institutions or private individuals, should have access to certain basic facts about an investment prior to buying it. To achieve this, the SEC requires public companies to disclose meaningful financial and other information to the public, which provides a common pool of knowledge for all investors to use to judge for themselves if a company's securities are a good investment. Only through the steady flow of timely, comprehensive and accurate information can people make sound investment decisions.

After the collapse of stock prices in 2000, a series of financial scandals involving Wall Street investment firms, companies such as Enron, and their corporate executives made the SEC even more vigilant.

The commission adopted a new rule in 2000 to prevent an inequitable distribution of information that might benefit large or well-connected investors at the expense of smaller investors or those less sophisticated. The fair disclosure rule, known as Regulation FD, aims to give everyone an equal chance to gain from stock market opportunities and avoid losses in market declines.

According to the SEC, "Regulation FD provides that when an issuer discloses material nonpublic information to certain individuals or entities—generally, securities market professionals, such as stock analysts, or holders of the issuer's securities who may well trade on the basis of the information—the issuer must make public disclosure of that information. In this way, the new rule aims to promote the full and fair disclosure."

INSTITUTIONAL AND INDIVIDUAL INVESTORS

In the United States and many other nations that rely on free-market capitalism to drive the economy, the ownership of stock equities—either directly or through mutual funds—is common. In 2002, the *New York Times* said an estimate from investment-industry research indicates half of all U.S. households own shares in companies or mutual funds. In the preceding 20 years, the proportion of households with equity ownership more than doubled.

Many individuals and families have built up investment portfolios in stocks and mutual funds through 401(k) plans offered by employers. Usually, an employer contributes a certain amount for each dollar that an employee puts in the plan. Some companies offer employee stock ownership programs, using a system similar to a 401(k) plan, that enable employees to buy stock in the employer at a discount.

Investor relations professionals agree that companies now must do a better job of informing individual investors about business plans, performance, and prospects. Many practitioners have been accustomed to focusing their communications efforts on institutional investors.

Compared with individual investors, institutional investors are small in number but huge in the volume of shares they own and trade. Institutional investors include pension funds, such as CalPERS (California Public Employees' Retirement System); mutual funds, such as the Vanguard Group; insurance companies, such as Prudential; and similar large financial organizations.

The value of institutional holdings is immense. For example, CalPERs alone owned 523,100 shares of AT&T Corporation at midyear 2002, with a market value of about $5.6 million. The pension fund held almost $100 billion in total equities.

PAYING ATTENTION TO INDIVIDUALS

A report issued by PricewaterhouseCooper in 2002 said that institutional investors own 62% of the shares in most large multinational companies, and individual investors own 38%. Individual ownership accounts for a higher proportion of smaller companies' shares and probably is close to half of the shares of all public companies.

Investor Relations Business, a twice monthly magazine for investor relations and public relations professionals, has said that companies should use their Web sites more effectively to build relationships with their individual investors.

"Although individual investors prefer to get information directly from the web site of the company they want to invest in, in many cases the IR section is not up to date," the magazine said.

ADDITIONAL READINGS

Droms, William G. (1997). *Finance and accounting for non-financial managers*. Reading, MA: Addison-Wesley.

Hermann, Keith R. (2001). *Visualizing your business: Let graphics tell the story*. New York: Wiley.

Kurtz, Howard. (2000). *The fortune tellers: Inside wall street's game of money, media and manipulation*. New York: The Free Press.

Walton, Wesley S., & Joseph M. Lesko. (2002). *Corporate communications handbook: A guide to press releases and other informal disclosure for public corporations*. New York: Clark Boardman Callaghan.

CASE 21. THE COMMUNICATIONS COMPANY THAT DIDN'T COMMUNICATE: WORLDCOM FACES A WORLD-RECORD BANKRUPTCY AND LEADERSHIP SCANDAL

In the 1980s and 1990s, under the leadership of CEO Bernie Ebbers, WorldCom grew into the second-largest telecommunications company in America. Then, in 2002, the corporation filed the largest bankruptcy in history after losing more than $120 billion of equity in 3 years. Ebbers himself was named as part of a $4 billion fraud case.

The story of the company may in essence be the story of its CEO and his interactions with board members and employees. Pai Sarkar, writing in the December 27, 2002, *San Francisco Chronicle*, concluded: "It was just one man, one company, one downfall. But in the grander scheme of men and companies and downfalls, Bernie Ebbers of WorldCom stuck out as a glaring example of what went wrong with corporate America in a year defined by greed and deceit—and the loss of public trust." As such, it illustrates the need for truthful, timely communication with board members, shareholders, employees, creditors, analysts, and regulators.

Bernie Ebbers Builds a Network

Ebbers was a charismatic CEO, known for his personal Christian faith and charity work. Born in Edmonton, Canada, he was raised in New Mexico where his father was a business manager for a Christian mission. Reports say Ebbers flunked out of the University of Alberta and Calvin College before enrolling at Mississippi College, where Ebbers said his life changed. He graduated in 1967 and went to work as a teacher and coach in a small town south of Mississippi's capital, Jackson. He then founded a small chain of hotels, working with two friends who later sat on the WorldCom board.

In 1983, he and several other businessmen took advantage of the AT&T telephone breakup and started a company that would resell bandwidth, the data-carrying capacity of telephone lines, to small businesses. Sensing an opportunity, he bought 75 companies in the next 15 years. He took his company, Long Distance Discount Service, public in 1989. It was reported that Ebbers boasted that LDDS never grew at less than 16%.

He encouraged employees to buy stock options, a practice that would continue throughout his career. His practice of offering large personal loans to key employees in order for them to buy stock was well known. He also became known as not being involved in the actual operations of the telecommunication industry, but intensely interested in the possibilities for mergers and acquisitions within it.

In the early 1990s, Ebbers began to buy companies that owned fiber-optic lines so that he could move data on his own lines. In August 1994, he bought Wiltel, a Tulsa, Oklahoma, company that owned the fourth-largest fiber network in the

United States, and renamed it WorldCom. That enabled him to take advantage of the burst of interest in the Internet during the mid-1990s.

By 1997, WorldCom owned 20% of the Internet fiber network, and the corporation grew like wildfire. The stock value attracted investors who put all their funds in the one stock. On June 21, 1999, WorldCom stock reached a high of $64.50 per share, and Ebbers was listed by *Forbes* as among the richest men in the world, ranking his personal fortune at some $1.4 billion. Ebbers reportedly enjoyed his wealth. He paid $47 million to buy the largest working ranch in Canada, a half-million acre spread with cattle, a fishing village, and a heavy-equipment dealership.

In 1997, Ebbers made his boldest move, buying MCI's residential and long-distance telephone service for $37 billion. Yet, he sold off its Internet network when faced with federal regulators' protests about fears of limiting fiber-optic competition. A 1999 attempt to merge with Sprint was blocked by American and European regulators. At the same time, growth in the Internet dropped by 90%. Stock values dropped. Ebbers' fortune also dropped; he was forced to sell 3 million shares of his WorldCom stock in October 2000 to raise $84 million to pay off investment debts.

Ebbers prepared to sell more shares in January 2002. The WorldCom board, afraid that such a sale would drop the stock value even further below the $9.80 it was then valued at, loaned Ebbers more than $400 million at 2.2% interest.

Reaction to this arrangement created outrage among other investors who had seen their share values drop precipitously. In March, the SEC requested information related to WorldCom accounting procedures and loans to officers. Ebbers resigned in April, taking with him a $1.5-million-a-year pension.

Investigation Reveals a Tangled Network of Accounting

That might have ended the story, had not an investigation revealed other problems. Reports in June 2002 documented that the company had designated $3.8 billion as assets instead of expenses to cover a net loss for 2001 and the first quarter of 2002, and chief financial officer (CFO) Scott Sullivan was fired. Following an internal audit, WorldCom admitted inflating earnings over a period dating back to 1999. For example, it claimed that the costs of leasing telephone lines from other companies were capital investments. It would later argue in court that its internal accounting records were so confused that it was impossible to verify or balance them. (Subsequently, the SEC asserted the improper bookkeeping had totaled more than $9 billion.) The corporation began laying off thousands of employees in June 2002.

The new CEO, John Sidgmore, held a press conference in Washington to apologize for the accounting scandal. He said the company hoped to avoid bankruptcy. However, WorldCom filed for Chapter 11 bankruptcy July 21, 2002, listing $103.9 billion in assets. The corporation owed $67 billion to its creditors. Shares traded at less than $1 by the end of that year. Sidgmore resigned as CEO in September.

Two corporate officers, including CFO Scott Sullivan, were charged in August 2002 by federal officials with securities fraud and filing false statements with the

SEC. In September, the corporation's former controller pleaded guilty to three counts of conspiracy, securities fraud, and making false statements to the SEC. The next month, the former accounting director pleaded guilty to two counts of securities fraud and conspiracy.

Rebuilding a Network for Leadership

In November, WorldCom reached a settlement with the SEC. In December, federal judges approved the hiring of new CEO Michael Cappellas, former Hewlett-Packard president.

The board of directors was also reformed after six directors resigned. The board had included the former head of the National Association of Securities Dealers, the chairman of Moody's Investors Service, and the dean of the Georgetown University Law Center, along with several company chief executives. A report compiled by a committee of new directors said the previous board had been given information that "was both false and plausible." The board had met infrequently, sometimes only 3 to 5 hours a year.

Its operations changed dramatically after the reorganization. New CEO Capellas told the *Washington Post*, "The company has already implemented many of the proposed corporate reforms, but we know we have to do even more to regain public trust." The *Washington Post* described how the new board considered buying remaining shares of Digex Inc. It had been given a detailed report from its investment bankers and a presentation from the corporate development team, and the Digex chairman was available to answer questions. The directors then met privately to discuss the $18 million purchase. The *Post* said the last time WorldCom had considered a deal to buy the corporate "parent" of Digex, Intermedia Communications, the board approved the $6 billion acquisition after only 35 minutes of discussion. Board members had been given no written material to review, and some were not told that such an acquisition was due for a vote until 2 hours before a convened conference call.

The federal monitor, Richard C. Breedon, a former SEC chairman, required the new board to meet at least 10 times a year and to replace at least one member every 12 months. No director would be allowed to remain on the board more than 10 years. With the exception of the CEO, directors were required to have no outside ties to the company. Pay for directors was boosted to $150,000 a year, but they were required to take at least 25% of the salary in stock. Stock options would not be granted to employees and board members. Instead, they would be granted restricted company shares with rules limiting when they could be sold. The cost of the stock grants would be included in profit-and-loss statements.

The reformed corporation took out a full-page advertisement in leading U.S. newspapers in December 2002 to offer what it called a "Summary of Progress." The ads' headline proclaimed, "WorldCom Wants You To Know: From governance to finances, quality of service to customer commitment, we've made significant progress. And we're just beginning." It touted the hiring of a new CEO and new independent board members, the generation of more than $1 billion in cash and available financing, the meeting of service benchmarks, and its ability to retain customers and to attract new ones. More information, the ad said, would be available on the corporate Web site at www.worldcom.com/update.

By April 2003, WorldCom announced a reorganization plan to erase most of its debt and to rename itself after its long-distance unit, MCI. Headquarters for the corporation would be moved to Ashburn, Virginia. The corporation agreed to pay investors $500 million to settle civil fraud charges and a $750 million settlement with federal regulators. According to the *Washington Post*, the corporation emerged from bankruptcy with $4.6 billion in cash.

In August 2003, Ebbers was arraigned and charged by the state of Oklahoma on 15 fraud counts. He pleaded innocent to the charges. Four other executives were charged by the state. Federal investigations continued.

QUESTIONS FOR REFLECTION

1. Working with a powerful CEO can pose challenges for public relations practitioners and others responsible for communicating truthfully within and outside a corporation. What practices might have addressed some of these challenges successfully?
2. How much knowledge of sound business practices is required for the effective practice of investor relations by public relations professionals?
3. How do corporations faced with such scandals regain public trust?

Sources for this case include Catan, T., Kirchgaessner, S., Ratner, J., & Larsen, P. T. (19 December 2002), "Before the fall: How, from the outset, Bernie Ebbers' character and business methods sowed the seeds of disaster," *The Financial Times*, p. 17; Cohn, D., & Herera, S. (28 August 2003), "Former WorldCom CEO Bernie Ebbers to turn himself over to Oklahoma authorities next week to face charges of fraud," *CNBC Business Center*; (4 September 2003), "Former WoldCom CEO pleads not guilty," *Washington Post*, p. E2; Hilzenrath, D. S. (16 June 2003), "How a distinguished roster of board members failed to detect company's problems," *Washington Post*, p. E1; Reuters and washingtonpost.com (5 August 2003), *Timeline of history of WorldCom*, www.washingtonpost.com; Rovella, D. (13 August 2003), "Enron, WorldCom chiefs may never be charged," *The New York Sun*, p. 9; Sarker, P. (27 December 2003), "Year in Review: People in crisis: WorldCom Unravels; Ex-CEO Bernie Ebbers flew high, fell hard and took the telecom giant with him," *San Francisco Chronicle*, p. B1; Staples, D. (1 August 2002), "God, markets, mergers and money: Part I: Edmonston's Bernie Ebbers rose from milkman to herald of the new economy," *Ottawa Citizen*, p. F2; Stark, B. (28 June 2002), "WorldCom begins laying off employees," ABC News "World News Tonight"; Stern, C. (8 September 2003), "Hoping to shed a scandal," *The Washington Post*, p. E1; Stern, C. (6 November 2002), "SEC case against WorldCom grows," *The Washington Post*, p. E1; Stern, C. (16 September 2003), "WorldCom tells of snarled records," *The Washington Post*, p. E1; and (16 December 2002), "Summary of Progress," WorldCom Advertisement, *The Atlanta Journal-Constitution*, p. C5.

CASE 22.   APPEARANCES OR SUBSTANCE: WHICH IS MORE IMPORTANT?

Martha Stewart built a successful international business on the canons of style. Through her books and magazines and television programs, she taught a mostly middle-aged, middle-income audience how to prepare foods that look as great as they taste, how to color-coordinate bath accessories for highest appeal to eye and touch, and how to furnish the family room so that it unites functionality and fashion.

Her focus on perfecting domestic details and controlling each element of graceful living invited parody and lampooning on late-night television, but it also made her popular with millions and made millions of dollars for her as well. Just when she reached the pinnacle of success, she seemed to forget how much appearances count or, perhaps, how easily appearances are misinterpreted.

Raised in a New Jersey family of six children, Martha began her business career as a stockbroker after graduating from Barnard College. Later, she set up her own catering business and won a reputation for staging parties of insuperable taste. From this experience, she wrote *Entertaining*, a book that has sold more than a half-million copies since its first printing in 1982.

Buying Her Own Magazine

Working with Time Warner, she launched *Martha Stewart Living* magazine in 1991 and built up its circulation as editor. In 1997, she bought out her corporate partner's interest and gained control of the publication. At about the same time, Kmart began selling a wide selection of Martha Stewart-brand merchandise that ranged from bath towels to garden trowels. By then, the Martha Stewart media empire had grown to include a syndicated newspaper column, regular appearances on CBS-TV's *Early Show*, her own cable television programs, and more.

The business grew around her personal interests, her talents, her public personality, a winning smile, and dogged determination. She worked extraordinarily hard and received a queen's reward when her company went public in 1999. The IPO of common stock in Martha Stewart Living Omnimedia Inc. began trading at $18 a share on October 19 and raised $149 million in equity capital. On the day of the IPO, Ms. Stewart was present at the New York Stock Exchange to see her company's stock symbol, MSO, appear on the Big Board for the first time. The stock soon rose to $36 in the euphoric securities market of 1999 before settling into the $20s.

Here's how the company has described itself:

> Martha Stewart Living Omnimedia Inc. is a leading provider of original how-to content and products for the home. We leverage the well-known "Martha Stewart" brand name across four business segments—publishing, television, merchandising and internet/direct commerce—and provide consumers with the how-to ideas, products and other resources they need to raise the quality of living in and around their homes.

Our two primary strategic objectives are to provide our original how-to content and information to as many consumers as possible and to turn dreamers into "doers" by offering our consumers the information and products they need for do-it-yourself in-genuity—the "Martha Stewart" way.

The Company Martha Keeps

Three months after the IPO, *Business Week* published a cover story on Martha and her triumphs. The magazine pointed out that the company, though known by its fa-mous founder's name, was led by a management team of broad experience and deep talent.

The president was a former McKinsey & Company consultant and Cablevision Systems Corporation executive. The editor-in-chief had worked for the *New York Times* and *Travel & Leisure* magazine. The creative director had been a publishing executive before joining Stewart in 1990. The chief financial officer had led an IPO at a recording company. Altogether, the staff consisted of more than 400 peo-ple with bright ideas about cooking, crafts, holidays, weddings, babies, and other essentials of the domestic arts.

Yet, Martha was the face, voice, and inspiration known best by customers, in-vestors, and the media. The brand was Martha Stewart, and she was the brand. The two were truly inseparable. Conveniently, the linked identity offered a ready plat-form for expansion into new media ventures and markets. In 2000, *Business Week* pointed out that it also represented a source of risk:

"While the company is now playing up other talent—and taking out massive in-surance policies on its ubiquitous chief—Stewart remains the walking, talking personification of her brand," the business weekly said. "No wonder investors are worried about the fate of their stock if Stewart should, say, choke on a bad batch of butter cream."

A Promising Financial Performance

Investors may have worried about overreliance on Martha Stewart's image, but MSO shareowners certainly relished the company's early financial performance. For the company's first full year of operation as a public traded entity, the 2000 an-nual report listed revenues of $285.8 million dollars and $37.3 million in income before income taxes. Revenues were 23% higher than the preceding year's, and in-come before income taxes was up 63.3%. Overall, prospects looked delicious.

A stock analysis posted on The Motley Fool Web site (www.fool.com) in May 2001 echoed the upbeat rhythm for the company, but it too noted the risk of hitch-ing your future to a single star.

"What happens to the company when there's no Martha?" the author asked. "This is a risk investors should weigh heavily, but I feel her spirit will live on years after her departure."

Newsweek magazine put Martha Stewart on its cover when a federal investigation of insider trading began.

Scent of Scandal

Both *Business Week* and *The Motley Fool* pinpointed the source of the risk, but neither divined its true nature. It wasn't Martha's inevitable exit that presented the problem but rather her imminent entanglement in a prolonged stock scandal and her method of dealing with it. To some, she appeared arrogant in avoiding questions about the problems, contradicting her axiom that appearances count.

The public first became familiar with the issue when news broke on June 6, 2002, that federal investigators were looking into her sale of ImClone common shares on December 27 of the preceding year.

ImClone Systems Inc. was a small biotechnology company with a promising new cancer drug under review at the FDA. On December 26, the ImClone chief executive, Samuel Waksal, learned that the FDA was likely to reject the drug, an action sure to hurt the value of his company's stock. In violation of federal securities regulations, Dr. Waksal attempted to sell his shares before news of the rejection became public and, according to the SEC, warned his daughter and father to do the same.

Martha Stewart, who owned about 4,000 shares of ImClone, was a good friend of Dr. Waksal. She sold out her investment at $58 a share on the same day that the Waksals sold large blocks of shares. After the stock market closed the following day, news about the FDA rejection was released to the public for the first time. The stock dropped to $46.46 when trading resumed. By selling ahead of the news, Ms. Stewart received about $43,000 more than she might have later—a year's income for many families but not a large sum for such a wealthy businesswoman.

An Insistence of Innocence

A congressional subcommittee began investigating suspicious trading in ImClone stock and learned about Martha Stewart's sale of shares from the drug company's attorneys. Phone records of Ms. Stewart, her broker, and Dr. Waksal were examined for evidence that information might have been passed along illegally. The records showed that Ms. Stewart had returned a call from her broker, sold her stock, and then placed a call to Dr. Waksal's office and left a message asking him to call her back, which he did not do.

Ms. Stewart told her company's staff, board members, and large shareholders that she had done nothing wrong, and she answered questions about the transaction. She issued a statement on June 12 to say that she had no inside information on ImClone and sold the stock under conditions prearranged with her broker. She said they had agreed to sell if the price dropped to $60. In fact, the *Wall Street Journal* acknowledged that she cooperated—up to a point.

"Although early on, Ms. Stewart provided a detailed explanation of her stock trade, she hasn't elaborated publicly since investigators started questioning her story," the newspaper said. The questions stemmed from inconsistencies between Martha's version of events and those of others involved. The *Journal* article's headline read, "Martha Stewart: Project for July Is Image Repair."

Other publications also focused on her public relations dilemma. A *New York Times* headline said, "Stewart's Image Woes Hurt Shares of Company," and the *PR Reporter* newsletter devoted its front page to her on July 15, 2002, under this headline: "Martha Stewart—Another Casualty of Plummeting Public Trust in Business."

Bad Company in Business Headlines

As the newsletter headline suggested, disclosures about her timely stock sale first appeared in a season where headlines about big-business misbehavior had become commonplace. Senior executives at Enron, Arthur Andersen, WorldCom, Adelphi, Global Crossing, and other companies had gained media attention for the use of misleading—and, in some cases, illegal—financial devices. Reports suggested that Martha might be another business bigwig with something to hide.

As the news media pressed harder for answers, Martha grew firmer in resisting them. She dodged reporters by using a private entrance and service elevator when they staked out a building where she was scheduled to appear. During her regular culinary appearance on *The Early Show*, Martha kept chopping vegetables when the show's anchor posed questions about the ImClone trade. Her reply was, "I want to focus on my salad."

Martha Stewart Living Omnimedia hired a strategic public relations firm at the end of June to help with the new distractions caused by the media attention, and Martha got a lot of unsolicited public relations advice as well in the news columns. Some of the kibitzers told her to go public and fight back. Others said a public fight would simply cause more damage. Some suggested that she tell everything and hold back nothing. A few said no one could know the best course to take.

In the month after Martha Stewart's name was linked to the ImClone scandal, MSO shares lost 39% of their value, dropping to $11.67 on July 3.

A Bad Situation Gets Worse

One year after Martha Stewart was first linked to the ImClone investigation, a federal grand jury indicted her on five criminal counts of securities fraud, conspiracy, and making false statements. In a separate civil case, the SEC charged her with insider trading.

Ms. Stewart relinquished her posts as chairman and chief executive officer at her company but remained a member of the board of directors and assumed the title of chief creative officer.

The day following the indictments, she took out a full-page ad in *USA Today* asserting her innocence and launched a personal Web site, www.marthatalks.com, on which she offered an open letter responding to the charges. It said:

To My Friends and Loyal Supporters,

After more than a year, the government has decided to bring charges against me for matters that are personal and entirely unrelated to the business of Martha Stewart Living Omnimedia. I want you to know that I am innocent—and that I will fight to clear my name.

I simply returned a call from my stockbroker. Based in large part on prior discussions with my broker about price, I authorized a sale of my remaining shares in a biotech company called ImClone. I later denied any wrongdoing in public statements and in voluntary interviews with prosecutors. The government's attempt to criminalize these actions makes no sense to me.

I am confident I will be exonerated of these baseless charges, but a trial unfortunately won't take place for months. I want to thank you for your extraordinary support for the past year—I appreciate it more than you will ever know.

The Web site turned out to be quite popular. It got 2 million hits on the day it appeared and logged nearly 13 million within its first 6 weeks of existence. In the same period, more than 60,000 visitors used its interactive features to offer messages of support.

Yet the ongoing investigation and media attention hurt the financial performance of Martha Stewart Living Omnimedia. In the first half of 2003, the company lost $3.58 million, compared with a profit of $6.51 million in the first 6 months of 2002. In a statement accompanying the earnings figures, the company suggested a gloomy prospect.

"We believe that the Martha Stewart Living core brand will continue to be under pressure until resolution of Martha Stewart's personal legal situation," the statement said.

Suspicions Engendered

From the day that Martha Stewart's name first appeared in news accounts of the ImClone episode, some people—friend and foe alike—suspected that Martha's gender was partially responsible for attracting the attention of federal prosecutors. They pointed out that she had competed aggressively in an arena usually dominated by men, that she had acquired a reputation as a demanding and successful leader, and that she fought back defiantly rather than retreat demurely. Perhaps to neutralize such claims, the U.S. Attorney responsible for the case appointed a woman as lead prosecutor. The federal prosecution succeeded. On Friday, March 5, 2004, a jury of eight women and four men found the business executive guilty of obstructing justice and making false statements to government investigators about the sale of ImClone stock. Ten days later, she resigned from her positions as chief creative officer and a director of the company and assumed a new title as founding editorial director.

QUESTIONS FOR REFLECTION

1. Some public relations practitioners said that Martha Stewart should have apologized for bad judgment—even if she did nothing illegal—as soon as insinuations of inside trading surfaced. Would such a course have saved her reputation?

2. How can a company that seems inseparable from its founder—such as Martha Stewart, Oprah Winfrey, Donna Karan, Bill Gates or, in an earlier time, Walt Disney—protect itself from a catastrophe that might befall the human symbol of the company?

3. Martha Stewart mostly avoided the media for more than a year after federal investigators took an interest in her affairs. What would you have advised her to do during this period?

4. Some people said that interest in Martha Stewart's problems was an example of *schadenfreude*, a German word meaning malicious satisfaction in the misfortune of others. Do you agree?

Information for this case was drawn from the following: the Martha Stewart Living Omnimedia Web site at http://www.marthastewart.com/; Martha Stewart's personal Web site at http://www.marthatalks.com/; Brady, D. (17 January 2000), "Martha Inc.: Inside the growing empire of America's lifestyle queen," *Business Week*, p. 62; Cohen, L. (7 July 2003), "U.S. wants 'gender card' out of Stewart case," *The Wall Street Journal*, p. C1. Hays, C., & Pollack, A. (4 July 2002), "Stewart's image woes hurt shares of company," *The New York Times*, p. C1; (15 July 2002), "Martha Stewart—Another casualty of plummeting public trust in business," *PR Reporter*, p. 1; Rose, M. (2 July 2002), "Martha Stewart: Project for July is image repair," *The Wall Street Journal*, p. B1; and Trigg, M. (8 May 2001), "Martha Stewart Living Omnimedia; A stock for Mom," The Motley Fool, http://www.fool.com.

CASE 23. CONSULTING COMPANY GETS NEW NAME AND NEW OWNERS

Accenture topped the list of the world's largest management and technology consulting companies at year-end 2001 even though 15 months earlier no one had heard its name. Traded on the NYSE under the symbol ACN, the company's closing price on the last day of the year was $26.92. More than 920,000 common shares of ACN were bought and sold that day, a slow session on the NYSE. Any investors who'd bought ACN 3 months earlier had doubled their money.

The story of Accenture's origin combines sibling strife, economic prophecy, and financial rewards in a tale that might fascinate psychologists and astrologers as much as it does investor relations professionals.

In 1953, an accounting firm known as Arthur Andersen undertook its initial management consulting project by helping General Electric with the installation of the first computer for business applications. Already 40 years old when the project began, Arthur Andersen ranked as one of the largest and most influential accounting firms in the United States. Corporations hire independent accountants for professional help with taxes, financial decisions, and auditing.

Because consulting could lead to new accounting clients and offer the promise of its own growth, Arthur Andersen set up a team to identify and manage consulting opportunities in 1953. At first, the consulting business grew slowly, but it was generating more than 20% of the firm's annual revenues by 1980 and 40% by 1988.

Consulting Partners Gain Clout

Like most accounting firms, Arthur Andersen was owned by its partners, and most partners earned their positions by obtaining new clients and keeping existing clients satisfied. The partners, as owners, managed the business and shared the profits among themselves. As prospects in consulting rose on a tide of growth, accountants felt pressures in pricing and litigation. Price competition sharpened as the accounting profession consolidated into a few major rivals, and lawsuits multiplied as investors held independent auditors liable for the accounting sins of the auditors' clients.

In 1989, the entire company was restructured, acknowledging the importance and potential of the consulting business. Andersen Worldwide was created as parent of two separate and independent units: Arthur Andersen to focus on auditing and accounting; Andersen Consulting to develop its practices in systems integration, manufacturing processes, finance, and government.

The following year, the Arthur Andersen accountants set up a consulting practice within their unit despite the resentments they might expect from Andersen Consulting colleagues and the confusion it might cause among clients. Some business journalists have pointed to this event as a clear signal that the two major divisions of Andersen Worldwide were on a collision course.

For most of the 1990s, Andersen Consulting benefited handsomely from an extended period of business prosperity and technological innovation. Clients wanted the consultants' guidance in adopting technology for corporate functions ranging from human resources to logistics, in adapting the Internet for business efficiencies, in managing the movement of raw materials and finished products in a global economy, and more.

A Strained Relationship

In 1997, the strains between the consultants and auditors surfaced publicly when the Andersen Worldwide partners voted to select a new CEO. The accountants wanted someone from Arthur Andersen in the top job, and the consultants preferred someone from Andersen Consulting. At the time, the consulting division outproduced the accountants in revenue and profit and was growing faster as well, but the accountants dominated the governing board. The consultants complained that their performance subsidized the accounting division and its competing consulting business.

Under the firm's rules, a CEO candidate needed two thirds of the partners' votes to win, and neither of the first two candidates—one from accounting and the other from consulting—attracted enough support to get the job.

Before the end of the year, Andersen Consulting announced that it wanted to split away from Andersen Worldwide and set up operations as an independent shop. However, the partnership agreement required any seceding group to buy its freedom with a payment equal to 150% of annual revenues. For the Andersen Consulting, the amount would have been about $14 billion. The consultants said that Arthur Andersen already had violated the agreement by setting up a competing consulting business.

Mediation Settles Issue

Andersen Consulting took the dispute to the International Chamber of Commerce and asked for arbitration to settle the issue. After more than two years of argument, the arbitrator decided in August 2000 that the consultants could have their divorce. However, he required Andersen Consulting to pay the accountants $1 billion in regular installments and to stop using the Andersen name by New Year's Day.

The consultants were delighted with the ruling but surprised to have only 4 months for the process of selecting a new name and developing a new identity program. Because arbitration had taken so long, they'd had time to consider rebranding the consulting practice as a future goal, but they had not expected to do it immediately.

With the ruling in hand, they hired a strategic brand identity firm and got busy. As part of the process, they encouraged Andersen Consulting employees to suggest names and received about 2,700 possibilities, eventually choosing one offered by a senior manager in the Oslo, Norway, office.

The new name—Accenture—suggested *accent on the future*. Before adopting it, they made sure that it was not already taken, had no offensive meanings in unfamiliar languages, and would be available as a Web site address—www.accenture.com. The new name was announced in October 2000, and its adoption was effective on January 1, 2001.

Replacing Andersen with Accenture in the minds of 20,000 client executives, 70,000 consulting employees, and hundreds of thousands of potential clients was a tall order. In addition, the consultants had 137 offices around the world to remark.

As soon as the new name was selected, they began a public relations and advertising campaign to create awareness of Accenture and establish understanding of its mission. The company put a $175 million budget behind the effort and by New Year's Day had gained a wide measure of familiarity for its new name.

Plans for IPO

Eight months after emancipation through arbitration, the Accenture partners voted to begin the process that would convert the company into a public stock corporation. They hired two investment banking firms, Goldman Sachs Group and Morgan Stanley Dean Witter & Company, to lead the underwriting group that would handle the IPO of ACN shares.

In planning this initial public offering, Accenture expected to sell 115 million shares at $14 apiece in July 2001 and raise $1.6 billion. Customarily, underwriters begin work long before the date of the IPO to make sure that there are enough investors interested in the shares to ensure a successful sale on the day they become available.

To discourage aggressive promotion, the SEC imposes what's called a *quiet period* on companies issuing new shares. The period begins when a company files a registration statement with the SEC outlining its offering. It ends, according to the SEC, when "SEC staff declares the registration statement 'effective.' " Many investor relations professionals say the quiet period ends 25 days after the shares first begin trading.

During the quiet period, a company may continue to issue the kinds of news releases and other announcements that it would make in the normal course of operations, but most avoid statements that would color interpretations of a stock's future value.

A Successful Offering

On July 19, Accenture sold its IPO at $14.50 per share through the underwriting group, and the shares' closing price on the NYSE that day was $15.17—a gain of 4.6%. Public investors ended up with 115 million shares—12% of the company.

The Accenture partners received shares accounting for 82% of the company, and employees and retired partners received 6%.

Months later, shareowners could appreciate even more the company's unexpected race through the name development process and its heavy push to boost awareness of the Accenture identity and mission. The Andersen name was tarred by scandal, and Arthur Andersen began folding its operations after client Enron Corporation was disgraced by financial disclosures and accounting irregularities.

In 2001, the PRSA gave its Public Relations Professional of the Year Award to James E. Murphy, Accenture's global managing director of marketing and communications. It honored his work in managing the rebranding project.

QUESTIONS FOR REFLECTION

1. Does the name for the new firm, Accenture, convey what the company does?
2. If Andersen Consulting had been allowed to keep using the Andersen name after its split from Andersen Worldwide, would you have recommended changing it when the Arthur Andersen auditors were tainted in the Enron scandal?
3. What kinds of public relations activities would you have used to create and build awareness of the new name?
4. Why are companies careful about what they say during the SEC-mandated quiet period?

Information for this case was drawn from the following: the Accenture Web site at http://www.accenture.com; (1 September 2002), "Accenture Ltd.," *Hoover's Company Profiles*; Barker, R. (9 July 2001), "Accenture partners take the cake," *Business Week*, p. 116; (10 December 2001), "Accenture's Murphy wins PRSA accolade," *Investor Relations Business*, p. 1; Brown, K. (27 October 2000), "Andersen Consulting chooses Accenture," *The Wall Street Journal*, p. B6; Fattah, J. (June 2001), "A giant's rebirth," *Adweek Magazine's Technology Marketing*, p. 44; and McMaster, M. (March 2002), "What's in a name?" *Sales and Marketing Management*, p. 55.

CASE 24: CASE OF THE MISFIRED MEMO

Fortune magazine's list of the 100 Best Companies to Work for in America ranked Cerner Corporation at No. 54 in January 2001, a repeat appearance for the Kansas City-based developer of health care software. Later the same month, the company added to its laurels with news of a record-setting fourth quarter, which capped a successful year. Cerner employees had plenty to be proud of.

Cerner Corporation's CEO drew criticism when he complained that his headquarters' parking lots had too many empty spaces early and late on weekdays and on Saturdays, too.

Two months later, the company grabbed national attention again—this time for a bad-tempered e-mail message that the company's chief executive expected only Cerner managers would see. In it, he threatened to trim jobs and benefits if productivity did not rise. Someone anonymously posted the message on a public Internet site, and alarm spread not just through the Cerner workforce but also into the investment community. The stock market's valuation of Cerner dropped by $270 million in 2 days, prompting a *New York Times* article that was headlined "A Stinging Office Memo Boomerangs."

An Unhealthy Environment?

Here is what the CEO, Neal Patterson, put in the e-mail that he sent to some 400 managers. The message's unusual capitalization, from Mr. Patterson's original, draws attention to the Cerner custom of referring to the company's 3,100 workers as "associates."

> We are getting less than 40 hours of work from a large number of our K. C.-based EMPLOYEES. The parking lot is sparsely used at 8 a.m.; likewise at 5 p.m. As managers—you either do not know what your EMPLOYEES are doing; or you do not CARE. You have created expectations on the work effort which allowed this to hap-

pen inside Cerner, creating a very unhealthy environment. In either case, you have a problem and you will fix it or I will replace you.

NEVER in my career have I allowed a team which worked for me to think they had a 40-hour job. I have allowed YOU to create a culture which is permitting this. NO LONGER.

Emphasizing his expectation of long workdays, Mr. Patterson noted, "The pizza man should show up at 7:30 p.m. to feed the starving teams working late." He said that the employee parking lot should be "substantially full" at 7:30 a.m. and 6:30 p.m. on weekdays, and on Saturday mornings it should be half-full.

"You have two weeks. Tick, tock," his e-mail message warned.

Offensive or Aggressive?

Some employees were shocked and offended by the CEO's unusually harsh language, whereas others simply chalked it up to his bluntly aggressive leadership style. After earning a master of business administration degree from Oklahoma State University, Mr. Patterson had worked for the Arthur Andersen auditing firm for 6 years. With two colleagues, he founded Cerner in 1979 to develop automated health care information systems, particularly for application in clinical laboratories. All three founders stayed active in the business, and Mr. Patterson received credit for leading the company's remarkable growth and innovation over its first 20 years.

In information for investors, the company explained, "Cerner Corporation is taking the paper chart out of healthcare, eliminating error, variance and unnecessary waste in the care process. With more than 1,500 clients worldwide, Cerner is the leading supplier of healthcare information technology."

Outside the company, management experts pointed out that Mr. Patterson's e-mail memo to managers did not say what—besides long hours—he was expecting from employees. They also noted that his threats could lead to higher turnover and difficulty in recruiting.

Financial Uncertainty

In the financial markets, many investors were not sure what to make of the e-mail message. Some wondered if Cerner was experiencing performance problems that would affect first-quarter results, and so they reacted to the uncertainty by hurriedly selling shares and driving down the price of the stock.

A business columnist in Cerner's hometown newspaper, *The Kansas City Star*, said the stock price might recover quickly, "but there is no denying that the harm done to company stakeholders has been as grave as it was unnecessary. As such, Patterson's misstep offers an important lesson for top execs everywhere."

Patterson himself was surprised by the firestorm that he had ignited, and he soon followed up with an apology to employees and with a message that was posted on the company's Web site. The message acknowledged that his original complaint applied only to "a small number of associates."

"My intent with the e-mail," he wrote, "was to issue a direct challenge to our front-line managers to set a minimum level of work effort for every one of their team members. And that I, as the CEO, would hold them accountable for this result …. My biggest concern was that it had been distributed beyond the list of managers to many, if not all, of our Cerner associates."

Success Uninterrupted

In what some might see as a happy ending to an unhappy episode, Cerner again achieved record results in the first quarter. Only 5 weeks after Patterson's blistering e-mail message, the company issued a glowing report on revenues and earnings and commented positively on opportunities for the remainder of the year. Nowhere in the company's earnings announcement was there a hint of any productivity problem.

Cerner's revenues for 2002 were $752 million, an increase of 39% from the $542 million of the preceding year. Net earnings (before nonrecurring items) were $52 million in 2002, an increase of 51% from the $34 million earned in 2001.

Although the company's financial results continued to improve after the misfired memo, *Fortune*'s list of the 100 Best Companies to Work for in America did not mention Cerner in 2002 or in 2003.

For public relations professionals, Cerner's experience offered lessons in both employee relations practices and investor relations sensitivities. Moreover, it showed that successful management of different public relations functions is often highly interdependent. Material intended for employees may affect investors, and vice versa.

QUESTIONS FOR REFLECTION

1. What are the benefits and risks of using e-mail to deliver a confidential message to a group of individuals? Would a traditional memo distributed on paper pose the same risks?
2. What should you do if you know that a key message aimed at one important group will disturb or alienate another?
3. How should senior managers tell rank-and-file employees that organizational performance is not satisfactory?
4. How should rank-and-file employees express concerns to senior managers?

Information for this case was drawn from the following: the Cerner Web site at http://www.cerner.com/aboutcerner/newsroom_3a.asp?id=783; Burton, T., & Silverman, R. (30 March 2001), "Lots of empty spaces in Cerner parking lot get CEO riled up," *The Wall Street Journal*, p. B3; Hayes, D., & Karash, J. (24 March 2001), "Harsh e-mail roils Cerner," *The Kansas City Star*, p. A1; Heaster, J. (28 March 2001), "Executives, heed lesson from Cerner," *The Kansas City Star*, p. C1; Stafford, D. (29 March 2001), "Shattering the illusion of respect," *The Kansas City Star*, p. C1; and Wong, E. (5 April 2001), "A stinging office memo boomerangs," *The New York Times*, p. C1.

It's What We *Do* in Investor Relations That Matters

Louis M. Thompson, Jr., president and chief executive officer,
National Investor Relations Institute

Based on more than 30 years in public and investor relations, I've not seen corporate America faced with a challenge as serious as we are dealing with today in restoring investor and public trust and confidence. I believe that we have entered an era where our mantra should be—"What we *do* is more important than what we *say*."

And, corporations are not alone in this effort to build greater trust in the minds of individual investors—who I believe will be the final arbiters in determining whether we have accomplished this daunting task. A 2002 survey by Opinion Research Corporation found investors get most of their information through intermediaries they don't trust (i.e. brokers, analysts, companies and the media). They believe brokers and financial analysts have conflicted interests and that corporate executives are greedy. They believe reporters don't understand business and are biased and that the government was late to the game in dealing with the accounting scandals and is influenced too much by business.

If that is where we start, we have a lot of work to do. One theme emerging from the many conferences and symposia on restoring investor trust that overrides all others is that behavior is far more important than mere compliance with the rules. Following a legalistic, risk-averse approach will not bring investors back to the market fast enough. Companies that are willing to be leaders by demonstrating strong ethical behavior and by putting the investors' and the public's interests before their own will ultimately be rewarded. And public relations people need to remember that straightforward, honest, and transparent communication is in. Spin is out. Again, it's what we *do*, not what we *say* that counts.

Louis M. Thompson, Jr., is president and chief executive officer of the National Investor Relations Institute (NIRI), a professional association of more than 4,700 members representing over 2,500 publicly held companies. Mr. Thompson served in a variety of public relations positions before joining NIRI in 1982, including that of Assistant White House Press Secretary to President Gerald R. Ford. He earned a B.S. degree in journalism and an M.S. in journalism and mass communication from Iowa State University, where he currently serves as Vice Chairman of the Greenlee School of Journalism and Communication Advisory Committee.

7

Stakeholders: Members and Volunteers

Of all stakeholder relationships, those that nonprofit organizations have with members or volunteers may be at the same time the most tenuous and the most necessary. Stakeholders who enter into a relationship with a nonprofit group, whether it is an alumni association, a professional group, or a social service agency, usually have some need or goal that motivates their joining, donating, serving, or attending. Yet that need or goal is usually self-directed, meaning that if it is not satisfied or supported, the individual will find another source for satisfaction or motivation. Similarly, most, if not all, membership or volunteer-based organizations have needs or goals as well. In order to address their missions, most often the need is financial, with the organization heavily dependent on donations to maintain activities or services. The need may also be for staffing, where in essence the volunteers are functioning as quasi-employees of the organization. Such great pressures may tempt organizations to exploit donors, volunteers, or clients or to forego truthful disclosure when puffery or evasion may bring quicker returns.

The relationships between such organizations and their stakeholders are best maintained when they are founded on mutual trust built and maintained through meeting mutually recognized needs and interests. Organizations with a clear sense of their mission and an articulation of how the stakeholders are aligned with that mission are the most likely to succeed in building those types of relationships. However, no matter how lofty the expressed mission and purpose statement of an organization may be, the most pertinent factor in determining an ongoing relationship is found in satisfying the donor's, volunteer's, or member's multiple motivations as well as the overall objectives of the group. For example, donors may be highly sympathetic to the mission an organization has to offer support services for cancer patients in their area. An altruistic desire to help those in need may drive donors to offer financial support. Yet, donors may also be highly motivated by the need to obtain documentation of their giving so they may use it to reduce income tax liabilities, or they may be motivated by the desire to gain recognition for their donations as when a building or center is named in their honor.

Such multiple motivations are to be expected—and indeed encouraged. Individuals are far more likely to continue a costly relationship such as this when they are given multiple incentives or rewards. The public relations pay-off for "catching someone doing good" may also serve as incentive for recruiting others to awareness or activity. Practitioners may face the challenge of balancing their interactions with members or volunteers who have offered different levels of support to the organization. On a practical note, practitioners will need to develop ways of expressing appreciation for large and small levels of support so that neither group feels slighted, while also maintaining ways for both groups to offer input and feedback.

Organizations also are dependent on increased involvement. Donors who may have offered initial small gifts or pledges, for example, may later become major donors or may become active volunteers. Volunteers may become so committed to the service or mission of the organization that they invest not only their time and talents, but also their financial resources. Individuals who find their own involvement to be rewarding will also become great ambassadors for the involvement of their friends or associates. Everyone within such an organization will benefit if the expressed and unexpressed motivations of donors, members, and volunteers are recognized, acknowledged, and authenticated by leadership within the organization.

COMMUNICATING WITH VOLUNTEERS AND MEMBERS

Practitioners are often charged with the details of developing and deepening relationships between members and volunteers and organizations. This may entail the detailed work of maintaining data files with names, addresses, and personal histories. The tracking may also involve recognition, matching levels of involvement with appropriate rewards: receipts, thank-you letters, certificates, plaques, T-shirts, pins, invitations, and even planning annual special celebrations.

The task of informing these stakeholders may also fall to the practitioner. Print and digital newsletters, direct mail, magazines, Web sites, personal visits, telephone calls, meetings, and special events may all be utilized by practitioners committed to ensuring that members and volunteers are kept up to date about the activities and accomplishments of the organization. If the relationship is to deepen, such regular contact is vital.

However, it is also critical for the practitioner to devise means for soliciting input from the stakeholder so that it does not appear that they are exploited for the resources they can bring with them to the organization. Such methods may be informal: debriefings after a special project or events or occasional visits by a representative board. For example, many colleges and universities maintain alumni councils that gather once or twice a year to plan alumni events but also to respond to questions or to ask questions of administrative leaders. The growing popularity of e-mail has made it easier for organizations to design links from a Web site for questions or comments to be directed to public relations or management personnel.

More formal methods for stimulating may also be utilized. Surveys or focus groups may yield important results. In-depth interviews are also helpful in obtaining the opinions and attitudes of stakeholders. Members or volunteers who are empowered to affect change by offering their insights will be far more likely to continue the relationship than those who are not allowed to become part of the strategic enterprise of the organization.

However the feedback and/or input is generated, sharing some of that with other members or volunteers underscores the seriousness with which the practitioners and management are considering it. Having a "letter to the editor" section in the organization's magazine or a question-and-answer period at monthly or quarterly meetings with responses stressed and demonstrated are just some ways that management may demonstrate its commitment to the two-way communication flow.

SPECIAL CONCERNS

The relationships are not always positive or easy. Some membership groups become so closely knit that they are not open to newcomers or to input from newcomers. Balancing organizational commitment, which is a positive attribute of these relationships, with a need to maintain openness may demand action from the practitioner. For example, what orientation is offered to newcomers? Involving veterans in that process may help demonstrate the need for inclusion. Occasionally, some gifts of involvement, time, or money come with implicit or explicit conditions. Practitioners may need to lead management to establish and then should publicize policies concerning such gifts and the like before sensitive situations develop.

Policies for recruiting and involving members and volunteers need to be developed to help manage other issues as well. Will volunteers be required to complete specialized training? The organization may need to establish standards for dependability and performance; even though the volunteer is not an official employee, there may need to be some method for ensuring that they meet the requirements of the various tasks. Legal issues involving liability and privacy should also be addressed. Using the image of a volunteer or member in a publication may require signed consent, for example, and certainly using the image of a nonprofit's client might require such. Membership organizations may need very detailed descriptions as to who qualifies. If there are educational or geographic or accomplishment requirements, for example, they need to be publicized clearly.

Practitioners and their organizations should also have policies established that address the ethical and legal concerns of clients or volunteers. For example, how may the service accomplishments of a health care organization be publicized without invading the privacy of clients or patients or their families? In a litigious culture, volunteers or the organization may require specialized education about the legal issues involved in their activities. Agencies that solicit donations for children or other protected groups may need policies regarding volunteer access to knowing the identities or other private information about those in the groups. One temptation in fund raising may be to overly emotionalize or caricature those who benefit from the donations. In a nonprofit environment filled with organizations that may all have equally worthy missions and yet must vie against each other for the available time, money, and effort of volunteers and members, practitioners may find the competition so tough that it may be easy to argue that "the end justifies the means." However, whether the practitioner is one within a nonprofit organization or one within an agency contemplating charitable pro bono work, ethical practice would be characterized by a commitment to contextually truthful presentation of information that treats donors and the recipients of services with the same levels of dignity and respect.

ADDITIONAL READINGS

Austin, Erica Weinstraub, & Bruce E. Pinkleton. (2001). *Strategic public relations management. Planning and managing effective communication programs.* Mahwah, NJ: Lawrence Erlbaum Associates.

Bonk, Kathy, Henry Griggs, & Emily Tunes. (1999). *The Jossey-Bass guide to strategic communications for nonprofits.* New York: Jossey-Bass.

Kelly, Kathleen S. (1996). *Effective fund-raising management.* Mahwah, NJ: Lawrence Erlbaum Associates.

Radtke, Janel. (1998). *Strategic communications for nonprofit organizations: Seven steps to creating a successful plan.* New York: Wiley.

CASE 25.   DESIGNATED DONATIONS? THE AMERICAN RED CROSS AND THE LIBERTY FUND

September 11, 2001: Virtually every household in the United States and many across the globe shared in the fear, the anger, the disbelief, and the sorrow resulting from the terrorist attacks on Washington, DC, and New York City. Many wanted to do something to reach out to the thousands of victims and their families and to offer assistance to those who were actively giving support.

Creation of the Liberty Fund

The American Red Cross quickly responded to the disaster and perhaps just as quickly created the Liberty Fund, a special opportunity for donations that would go to support the aid and recovery efforts. The creation of a special fund was unexpected. Traditionally, when soliciting funds, the Red Cross had asked donors to give to its Disaster Relief Fund where money raised could be used in connection with whatever disasters that arose.

By the end of October, the Liberty Fund had received $547 million in pledges. The Associated Press (AP) reported that the Red Cross had spent more than $140 million on terrorism-related efforts. Nearly $44 million was used through the Family Gift Program to help cover the costs of housing, food, child care, and other expenses for more than 2,200 affected families in New York and Washington. The *Toronto Star* reported on November 7 that victims' families had received an average of $25,000 for 3-months' living expenses from the fund, meaning that only about one third of the amount raised in the Liberty Fund had gone directly to victims and their families. The AP said about $67 million was spent on immediate disaster-relief needs such as shelter, on-site food, on-site counseling, and other support for victims' families and rescue workers. More than $11.5 million went to blood-donor programs, $14.7 million to nationwide community outreach, and another $2.5 million to indirect support costs.

Too Much Support?

There was just one problem, however. The Red Cross said it did not need all the money in the Liberty Fund to help address the needs. Red Cross CEO Bernadine Healy reported that $200 million of the Fund would be used to support other Red Cross efforts, an announcement that spawned a negative uproar and prompted two congressional hearings. When donors found out that up to half of the Liberty Fund was going to be used to support other projects, national reaction was swift. Some people felt they had been misled. They had given money believing it would be used to support the victims or the survivors of the disasters, and they wanted the funds to be used in that way.

The uproar led to changes at the Red Cross. Dr. Healy resigned as CEO on October 26, citing differences with the governing board. She was allowed to keep the title of president until the end of 2001.

Harold Decker, who had served as the organization's deputy general counsel since February 2001 and general counsel since September 2001, was named interim CEO in October. One of his first actions was to announce that as of October 31, the Red Cross would cease soliciting donations for the Liberty Fund. Contributions received from that point on would be added to the group's Disaster Relief Fund unless donors specifically targeted the Liberty Fund for their donations. Accounting firm KPMG was also hired to audit the Liberty Fund.

In the November 14, 2001, release announcing the change, Decker said:

> Americans have spoken loudly and clearly that they want our relief efforts directed at the people affected by the Sept. 11 tragedies. We deeply regret that our activities over the past eight weeks have not been as sharply focused as America wants, nor as focused as the victims of this tragedy deserve. The people affected by this terrible tragedy have been our first priority, and beginning today, they will be the only priority of the Liberty Fund.

David T. McLaughlin, chair of the Red Cross Board of Governors, said in the release:

> The people of this country have given the Red Cross their hard-earned dollars, their trust and very clear direction for our September 11 relief efforts. Regrettably, it took us too long to hear their message. Now we must change course to restore the faith of our donors and the trust of Americans and, most importantly, to devote 100 percent of our energy and resources in helping the victims of the terrorist attacks.

Former Senate Majority Leader George Mitchell was named as the "independent overseer" of the fund in January 2002. The former senator had become known for his leadership in the negotiations to foster peace in Ireland and in the Middle East. He was charged with helping to develop a plan for how the Liberty Fund monies would be spent. Mitchell led the group to declare that 90% of the $360 million dedicated for victims would be spent by the first anniversary of the attacks, with the remainder to be earmarked for long-term aid.

The Red Cross also created a "Celebrity Cabinet" in February 2002 to promote its work. Celebrities such as Jennifer Love Hewitt, Mike Piazza, and Jane Seymour were included in the first group.

New guidelines for the Liberty Fund were developed. Families who had members killed or seriously injured in the attacks were to receive financial support through the Family Gift program for 1 year, an extension of the initial 3-month funding period. The remaining needs of the families will be studied, the Red Cross said in a November 2001 release; it may be that financial support would be needed even longer. The names of the 25,000 families it had supported will be shared in a database with other relief agencies in an effort to help coordinate relief.

In addition to its decision to extend longer-term help to victims' families, the Red Cross said it would charge operating costs for the Liberty Fund and such services as the toll-free information lines to the interest earned on the fund balance, rather than directly to the Fund itself. An additional 200 caseworkers were being hired, and more full-time staff members were moved to the Long-Time Disaster Recovery Unit.

The Red Cross says it expected to spend about $300 million in 2003 to further these efforts, and the remaining $200 million-plus would be held in trust for later help to victims. The Red Cross said it was also contacting the victims of the postal-anthrax attacks and that it had already given money to the families of three anthrax victims.

The Changes Prompt Praise and Criticism

According to a Red Cross news release on November 14, 2001, the Oversight and Investigations Subcommittee of the U.S. House Energy and Commerce Committee endorsed the Red Cross's decision to use all the Liberty Disaster Fund donations to support the needs of people affected by the terrorist attacks. Appearing with the Red Cross officials, Committee chair Rep. James C. Greenwood (R-Pa.) was quoted on National Public Radio's (NPR) *All Things Considered* endorsing the changes. He said this was a "first-rate response" from the group.

Other members of the Oversight Committee promised continuing scrutiny, however. Rep. Bart Stupak (D-Mich.) said the news conference alone was not enough. He told *All Things Considered* on NPR: "This is really just the beginning of it. We will continue our oversight of the American Red Cross. We'll continue to make sure that donors' intent and wishes are followed through."

Reacting to the controversy, Daniel Borochoff, president of the American Institute of Philanthropy, a charity-watchdog group, told Knight-Ridder Washington Bureau reporter Kevin Murphy, on November 15, 2001, that when the Red Cross set up the Liberty Fund, "The message in most people's minds was that 100 percent would go to victims' families and relief work." The earlier decision to use the Fund to help support other Red Cross efforts may offer a lesson, however. "People understand the important role the Red Cross plays in disaster relief, but I think it will lead to some healthy skepticism. It won't be enough for them to say, 'give us some money for this disaster.' People will want to know how much do you really have, how much do you need, what are you doing with it?"

Paul Clolery, editor-in-chief of the *NonProfit Times*, a bimonthly trade paper, told Knight Ridder, "It is the first time I know of that they set up a separate fund, and therein was their huge mistake." Before when they responded to disasters with appeals, "They always couched it in phrases like 'for this and other disasters,' which is the correct way because you never know how much money you are going to need."

Lasting Changes at the Red Cross

Following this controversy, the Red Cross said it would remove references to a specific crisis from its advertising, and that it would make a public announcement at the point when it had received enough money to cover a relief effort. A system for double-checking to ensure that designated gifts are used where the donor intended would also be instituted, NPR reported in June 2002. According to a June story in the *Atlanta Journal-Constitution*, all disaster-related appeals would contain this statement: "You can help the victims of (this disaster) and thousands of other disasters across the country each year by making a financial gift to the American Red Cross Disaster Relief Fund, which enables the Red Cross to provide shelter, food, counseling and other assistance to those in need."

Donations to the general Disaster Relief Fund also dropped in the months following the terrorist attacks. Chief Financial Officer Jack Campbell told the AP in October 2001 that the disaster fund held only about $26 million as of September 30, whereas its target goal had been about $57 million. In March 2002, the *Dallas Morning News* reported that the Wise Giving Alliance of the Better Business Bureau had removed its seal of approval for the Red Cross, saying it would not be restored until the charity demonstrated it was meeting all standards for good management. However, Alliance President Art Taylor commended the changes in fund-raising announced in June by the Red Cross. He was quoted in the *Atlanta Journal-Constitution* in June, saying, "We believe that donors, beneficiaries and the charity itself all benefit when there is a clear understanding of how donations will be used."

Giving to chapters across the country was affected by the controversy. "There are 1,100 chapters across the U.S., and we're all suffering to some degree from the national negative publicity about the organization," Greg Hill, director of communications and marketing at the Dallas chapter told Todd Gillman of the *Dallas Morning News*. "And whether it's justified or not doesn't matter." The St. Louis chapter cut 14 jobs and closed two offices after a drop in donations, and chapters from North Carolina to Maine reported troubles in fund raising.

At the national headquarters, some 30 communication and marketing department employees were expected to be laid off by summer 2002, according to *PR Week*, and a hiring freeze was in place while an internal reorganization was being led by interim CEO Decker.

Yet by March 2002, Red Cross national spokeswoman Devorah Goldberg told the *Dallas Morning News:* "It's obviously settled down quite a bit …. Controversies come and go. We respond to more than 67,000 disasters every year. We're still there, we're still serving communities nationwide."

In August 2002, the Red Cross named Rear Admiral Marsha Evans as CEO. Evans had been heading the Girl Scouts of the USA.

Darren Irby, the Red Cross director of external communications, told *PRWeek* in August 2002: "Some people criticized us for not being as up front as we could be about where their donation was going, so we took a real hard look, and our commitment now is to be the leader in transparency and accountability." Irby said tactics needed included clearer and simpler statements about how donations will be used because most Americans don't understand the work of charities. He also said recruiting more third parties to speak for the organization and better cross-training of volunteers would help. "All we can do is be a leader in responding to the lessons we learned, and hope that other nonprofits will learn from that," Irby told *PRWeek*.

Yet, controversy arose again in spring 2003 when tax documents released by the Red Cross showed that during her last 6 months of employment as CEO and president of the Red Cross from July through December 2001, Healey had received some $1.3 million in deferred compensation, almost $300,000 in salary, an additional $228,929 in severance pay, $50,000 in expense allowances, and $5,622 in benefits. The documents showed that her chief of staff Catharine "Kate" Berry, who was fired 11 days after Healy's resignation, received $73,602 in salary and benefits, $132,509 in severance pay, and $403,473 in deferred compensation during that time period. The compensation Healy received during the last 6 months of 2001 was more than twice what she had received during her first 22 months at the Red Cross and were above the highest salary of $690,000 listed by *The Chronicle of Philanthropy*'s October 2002 report, which said 34 of 282 large nonprofits paid their CEOs more than $500,000.

Other September 11-Related Charities Also Come Under Criticism

The Red Cross was not the only charity to be questioned about its disbursement of terrorism-related donations, however. According to a report in the June 23, 2002, *New York Times*, the Sept. 11 Fund, a joint project of the New York City United Way and the New York Community Trust, had distributed less than half of the $456 million it had received. The Robin Hood Relief Fund in Manhattan had $23 million in undistributed donations, the World Trade Center Relief Fund had $29 million of the $65 million remaining, and the Uniformed Firefighters Association was reported to be negotiating about how to distribute its $60 million. Many of the charities' leaders report that the immediate needs of victims have been met and they are now dealing with how to finance the longer-term needs such as mental-health counseling and job training.

QUESTIONS FOR REFLECTION

1. What characterizes a mutually beneficial relationship between a charitable organization and its donors or members? What duties or responsibilities do nonprofits or charities owe to their donors and their clients?

2. What responsibility do governments and regulators have in overseeing the operations of nonprofit, fund-raising organizations?

3. Identify some of the ethical and managerial responsibilities of the leaders of nonprofits or charities.

4. What environmental factors may have contributed to this crisis for the American Red Cross?

Information for this case came from the following: Blaul, B. (30 October 2001), "American Red Cross names Harold Decker interim CEO," American Red Cross Release, *PR Newswire*; Irby, D. (14 November 2001), "Members of Congress praise Red Cross for policy changes with Liberty disaster fund," American Red Cross Release, *PR Newswire*; Flaherty, M. P., & Gaul, G. M. (19 November 2001), "Red Cross has pattern of diverting donations," *The Washington Post*, p. A1; Gillman, T. J. (11 March 2002), "Red Cross faces continuing queries about Sept. 11 funds," *The Dallas Morning News*; Irby, D. (14 November 2001), "Red Cross announces major changes in Liberty Fund," American Red Cross News Release, *US Newswire*; Mollison, A. (6 June 2002), "Red Cross changes the way it solicits funds," *The Atlanta Journal-Constitution*, p. A14; Mollison, A. (19 April 2003), "Red Cross chief got $1.9 million gold parachute," *The Atlanta Journal-Constitution*, pp. A1, A13; Murphy, K. (15 November 2001), "Charity watchdog agency wants Red Cross to be more candid about donations," *Knight Ridder Washington Bureau*; Quenqua, D. (25 August 2002), "Cross purpose," *PRWeek*, p. 19; Rabin, P. (6 May 2002), "Red Cross reorganization results in comms cutback," *PRWeek*, p. 2; (15 November 2001), "Red Cross 'correction' redirects reserve funds," *The Washington Times*; Seabrook, A. (5 June 2002), "American Red Cross makes changes in money solicitation," NPR *All Things Considered*; Seabrook, A. (14 November 2001), "Red Cross announces all donations to its Liberty Fund will be used for victims of Sept. 11," NPR *All Things Considered*; Strom, S. (21 June 2002), "Charitable contributions in 2001 reached $212 billion," *The New York Times* online; Strom, S. (23 June 2002), "Families fret as charities hold a billion dollars in 9/11 aid," *The New York Times* online; Strom, S. (2 February 2003), "With a lawsuit pending, charities are divided over disclosure," *The New York Times* online; Superville, D. (30 October 2001), "Red Cross to cease solicitations for Sept. 11 disaster relief fund, introduces interim CEO," *Associated Press*; (27 December 2001), "Mitchell heads WTC Red Cross fund," United Press International; Walker, W. (7 November 2001), "U.S. Red Cross may double victims' payout," *Toronto Star*, p. A8; and Zepeda, P. (3 February 2003), "Senator Mitchell praises Red Cross for its 'excellent service to America,' " News Release at www.redcross.org/press/.

CASE 26.   "ONLY IN SASKATCHEWAN": GOVERNMENT CAMPAIGN SOLICITS YOUTH TESTIMONIALS ABOUT LOCAL OPPORTUNITIES

There is no need to leave Saskatchewan to find opportunity. We need to let opportunity find us here, because it is here. We just need to realize that.

Many Saskatchewan youth believe that the grass is greener in other provinces or countries. I tend to disagree. Saskatchewan has the resources and the people to create successful futures.

Perhaps the most convincing evidence in any persuasion campaign comes from firsthand testimonials such as these, which were drawn from prize-winning entries in the "Only in Saskatchewan" multimedia-contest promotional campaign. Obtaining such testimonials and evidence from volunteers was the focus of a contest and campaign sponsored by the province of Saskatchewan, Canada, which used the campaign in 2001–2002 to engage residents ages 8 to 24 who were willing to share their career dreams or success stories about living and working in Saskatchewan.

The goal of the contest and campaign was to encourage youth to remain in the province after completing their education by offering them a creative challenge to consider and to express their views about career and life opportunities in their area. The contest, announced in October 2001, encouraged young people to submit their "Saskatchewan success story" in a variety of media, including essay, video, artwork, or Web pages in either English or French. The entry deadline was in February 2002, and winners were announced in May 2002.

Prompting the Contest

From 1996 to 2001, the province of Saskatchewan, Canada, saw a net out-migration of 12,000 people age 15 to 29. The Canadian province, which has about 1 million residents and two large cities with populations of around 200,000 each, was perceived as having an image as a conservative, agricultural region with a relative lack of opportunity. Although out-migration slowed in the early 2000s, persuading younger residents that the province did offer social and career opportunities was the key objective of the contest sponsored by the department of Saskatchewan Industry and Resources, known as the Saskatchewan Economic and Co-operative Development during the campaign period. (The department works to promote a positive economic environment in the province.)

Brown Communication, a Saskatchewan-based agency, was hired to work with the department to develop and publicize the contest campaign.

Preparing for the Contest

Specific objectives for the campaign included soliciting more than 2,000 inquiries and a minimum of 500 entries from young people from a variety of geographic areas within the province, and to promote entrepreneurship among the young residents of Saskatchewan.

Key publics identified for the campaign included elementary, junior high, and high school students ages 8 to 18; college students, employees, and prospective young entrepreneurs ages 19 to 24; the parents of these two groups of young residents; educators, guidance counselors, and youth leaders; and through media coverage, the residents of Saskatchewan. Effort was also made to target aboriginal (native Indian, Métis, and Inuit) groups, a growing group of Saskatchewan residents.

The ad campaign incorporated edgy, contemporary design and text techniques for the restaurant table tents and posters that encouraged entries in the "Only in Saskatchewan" contest. (Courtesy of Saskatchewan Industry and Resources and Brown Communications.)

To test campaign plans and materials, Brown Communications organized five focus tests in different areas of the province targeted to residents ages 9 to 12, high school students, and workers ages 18 to 24. Although the campaign design and key messages tested well during the groups, small changes in plans were made, including stressing the $1,000 cash prizes and reducing the amount of text on the print materials.

The campaign's contest was subdivided into two parts. In Contest 1, school-age children ages 8 to 18 were asked to describe their Saskatchewan career dreams; there were individual categories based on narrower age groupings. In Contest 2, young adults ages 19 to 24 were required to submit their own Saskatchewan success stories, and the categories were divided by medium type (essay, artwork, and video/digital).

The total budget for the campaign was $178,000, which included agency fees, photography, printing, poster distribution, media placement costs, Web design, contest prizes, and related costs. Radio and print advertising and television PSAs were used to promote entries in the contests. Approval of marketing materials had to be obtained from senior government officials and politicians such as those on the Executive Council, the central communications body to the government of Saskatchewan that approves advertising and communications activities. Advertisements and promotions were scheduled through the first month.

Partnerships played a significant role in the campaign. Rawlco Radio, Saskatchewan's largest network of radio stations, promoted the contest on its radio shows, supplied prizes for various events, and contributed more than $25,000 of complimentary air time for radio advertisements about the contest. Local television stations ran the PSAs at no cost, at an estimated value of $53,000.

Washroom miniboards and table-tent cards were placed in popular restaurants and bars. Industry and Resources staff worked with the Department of Education to distribute information packages and posters through the school system. Promotional posters were displayed in libraries, offices, restaurants, bars, malls, and other public locations. A national youth magazine, *Realm,* ran a feature on the campaign. Testimonials were received and published in a supplement that went out in both of Saskatchewan's major daily papers, the *Saskatoon StarPhoenix* and the *Regina Leader-Post.*

The department of Industry and Resources established a contest Web site (www.onlyinsask.ca) and set up a contest hotline with a toll-free number (1-86-ONLY-HERE) where people could request information kits or receive answers to questions about the contest. The Web site provided information on the contest and updates as they were announced.

The launch had to overcome a communication obstacle created when a by-election was called in Saskatoon days before the scheduled launch of the contest. Election laws mandated that no government advertising could be conducted during the days before an election. Saskatoon is Saskatchewan's largest urban center, and delaying the media placements and promotional activities pushed media placement from October into November/December, a particularly busy time for media. However, media outlets cooperated with the placements, despite the timing.

Seeking Success Stories

To launch the contest, advertisements profiled six Saskatchewan young people as "Saskatchewan success stories," selected based on their diversity and individual success stories. The six people profiled included an actress, a veterinarian, a young entrepreneur, an art director, a radio station manager, and a president of an information technology business. In the group of six, there was equal representation of male and female and the inclusion of both a First Nations and a Métis person. During the campaign, the young people profiled in contest were invited to speak and be guests at provincial and national conventions and conferences. They were interviewed by print, radio, and television.

A news conference held October 11, 2001, officially began the campaign. Three of the profiled "success" story personalities and more than 200 invited guests and interested youth attended the event. School children were bused in from around Regina to participate.

The lieutenant governor of the province served as the honorary judge for the contest. Other judges included the president of the Saskatchewan Chamber of Commerce, a past president of the School Trustees Association, three members of the Youth Provincial Action Committee on the Economy, and the president of the Conseil de la cooperation de la Saskatchewan.

Five hundred fifty-four entries were submitted from more than 40 different areas of the province, and each contestant received a certificate of participation. More than 200 people, mostly young people, were invited to attend the May celebration where the winners were announced. Winners in each of the various categories were awarded $1,000 in cash. There were several ties, with winners in those categories splitting the prize money. Ten Saskatchewan youths received cash awards, and another 14 received Honorable Mention awards of merit. Several of the grand-prize winners were then interviewed on radio talk shows, and various entries were displayed at the Saskatchewan Legislative Building for 2 weeks.

Premier Lorne Calvert said: "This contest gave our youth a chance to express how they feel about pursuing their career dreams in Saskatchewan, and the responses were quite inspiring. It was clear from the submissions that our young people really do love this province and they see it as a place of endless opportunities."

Media coverage of the contest campaign resulted in 48 mentions, 83% of which were positive and 4% were neutral. There were 9,500 unique hits on the contest Web site at www.onlyinsask.ca. There were over 300 calls to the toll-free contest hotline throughout the duration of the contest. The calls and hits came in from virtually all corners of the province.

QUESTIONS FOR REFLECTION

1. Why would a governmental body be interested in securing volunteers to help promote its goals?
2. What are the critical components of a mutually beneficial relationship between a state or provincial government and its residents?
3. What other tactics or strategies might be used by an organization that wants to elicit personal testimonials for use in promoting an idea or proposal?
4. When a governmental body chooses to engage in a public-information or persuasion campaign, it may face both legal and ethical questions. What should the parameters be for the ethical practices in such campaigns?
5. Competitions require strict procedures so that fairness and objectivity are maintained. Evaluate how this campaign worked to ensure the effectiveness of the contest.

Information for this case was drawn from the following: Ellis, Bob, "Youth Contest Appoints Judges," News Release, Saskatchewan Economic and Co-Operative Development (3 December 2001), www.gov.sk.ca/newsrel/releases/2001/12/03-909.html; Ellis, Bob, "Youth Contest Winners Announced," News Release and Additional Information, Saskatchewan Economic and Co-operative Development (15 May 2002), www.gov.sk.ca/newsrel/releases/2002/05/15-356.html; Entry, Gold Quill Competition, IABC, 2002; and Brown Communications Web site, www.browncommunications.com

CASE 27. COLOSSAL FOSSIL DOMINATES CHICAGO'S FIELD MUSEUM

Museums face powerful rivals—sports, movies, theme parks, and others—in the competition for family leisure time. To grab families' attention, museums need not only irresistible attractions but also the showmanship to spotlight them. The Field Museum of Chicago showed how to provide both in planning its permanent exhibit of Sue, the world's largest and best-preserved *Tyrannosaurus rex* fossil.

In the first hours after Sue was unveiled on May 17, 2000, more than 10,000 visitors filed past the fossil. The first day's success rewarded years of hard work.

The bones were discovered by Sue Hendrickson, self-taught field paleontologist for whom the fossil was named, in the Black Hills of South Dakota in August 1990. A six-member team of fossil hunters spent 17 days extracting the remains from the hillside where they'd rested since Sue the dinosaur took her last breath 67 million years ago. The skeleton included 90% of a complete set of 250 bones (adult humans have 206).

Eventually, the unassembled skeleton was scheduled for sale at Sotheby's auction house in New York in October 1997. Nine serious competitors entered the bidding, including the Field Museum. The Field had been established in 1893 as the Columbian Museum of Chicago and was renamed in 1905 to honor its first major benefactor, Marshall Field. Its threefold mission focuses on public education in natural science and natural history, collections in those same areas, and basic research in biology and anthropology.

Enlisting Partners

Realizing that a successful bid could exceed the museum's resources, Field President John McCarter enlisted the support of two major corporate sponsors, McDonald's and Disney, in July 1997. The three organizations were natural partners for the effort because all three focus their public relations programs on families with young children. In return for financial help, the two companies would receive exclusive rights to full-size replica casts of the skeleton.

At Sotheby's, the bidding started at $500,000 and ended 8 minutes later when the Field group won with an offer of $7.6 million. Including Sotheby's commission, the total cost was $8.4 million.

Once The Field acquired the bones and moved them to Chicago, a team of 10 experts began the 2-year process of cleaning, inspecting, repairing, and preserving them. The 2 years gave the museum and Sue's corporate sponsors time to develop public relations plans that would build anticipation ahead of the unveiling ceremony and gain maximum visibility in the days following it.

In June 1998, the museum opened the McDonald's Fossil Preparation Laboratory where visitors could watch experts preparing the bones for mounting. In

Florida, a second preparation lab was opened at DinoLand U.S.A. in the Walt Disney World Resort's Animal Kingdom Park.

Nine months later, the museum's Web site introduced an interactive Web camera, the SueCam, that Web users worldwide could use to follow the progress of the restoration. Although visitors could monitor the preparation of individual bones, the skeleton itself was assembled in secrecy to save the surprise of the exhibit's final appearance for the unveiling ceremony on May 17.

Preparing the Media for the Unveiling

Six months before the unveiling, a press kit provided reporters with the background they would need for opening-day news stories as well as for features in advance of the exhibit's formal introduction.

The kit included:

- A main news release briefly describing the fossil's discovery, the ceremony and Sue herself, supplemental exhibits, the scientific study of dinosaurs, and the sponsors' participation.
- A second release on McDonald's plans for two identical traveling exhibits that would take Sue replicas on a nationwide tour.
- A science backgrounder on what paleontologists already had learned from analysis of Sue and what more they hoped to learn from the study of fossils.
- A schedule with details on the unveiling and additional special events that would take place on the weekend immediately following the opening-day ceremonies.
- A fact sheet on the exhibition (e.g., subject, location, hours, museum admission fee).
- A second fact sheet on Sue the dinosaur (e.g., 41 to 45 feet long, seven-ton estimated live weight, one-quart brain cavity, gender undetermined).
- A timeline tracing Sue from birth and death in the Cretaceous Age to her debut in 21st-century Chicago.

In advance of the unveiling, the museum also provided the media with a full-color image of Sue alive and in the flesh, showing sculptor Brian Cooley's re-creation of the dinosaur's hungry face based on educated speculation concerning her musculature and hide.

Disney timed the theatrical release of *Dinosaur*, its computer-animated/live-action movie, to coincide with the opening events. A special screening was sponsored by the museum on the first Friday following the unveiling. Advertising and promotion of the movie in the weeks leading up to the museum ceremony also raised public anticipation of the new exhibit.

Waking Up With Sue

The unveiling ceremony itself was scheduled for 6 a.m. CDT on Wednesday, May 17—early for family attendance but ideal for television networks' morning shows, which reach millions of potential visitors. Despite the hour, the sunrise ceremony attracted big crowds. Dinosaur fans also watched the ceremony from home via the SueCam on the Field Museum Web site.

Describing the opening event, CNN said, "The 41-foot-long *T. rex* inspired instant awe from thousands who packed the Chicago museum for the unveiling of 'Sue,' one of the most talked about and debated dinosaur finds in history."

Noting the build-up for the debut, CBS News said: "With Hollywood-style razzle-dazzle, the reassembled skeleton went on display Wednesday for the first time. In advance of the opening at Chicago's Field Museum, dinosaur logos were plastered on T-shirts and city buses."

McDonald's public relations agency, Burson-Marsteller, estimated that media coverage of the event resulted in 750 million impressions worldwide.

From 10 a.m. to 3 p.m. on opening day, the museum offered a variety of interactive programs for visitors, from preschoolers on up, to engage them in learning more about paleontology and to turn the day into something more than a brief or long look at Sue. On the following Saturday and Sunday, the schedule included more events supporting the new exhibit, including a lecture by the paleontologist who was lead researcher on Sue, a performance of "Tyrannosaurus Sue: A Cretaceous Concerto" by the Chicago Chamber Musicians, a puppet theater showing the evolution of dinosaurs, and more.

The following month, Disney erected its full-size replica of Sue at DinoLand U.S.A. in Orlando, Florida, and McDonald's opened the first of its two traveling Sue exhibits in Boston at the Museum of Science.

McDonald's Sends Sue on the Road

For McDonald's, participation in the Sue project had a national objective of strengthening existing links to kids, families, and educators, and it had local objectives of boosting restaurant traffic during tour promotions and making deposits in "community trust" banks. Analysis of news reports indicated that McDonald's got the credit it had wanted—a generous company willing to give back to the community.

The traveling exhibition was a complete show. It included a 45-foot-long replica of Sue as well as interactive anatomical models that enabled visitors to manipulate the jaw, neck, tail, and forelimbs of a *T. rex*. Dinosaur fans could touch casts of bones and models of Sue's 12-inch-long teeth, see video explaining the fossil's restoration, and more. The tour schedule into 2004 included major metropolitan areas and smaller cities, such as Atlanta; Hays, Kansas; Honolulu; Los Angeles; Muncie, Indiana; and Seattle. McDonald's arranged for fossil hunter Sue Hendrickson to visit some of the cities on the tour, starting with Boston.

To take Sue's story into classrooms, McDonald's distributed the Colossal Fossil Education Program to more than 60,000 elementary schools in the United States. It included a 10-minute video, in-school lessons, and take-home activities exploring the science that led to Sue's discovery and that guided the skeleton's restoration. Burson-Marsteller said that 95% of the teachers they surveyed rated the overall program good or excellent.

Some Reservations Registered

In some news reports on Sue, journalists described two related issues that concerned natural scientists and others:

- The commercialization of museum exhibits through corporate sponsorships.
- The sale of fossil trophies to the highest bidder.

One paleontologist expressed concern to CBS that consumerism could put unhealthy short-term pressures on scientific decision making that has long-term consequences for the accumulation of knowledge. Another pointed out that the auction of fossils could put highly important finds into the hands of private collectors and make them unavailable for scientific examination.

However, some curators countered that corporate sponsorship enables museums to purchase geological specimens that they could not afford otherwise, and corporate objectives would invariably involve public display. Companies participate primarily to earn the goodwill of customers and other important publics. Often, the sponsors not only provide the money to acquire new exhibits but also promote them to raise awareness, encourage attendance, and win community respect.

For the Field Museum, a spike in attendance was one measure of success of the Sue exhibit. For all of 2000, the museum welcomed 2.3 million visitors, up 50% from the preceding year. The Field's director of exhibitions and education programs estimated half of the increase was attributable to Sue, the world's most complete *T. rex* and Chicago's most attractive museum exhibit of the year.

QUESTIONS FOR REFLECTION

1. Why would McDonald's and Disney agree to help finance a bid of almost $8 million for a dinosaur fossil? How would they expect to benefit?
2. The unveiling of Sue was held at 6 a.m. CDT to lure coverage by the TV networks' morning shows. Would you have scheduled a more family-friendly time?
3. Families with membership in the Field Museum ($80 in 2004) receive special benefits, such as free admission, members-only previews of special ex-

hibits, and an annual behind-the-scenes open house. How might the Field have involved member families in the Sue celebration?

4. Why are dinosaurs and fossils a natural draw for McDonald's target publics?
5. Some critics saw dangers in corporate sponsorship of museum exhibits. What are the risks?

Information for this case was drawn from the following: The Field Museum Web site at http:// www.fmnh.org/; Conklin, M. (4 December 2000), "Building momentum from the bones up," *The Los Angeles Times*, p. F8; Kinzer, S. (5 November 2002), "Museum's goal: Save the world's wild places," *The New York Times*, p. E1; (16 May 2000), "Massive *T. rex* invades Chi-town," CBS News, http://www.cbsnews.com; (accessed 27 June 2002), "McDonald's Sue T-rex sponsorship," *The Holmes Report*, http://www.holmesreport.com; (18 May 2000), "Monstrous *T. rex* is unveiled in Chicago," *The Los Angeles Times*, p. 16; Randolph, E., & Goldman, J. (5 October 1997), "Museum snaps up *T. rex* in historic sale," *The Los Angeles Times*, p. A1; and (17 May 2000), "Sue, the biggest *T. rex*, makes her public debut," CNN, http://www.cnn.com/2000/NATURE/.

CASE 28.   FOR EVERY GIRL, EVERYWHERE—GIRL SCOUTS PREPARE FOR THE 21ST CENTURY

It's not just about selling cookies. Today's Girl Scouts are seeking to engage an increasingly diverse group of girls in exploring the outdoor and the environment, learning practical skills through mentoring, promoting healthy life skills with peers, and exploring the arts and global diversity. Founded in 1912 by Juliette Gordon Low, the organization has grown to include about 11% of all available American girls in its programs, but it is now seeking to increase the number of members and volunteers from more diverse backgrounds.

The organization itself has been adapting to societal changes for years. The Girl Scout Research Institute was formed in 1999 to conduct original research and analyze other research to help the organization plan for the future. Recommendations from the Institute have led Scouts to focus on adding career components for its older members and offering badges in such areas as careers, economics, computer, space exploration, and mathematics for girls age 10 to 17.

Diversifying the Membership

National staff consultants have been working with the more than 900,000 Girl Scout volunteers to increase membership, particularly among Hispanic and Asian-American girls, girls with disabilities, and older girls; to recruit adult leaders from underrepresented groups; and to ensure that the programs offered the groups are contemporary and useful.

In 2002, the Girl Scouts launched a major outreach titled "For Every Girl, Everywhere," with a primary objective of increasing membership among the 17% of girls under age 18 in the United States who are Hispanic. Brochures were printed in Spanish as well as English. At the beginning of the campaign, only 6.6% of the Girls Scouts' almost 3 million members were Hispanic. The next stage of the campaign will be to reach out to increase membership among Asian girls.

Advertising Age reported in January 2002 that the Girl Scout organization had enlisted the help of San Antonio-based Cartel Group to help direct the outreach. They worked together to create a "Cultural Awareness Training Program," which sought to identify common ties between the organization and the Hispanic culture. The training program began with suggestions on how to develop a comfortable relationship between Scout leaders and the mothers of Hispanic children. Activities such as camping trips may be open to entire families, and other programs are open for brothers to attend.

The 317 Girl Scout councils in the United States, Puerto Rico, and the Virgin Islands are chartered by the national organization, but local councils are allowed to use different strategies to reach out to "every girl." For example, troops in the Northwest suburbs and Lake County area near Chicago have hopes of attracting about 7,000 new African American girls, 4,800 Hispanic girls, and 3,700 Asian American girls to their ranks. Organizers in DuPage County are offering scouting experiences for children of Hispanic migrant workers, and some troops are offering cultural experiences such as celebrating Kwanzaa.

The Girl Scout Council of Colonial Coast of Virginia is reaching out to Filipinos, after hiring a special consultant to spearhead these efforts. Outreach begins at the Philippine Cultural Center and at meetings of Filipino organizations. The Girl Scouts of Racine County, Wisconsin, have also hired a Spanish-language outreach coordinator. The Girl Scouts host a Latina Mother–Daughter series at the University of Wisconsin–Parkside; they are now seeking to work through Hispanic community leaders to attract Spanish-speaking leaders as well as girls interested in Scouting.

Partners Support Girl Scout Efforts

Girl Scouts has teamed with Unilever to develop the ME! self-esteem program targeting girls aged 8 to 14, with focus on girls from underprivileged communities. Integrating research from the Girl Scouts Research Institute, the new program offers a core curriculum of ME! booklets that were introduced by Olympic gold medalist and gymnastics star Dominique Dawes.

The curriculum is composed of three booklets: *uniquely ME! The Way To Be*; *uniquely ME! Inside & Out*; and *uniquely ME! The Real Deal*, each designed to target specific age groups. They include exercises about recognizing personal strengths, dealing with peer pressure, health and exercise, and understanding one's values and interests. They also focus on eating disorders, relationships, and stress. The booklets are available in English and bilingual English/Spanish versions.

Individual councils will offer supportive activities such as mentoring, community service, or sports. Unilever employee volunteers will serve as mentors, teach the curriculum, and participate in annual events. Unilever has set a goal of involving more than 60% of its workforce in the program.

Teaming with the Women's Sports Foundation, a project called GoGirlGo is helping Girl Scout volunteers and staff members mentor economically disadvantaged girls identified as having health risks, or those underserved by school and community sports programs and wellness initiatives. Grants have funded outreach activities such as these: Girls from three Indian reservations in South Dakota were provided an opportunity to learn basic karate moves and to relax through yoga. In Omaha, Nebraska, the local Girl Scout council offered intramural sessions that included soccer, basketball, golf, swimming, and personal nutrition and fitness. Interactive bilingual tools were used to help the residents of a San Diego teen detention center cope with real-life challenges like drug abuse, stress management, and eating disorders.

Through these and other ongoing sports programs, Girl Scouts can earn badges such as "Health and Fitness," "On the Court," "Sports Sampler," "Walking for Fitness," "Swimming," "Hiker," "Dance," and "On the Playing Field."

QUESTIONS FOR REFLECTION

1. Why would the Girl Scouts organization target membership from diverse groups? What are some of the challenges faced as organizations seek to expand their diversity?
2. What are some of the issues involved with attracting volunteers from diverse groups to serve as Scout leaders and mentors?
3. Why would corporations such as Unilever be interested in partnering with the Girl Scouts?

Information for this case was drawn from the following: The Girls Scouts of the USA Web site at http://www.girlscouts.org/; Foderaro, L. W. (25 December 2002), "Beyond crafts and cookies, Girl Scouts are prospering," *The New York Times*, p. A1; Franklin, K. (30 September 2001), "Scouts see promise in diversity; group launches appeal to Asian-American, Hispanic girls," *The Virginian-Pilot*, p. B1; (1 June 2001), "Girls Scouts of the USA," *Trusts & Estates*, p. S30; Hurt, J. (9 September 2001), "Scouts work on diversity bade," *Milwaukee Journal Sentinel*, p. Z1; Koropey, L. (18 September 2002), "Olympic champion Dominique Dawes teams up with Girl Scouts & Unilever to empower girls through progressing new self-esteem program," Release, *Internet Wire*; Mask, T. (16 January 2002), "Girl Scouts begin push to diversify their ranks," *Chicago Daily Herald*, p.1; and Taylor, C. P. (28 January 2002), "Diversity: Girl Scouts extend multicultural reach; All-American group seeks greater diversity," *Advertising Age*, p. 18.

CASE 29.   A NEW WAY FOR THE UNITED WAY OF THE NATIONAL CAPITAL AREA?

Investigations into administrative practices at the United Way of the National Capital Area affiliate have led to leadership resignations and a new system for board administration, while reminding affiliates across the country of the need for accountability to their donors.

United Way affiliates are typically administered by a director who acts as the CEO and other paid staff members who work with a board of directors composed of volunteers to form policies, lead fund-raising efforts, and make allocation decisions. The National Capital Area affiliate raises money for some 1,100 social-service agencies in the district as well as in its Maryland and Virginia suburbs. It has received donations through payroll deductions from some 350,000 workers and usually raises more than $90 million annually.

Capital Leadership?

Oral Suer had served as the affiliate's director for 27 years. He led in the creation of the affiliate from a merger of two others and then served as the affiliate's chief executive from 1974 to 2001. After his retirement in 2001, the United Way paid Suer a pension settlement of more than $1 million. He also received a $6,000-a-month consulting contract and was allowed to continue using an American Express platinum card the affiliate issues its executives.

Suer was succeeded by Norman O. Taylor, who later resigned on September 6, 2002, amid ongoing investigations into how the United Way affiliate had spent its donations. The investigations centered on practices during Suer's leadership. A federal grand jury and at least two federal agencies, including the federal Department of Labor, were reportedly investigating the group's financial management practices for possible financial mismanagement, including discriminatory pricing of services, excessive pension payments, and inflation of donation totals.

Following Taylor's resignation, Charles W. Anderson became the chief executive of the affiliate. His task was to help the organization settle its controversy and focus on revitalizing its fund-raising and service efforts.

Investigations Begin

Investigations into leadership compensation at the United Way first began in 2001 when the charity's general counsel was approached by board member Ross W. Dembling, who had questions about how donations were being spent. Dembling was told a few weeks later that his term on the board would not be renewed. News coverage about the incident raised questions, and an accounting firm was asked to audit the affiliate.

In May 2002, the affiliate reported that the audit found nothing significantly wrong in the way the United Way dealt with its finances. The audit report said it found a $1,800 discrepancy in the credit-card purchases of former affiliate executive Suer, but that he had repaid the affiliate for the amounts. Board member Anthony J. Buzzelli, who had overseen the audit, told the *Washington Times:* "The current management has been put under the microscope. The purpose of the report is to make sure that this management that is in place today is one that the public can trust." The audit also reported that reforms were put in place that mandated a competitive-bid policy for expenditures greater than $10,000 and prohibited sale of organization assets to employees or volunteers.

However, questions about the thoroughness of the audit soon were aired. The *Washington Post* said the auditor never interviewed a key executive, Kenneth Unzicker, who told an ethics panel following the audit that his attempts to report misgivings about ethical and accounting issues were "rebuffed or ignored by Norman Taylor and others in control of the organization." He said that Taylor had known of issues concerning credit-card abuses and the consulting contract for Mr. Suer. Critics said the accounting firm had been told to limit the scope of the audit to certain procedures.

The board of directors asked for an expanded audit, which was conducted by PricewaterhouseCooper LLP. In August 2003, the audit said former affiliate head Suer was accused of having taken more than $1.5 million in payments from the United Way, with the knowledge of a few board members. As far back as 1987, auditors said, Suer had received some $470,000 in advances from the United Way of the National Capital Area, and he had told auditors he was "embarrassed by the situation," according to an October 1987 memo by the auditor reported in the *Washington Post*. At the time, Suer had said he was taking steps to repay the affiliate through payroll deductions. The auditor's report said a few of the leading members of the board had tried to handle the financial matters privately, and apparently, the full board was never informed of the advances or the repayment agreement.

The audit said that in 1991 Suer had entered into a formal agreement to repay the more than $323,000 owed at that point by surrendering deferred compensation and having $5,000 a month deducted from his pay. He did not repay all of the money, however, and continued to receive more than his $196,000 annual salary, according to the audit. According to the *Washington Post,* the auditors said: "We found no footnote disclosure of this significant amount of recurring unpaid advances in UWNCA's financial statements. We also found no discussion of this issue in the Board of Director's [sic] meeting minutes." The affiliate had paid Suer some $1.4 million for unused holiday and sick pay and about $230,000 in retirement benefits, according to Associated Press reports. The *Washington Post* also reported that Suer had charged hundred of dollars on the corporate credit card at retailers and through mail-order catalogs during the 1999 holiday season without filing supporting paperwork for the purchases. Suer said the purchases were gifts for key executives and volunteers.

Responses to the Second Audit

In response to the findings of the second audit report, the board of directors for the affiliate was reorganized. Its 21 members meet monthly, rather than quarterly, and it must offer approval for affiliate activities. Employees are no longer paid for unused sick leave and vacation, and the salary and expenses of the chief executive office will be reviewed by the entire board. The affiliate's attorney said in the August 17, 2003, *Washington Post*: "There's nothing that happens now in this organization that isn't shared by all the board members and the management. The level of transparency is as high as I've ever seen at any organization."

It was also recommended that the United Way affiliate eliminate a third of its workforce, cut its budget by 41%, and select a new auditor. The task force recommended that some 30 staff positions be eliminated; during Taylor's tenure, staffing had grown from 67 to 90.

The affiliate filed a lawsuit against Suer, charging that he defrauded it of more than $1.5 million.

Focusing on Fund-Raising

The board then sought to emphasize that the problems had been solved. Donations in the 2002 campaign from the private sector had dropped from $45 million to $18 million, which meant that agencies that had depended on United Way support to serve clients were underfunded. The new leadership of the affiliate moved quickly to communicate that the problems had been identified and the affiliate reorganized. Anderson, the new chief executive, met with corporate executives to try to persuade them to support the United Way of the National Capital Area again. The audit was posted on the organizational Web site to allow open access to its findings.

The United Way of America Chief Executive Brian A. Gallagher told the *Post* on August 13, 2003, that the current leadership has "done everything that you would have hoped the former board and management would have done ... and now they've got to communicate effectively if folks are going to come back and trust them."

Other Impact?

Did the investigation in Washington, DC, affect giving to others of the 1,400 local affiliates? The *New York Times* said in September 2002 that the issue had "cast a shadow over the entire United Way." By April 2003, estimates predicted that the national United Way 2002–2003 campaign would raise as much as 4% less than had been raised during the 2001–2002 campaign. A few affiliates, such as Milwaukee and Birmingham, Alabama, saw increases in giving, but some affiliates in larger cities, such as Atlanta and Chicago, saw double-digit drops in giving. The *New York Times* reported that donations to the United Way had declined only once since 1971, in 1992 when William Aramony, then president of the United Way of

America, was indicted on charges of embezzlement and fraud. Aramony subsequently was sentenced to serve 7 years in federal prison after being convicted of defrauding the charity of more than $1 million.

However, new standards for accounting were adopted for the annual campaign, and some argue that the declines in giving could be attributed to those changes. Affiliate campaigns were no longer allowed to count the value of in-kind contributions. The drop in the stock market and a decline in other revenues may have affected people's abilities to give, although traditionally, economic downturns have not been reflected in United Way campaigns. Gary Godsey, president of the United Way of Dallas, told the *New York Times* that he had been assured by Dallas businesspeople that the scandal was not responsible for the downfall in Dallas fund-raising. "This is purely economic, and in Dallas, we've been particularly hard hit."

QUESTIONS FOR REFLECTION

1. How should a nonprofit, its board, and its staff interact? What are the most important responsibilities of these stakeholder relationships?
2. What are the ethical obligations involved in handling donations to a nonprofit service agency? What are the obligations that result from membership on a corporate or nonprofit board of directors?
3. What is the importance of open access to nonprofit records such as audits and financial reports? How does this correspond to the legal requirement for publicly owned companies to publish annual and quarterly reports?

Information for this case came from the following: coverage in *The Washington Post* by Whoriskey, P., & Salmon, J. L. (17 August 2003), "Dealings of charity executive concealed; United Way audit flagged issue in '87," *The Washington Post*, p. C1; Salmon, J. L., & Whoriskey, P. (13 August 2003), "Problems behind us, charity says; United Way partnership divides area employees," *The Washington Post*, p. B1; Whoriskey, P., & Salmon, J. L. (8 May 2002), "United Way credit charges described as holiday gifts; nonprofit to release audit in response to financial questions," *The Washington Post*, p. B1; and Whoriskey, P., & Salmon, J. L. (4 September 2002), "United Way audit omitted dissenter," *The Washington Post*, p. B1. Other information came from the following: Associated Press (12 August 2003), "Audit indicates millions in questionable expenses for former D.C. United Way leader," accessed through *LexisNexis Academic*; Johnston, D. C. (17 July 2002), "Grand jury is investigating United Way in Washington," *The New York Times*; Strom, S. (6 September 2002), "Director of the United Way in Washington steps down," *The New York Times*; Strom, S. (8 April 2003), "Usually resilient United Way now predicts a leaner year," *The New York Times*; and Taylor, G. (9 May 2002), "United Way audit clears managers," *The Washington Times*.

8

Stakeholders: Governments and Regulators

Few organizations in the United States escape the scrutiny and influence of government regulators. From jetliners 35,000 feet above the earth's surface to miners 5,000 feet below it, most organized human activity attracts government attention. Some agencies, such as the Federal Aviation Administration (FAA), become as well known as the companies they monitor. Others, such as the Mine Safety and Health Administration, are seldom seen or heard outside their own industry.

Regulatory agencies exist because elected federal, state, and local officials create them to develop and enforce rules needed to carry out the law. In most cases, regulations focus on protecting human health and safety, the natural environment, and the free-market economic system.

THE ROLES OF PRACTITIONERS

Public relations practitioners must understand the regulations that govern their organizations' activities and anticipate how the rules might affect their own plans or those of competitors. Knowing the rules will help practitioners:

- Contribute effectively to discussion, analysis, and strategic planning.
- Understand the consequences of both compliance and noncompliance.
- Anticipate how regulations may affect customers, employees, investors, and others.
- Interpret the potential effects of newly proposed rules.
- Prepare to explain adverse regulatory decisions.

For example, the Federal Trade Commission (FTC) announced in March 2003 that it would oppose Nestlé SA's acquisition of Dreyer's Grand Ice Cream Inc. because the combination would reduce competition in the gourmet-ice-cream segment. Despite the setback, the two companies publicly expressed their commitment to completing the deal. After 3 months of negotiations that were covered regularly in national media and watched closely by employees, they won FTC approval.

REGULATORY COMPLEXITIES

Complex regulations and high stakes have made pharmaceutical public relations a demanding specialty. The FDA strictly enforces its rules concerning the language that drug companies must use in describing the testing, efficacy, and side effects of products. News releases or other materials that run afoul of FDA rules may lead to delay, embarrassment, fines, or other sanctions.

Occasionally, regulatory agencies have overlapping responsibilities. For example, both the FTC and the Federal Communications Commission (FCC) were involved in establishing the National Do-Not-Call Registry in 2003, responding to industry objections and subsequent lawsuits, and implementing the new rules.

When the federal government establishes a regulatory agency, state governments often create their own corresponding agency to govern intrastate activities, and strong state regulatory structures are common in public service utilities, such as electric-power companies and telecommunications, and in the banking industry.

Some states have consistently adopted stricter rules than their federal counterparts in certain regulated activities, earning reputations as rule-making leaders and complicating the jobs of public relations professionals. For example, the California Air Resources Board has gained recognition for setting the nation's toughest auto emissions standards.

CRITICS OF REGULATION

Regulatory efforts have attracted a large number of critics who say they simply add to the costs of producing a product or service without providing an equivalent value in benefits. The operation of free markets, the critics say, would accomplish the same good effects that government rules do.

John Stossel, an investigative reporter for ABC-TV's "20/20" news program who's been honored five times for excellence in consumer reporting by the National Press Club, is one of the most tireless critics of government regulation. He explained his reasons in 2001 at a Hillsdale College seminar:

> When I started 30 years ago as a consumer reporter, I took the approach that most young reporters take today. My attitude was that capitalism is essentially cruel and unfair, and that the job of government, with the help of lawyers and the press, is to protect people from it. For years, I did stories along those lines—stories about Cof-

fee Association ads claiming that "coffee picks you up while it calms you down," or Libby-Owens-Ford Glass Company ads touting the clarity of its product by showing cars with their windows rolled down. I and other consumer activists said, "We've got to have regulation. We've got to police these ads. We've got to have a Federal Trade Commission." And I'm embarrassed at how long it took me to realize that these regulations make things worse, not better, for ordinary people.

The damage done by regulation is so vast, it's often hard to see. The money wasted consists not only of the taxes taken directly from us to pay for the bureaucrats, but also of the indirect cost of all the lost energy that goes into filling out the forms.

PROTECTING THE POWERLESS

Regulatory advocates respond that powerful corporations, highly motivated to minimize costs and well equipped with resources needed to prevail in disputes, would not adequately protect the health of workers or the environment if the government did not supervise them closely.

Here are brief descriptions of some of the most prominent federal regulatory agencies. The descriptions are adapted from materials the agencies have published.

Consumer Product Safety Commission (CPSC).   The CPSC protects the public against unreasonable risks of injuries and deaths associated with consumer products. The agency has jurisdiction over about 15,000 types of consumer products ranging from coffee makers to toys to lawn mowers.

CPSC activities include:

- Developing voluntary standards with industry.
- Issuing and enforcing mandatory standards and banning products if no feasible standard would adequately protect the public.
- Obtaining the recall of products or arranging for their repair.

Environmental Protection Administration (EPA).   The EPA mission is to protect human health and safeguard the natural environment on which life depends. In July 1970, the White House and Congress worked together to establish the EPA in response to the growing public demand for cleaner water, air, and land. Before formation of the EPA, the federal government was not structured to make a coordinated attack on the pollutants that harm human health and degrade the environment.

Equal Employment Opportunity Commission (EEOC).   The EEOC coordinates all federal equal employment opportunity regulations, practices, and policies. The commission also interprets employment discrimination laws, monitors the federal sector equal employment opportunity program, and provides funding and support to state and local fair employment practices agencies and tribal employment rights organizations.

Federal Aviation Administration.   The FAA is responsible for the safety of civil aviation. The FAA's major roles include:

- Regulating civil aviation to promote safety.
- Encouraging and developing civil aeronautics, including new aviation technology.
- Developing and operating the air traffic control system for civil and military aircraft.
- Developing and carrying out programs to control aircraft noise and other environmental effects of civil aviation.

Federal Communications Commission.   The FCC operates bureaus that process applications for licenses, analyze complaints, conduct investigations, develop and implement regulatory programs, and take part in hearings. Some of the bureaus are:

- Consumer and Governmental Affairs, which educates and informs consumers about telecommunications goods and services and invites public input to help guide the work of the FCC.
- Media, which regulates AM, FM radio and television broadcast stations, as well as cable and satellite distribution.
- Wireless Telecommunications, which oversees cellular and PCS phones, pagers, and two-way radios.
- Wireline Competition, which regulates phone companies that mainly provide interstate services through wire-based networks including corded and cordless phones.

Federal Reserve System.   The Federal Reserve, central bank of the United States, was founded in 1913 to provide the nation with a safer, more flexible, and more stable monetary and financial system.

The central bank's duties fall into four general areas:

- Conducting the nation's monetary policy.
- Supervising banking institutions and protecting the credit rights of consumers.
- Maintaining the stability of the financial system.
- Providing certain financial services to the government, public, financial institutions, and foreign official institutions.

Federal Trade Commission.   The FTC works to ensure that markets are vigorous, efficient, and free of restrictions that harm consumers. Experience demonstrates that competition among firms yields products at the lowest prices, spurs innovation and strengthens the economy. Markets also work best when consumers can make informed choices based on accurate information.

To ensure the smooth operation of the free-market system, the FTC enforces federal consumer protection laws that prevent fraud, deception, and unfair business practices. The commission also enforces federal antitrust laws that prohibit anticompetitive mergers and other business practices that restrict competition and harm consumers.

Food and Drug Administration.   The FDA is responsible for protecting the public health by assuring the safety, efficacy, and security of human and veterinary drugs, biological products, medical devices, commercial food supply, cosmetics, and products that emit radiation. The FDA advances the public health by helping to speed innovations that make medicines and foods more effective, safer, and more affordable and by helping the people get the accurate, science-based information they need to use medicines and foods to improve their health.

The FDA works to ensure that consumers have up-to-date, truthful information on the benefits and risks of regulated products. Its complementary roles are:

- Ensuring that the information companies provide about products is accurate and allows for their safe use.
- Communicating directly with the public concerning benefits and risks of products the FDA regulates.

Occupational Safety and Health Administration (OSHA).   OSHA's mission is to save lives, prevent injuries, and protect the health of America's workers. To accomplish this, federal and state governments work in partnership with the more than 100 million working men and women and 6.5 million employers covered by the Occupational Safety and Health Act. Nearly every working man and woman in the nation comes under OSHA's jurisdiction (with some exceptions such as miners and transportation workers).

National Highway Traffic Safety Administration (NHTSA).   NHTSA is responsible for reducing death, injury, and economic loss resulting from highway accidents. The agency sets and enforces safety standards for motor vehicles and vehicle equipment. NHTSA investigates safety defects in motor vehicles, sets and enforces fuel economy standards, helps reduce the threat of drunk drivers, promotes use of seat belts, child safety seats, and air bags, investigates odometer fraud, establishes and enforces vehicle anti-theft regulations, and provides consumer information on motor vehicle safety topics.

Securities and Exchange Commission.   The primary mission of the SEC is to protect investors and maintain the integrity of the securities markets. As more first-time investors turn to the markets to help secure their futures, pay for homes, and send children to college, these goals are more compelling than ever.

The world of investing is fascinating, complex, and potentially fruitful. Unlike the banking world, where deposits are guaranteed, stocks, bonds, and other securities can lose value. There are no guarantees. The principal way for investors to protect the money they put into securities is to do research and ask questions.

The main purposes of the laws creating the SEC can be summed up in two propositions:

- Companies publicly offering securities for investment dollars must tell the public the truth about their businesses, the securities they are selling, and the risks involved in investing.
- People who sell and trade securities—brokers, dealers, and exchanges—must treat investors fairly and honestly, putting investors' interests first.

U.S. Department of Agriculture (USDA).   The USDA's Food Safety Mission Area ensures that the commercial supply of meat, poultry, and egg products is safe, wholesome, and correctly labeled and packaged. The Food Safety and Inspection Service (FSIS) sets standards for food safety and inspects meat, poultry, and egg products produced domestically and imported. The FSIS inspects animals and birds at slaughter and processed products at various stages of production and analyzes products for microbiological and chemical adulterants. FSIS also informs the public about meat, poultry, and egg safety issues.

ADDITIONAL READINGS

Downs, Anthony. (1994). *Inside bureaucracy.* Long Grove, IL: Waveland Press.

Jung, Donald J. (2002). *The Federal Communications Commission.* Lanham, MD: University Press of America.

Labaree, Robert V. (2000). *The Federal Trade Commission: A guide to sources.* New York: Garland.

Wilson, James Q. (2000). *Bureaucracy: What government agencies do and why they do it.* New York: Basic Books.

CASE 30.   NEW INTERNET COOKIE RECIPE GIVES HEARTBURN TO DOUBLECLICK

Internet marketers have big appetites for cookies, but privacy advocates often find them not simply distasteful but dangerous. At DoubleClick Inc., a company that provides Internet services for advertisers, a new recipe for cookies caused so much indigestion that federal and state authorities decided to investigate DoubleClick's corporate kitchen.

On the Internet, a cookie is a small text file that's stored on your computer by many Web sites that you visit. The purpose? Like a serial number, a cookie can make your computer easily and uniquely identifiable to the Web site that created it—sometimes for marketing purposes and sometimes for access permission.

Web site operators hire DoubleClick to handle ad insertion and viewer measurement rather than do it themselves. Using computers called ad servers, DoubleClick inserts ads into the web pages of its clients, tallies usage of their Web sites, and analyzes usage patterns. DoubleClick technology can guarantee that the same ad isn't repeated for a Web site visitor, predetermine the order of ads in a series, and keep track of the number of unique visitors who access a Web site.

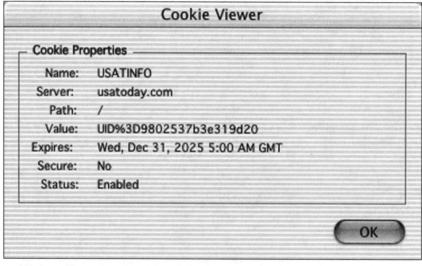

Magic cookies, written into a computer's memory by Web sites, contain a unique identifier, or value, and an expiration date. The cookie enables a Web site to recognize a computer each time it reconnects. (Illustration by L. Lamb.)

Recipe for Internet Cookies

Here's how the cookie process has generally worked:

1. You visit a Web site such as amazon.com or cnn.com. All types of organizations use cookies.
2. The Web site writes a small text file onto your hard disk. If your Internet browser is preset to accept cookies, you're not aware of this activity. (You can set browsers to refuse all cookies or accept only those meeting certain conditions.)
3. The text file contains both a unique number, assigned only to your computer, and an expiration date, which may be years away. The unique number could look something like iXxz@JB2ggkL ... IvYN3BofhQl.
4. Days or weeks later, you visit the same Web site again.
5. The Web site checks the cookie files on your hard disk, finds the one it wrote, and recognizes that iXxz@JB2ggkL ... IvYN3BofhQl is back for another visit.

As long as you don't erase the cookie and it hasn't reached its expiration date, the Web site that wrote the unique number will recognize your computer whenever it returns.

A single Web site may write several cookies to your hard disk, depending on how many pages or features of the Web site you access, and multiple cookies might enable a Web site to catalog your interests.

This data collection makes some privacy advocates uneasy and alarms others because the potential for misuse of personal information grows as detailed profiles are built up. For this reason, most Web sites post privacy statements that outline their policies on confidentiality and the sale of information to third parties.

Sharing Data Collected With Cookies

Some Web sites hire DoubleClick under arrangements that allow the sharing of cookie data from multiple Web sites. Through sharing, DoubleClick collects information on your usage patterns and analyzes it to learn your preferences. Knowing your preferences, DoubleClick calculates marketing scores that rank your probable interest in purchasing certain kinds of products or services and then delivers ads to you that match your preferences. This analysis, scoring, ad selection, and ad delivery happen instantaneously as you browse the Web.

For example, cookie analysis may show that consumers who buy mysteries are likely to drink more tea than average. If you access an online bookseller's listing for the latest Patricia Cornwell novel, an ad may appear on the same web page offering a collection of international teas. Knowing the person's name and address isn't necessary because the Internet provides a direct connection between the marketer and the individual consumer.

Even so, some marketers would prefer to know the name and address of the computer user who's associated with a cookie. Who is iXxz@JB2ggkL ... IvYN3BofhQl? A bookseller with that information could send a printed catalog of mystery novels to a computer user who accessed Patricia Cornwell titles but made no purchase. Intrusive? Undoubtedly. Ethical? Debatable.

Questions of Confidentiality

DoubleClick has been a leader in Internet advertising and technology services since the dawn of e-commerce, and for years its privacy statement had said that cookie data it collected would remain anonymous. Cookies inevitably become associated with individuals' names when computer users give personal information to Web sites to obtain free e-mail privileges, personalize news pages, gain access to password-protected Web sites, make purchases, and so on. When they do, they also consent to the Web site's policy concerning privacy—though most probably never read it.

DoubleClick began reconsidering its policy after acquiring Abacus Direct, a database firm that sells buyer behavior information on 90 million identifiable U.S. households. With modifications to its privacy and consent statements, Double-Click prepared to track the online habits of named—not anonymous—individuals and planned to sell the information to catalog marketers and others.

A tide of criticism swelled. A California woman sued the company in January 2000, asking the courts to stop DoubleClick from collecting personal details without permission and to require it to erase any records it had accumulated, and 12 more lawsuits soon piled on.

The FTC notified the company that an FTC inquiry into its data collection and ad serving practices was under way, and the attorneys general of 10 states also began similar investigations.

Five-Point Initiative on Privacy

Apparently surprised by the ferocity of its critics, the company announced a privacy initiative a few days later. Under the five-point initiative, DoubleClick pledged to:

- Use its www.privacychoices.org Web site and full-page ads in the *New York Times* and other major newspapers to inform online users about privacy rights and the ability to opt out of cookies.
- Adopt a new policy requiring all Web site operators using DoubleClick technology to have a clear and effective privacy policy governing their sites.
- Engage independent auditors to verify the company's compliance with its privacy commitments.
- Establish an advisory board of consumer advocates, security experts, and online privacy authorities to guide the company in improving the clarity of privacy policies.
- Hire a chief privacy officer to ensure adherence to privacy policies.

Some privacy critics applauded the initiative as a good start, but others said that the changes were mostly cosmetic and left untouched the fundamental problem—surreptitious recording of user behaviors into a massive library of personal information.

DoubleClick insisted that it was doing nothing wrong and issued a statement by the company's president, Kevin Ryan, just 3 days after announcing its five-point initiative.

"We are confident that our business policies are consistent with our privacy statement and beneficial to consumers and advertisers," he said. "The FTC has begun a series of inquiries into some of the most well-known web companies, including DoubleClick, and we support their efforts to keep the Internet safe for consumers."

Critics Pile On

Critics did not let up. The Electronic Privacy Information Center and the Center for Democracy & Technology complained that many privacy statements, even those of some prominent online retailers, were misleading and often ignored by Web site operators. Consumer advocates said that DoubleClick should directly ask Internet users for permission to record data.

A *Business Week* editorial warned: "The hope that the Internet could police itself on privacy is quickly fading, as new invasive technology generates an ominous flood of intrusions ... DoubleClick Inc., the biggest Internet ad placement company, unleashed a storm of controversy by profiling thousands of web surfers by name—without their explicit consent."

The editorial noted that some members of Congress were considering legislation to regulate the use of cookies and that the European Union already had imposed limits on the collection of personal data in its 15 member nations.

Doubleclick Acknowledges Mistake

After more than a month of complaints and castigation, the CEO of DoubleClick, Kevin O'Connor, acknowledged that the company had started down the wrong path and was ready to backtrack. He said on March 2:

> Over the past few weeks, DoubleClick has been at the center of the Internet privacy controversy. During this time, we have met and listened to hundreds of consumers, privacy advocates, customers, government officials and industry leaders about these issues. The overwhelming point of contention has been under what circumstances names can be associated with anonymous user activity across Web sites.

> It is clear from these discussions that I made a mistake by planning to merge names with anonymous user activity across Web sites in the absence of government and industry privacy standards.

> Let me be clear: DoubleClick has not implemented this plan and has never associated names, or any other personally identifiable information, with anonymous user activity across Web sites.

We commit today that, until there is agreement between government and industry on privacy standards, we will not link personally identifiable information, to anonymous user activity across Web sites.

Over the next 30 months, the FTC closed its inquiry into the company's operations; a federal court approved a settlement that DoubleClick reached in the Internet users' lawsuits, subsequently combined into a single federal case; and the company reached agreement with the attorneys general of 10 states, ending their investigation.

In none of the cases did DoubleClick admit any wrongdoing, and the company was required to do little beyond its original five-point initiative. In effect, the agreement with the states made the initiative legally binding rather than simply voluntary.

QUESTIONS FOR REFLECTION

1. Do you think that most people use the Internet with the expectation that their privacy—which sites they visit and how often—will be respected and protected?
2. Some Internet users like cookies because they can make the Internet easier to use if you repeatedly visit the same site. Others object to the invisible collection of data. Can the two viewpoints be reconciled?
3. Why is the FTC interested in Internet cookies?
4. What are the most recent controversies concerning Internet privacy? Do they resemble the DoubleClick issue?

Information for this case was drawn from the following: the DoubleClick Web site at http://www.doubleclick.com/us/about_doubleclick; Teinowitz, I., & Gilbert. J. (31 January 2000), "Online privacy disputes reach FTC panel, courts," *Advertising Age*, p. 92; Gray, D. (28 January 2000), "DoubleClick sued for privacy violations," IDG News Service; Miller, G. (3 February 2000), "Ad firm's practice seen as threat to net anonymity," *The Los Angeles Times*, p. A1; Dreazen, Y. (18 November 2002), "The best way to ... guard your privacy," *The Wall Street Journal*, p. R4; Green, H. (23 April 2001), "Commentary: Your right to privacy: Going ... Going ...," *Business Week*, p. 67; Sullivan, B. (24 May 2002), "Privacy groups debate DoubleClick settlement," IDG News Service; Schwartz, J. (17 October 2002), "Consumers face tricky maze in guarding privacy," *The New York Times*, p. C1; Green, H., Alster, N., Borrus, A., & Yang, C. (14 February 2000), "Privacy: Outrage on the web," *Business Week*, p. 111; and (28 February 2000), "Time to move on Internet privacy," *Business Week*, p. 142.

CASE 31. "WORKING TOGETHER TO BRING PEACE": SAUDI ARABIA SEEKS TO IMPROVE ITS U.S. IMAGE

The commercial proclaimed: "We are separated by three oceans.... one language .... But we share the same desires ... the same dreams ... the same joy ... the same pain ... and the same hope that we can make our world a safer place. Together."

The advertisement, which aired in 14 American markets, was part of a multimillion-dollar public relations campaign financed by the Saudi Arabian government in an attempt to improve the image of the country among Americans and their leaders.

Post-September 11 Concerns

The image of Saudi Arabia had apparently been damaged by fears about terrorism and anti-U.S. sentiment. Fifteen of the 19 hijackers who attacked U.S. targets on September 11, 2001, were Saudi citizens. Reports that emerged following the attacks contained allegations that a Saudi princess had inadvertently given money to the terrorists. Security measures imposed following the attacks had led to the screening of visa applicants from the Middle East and intensive scrutiny of Arab charitable organizations within the United States; these actions heightened concerns about relations between the longtime allied countries. A Gallup opinion poll 5 months following the attacks found that negative opinion of Saudi Arabia was up to 64%, rising from the 46% of Americans who held unfavorable positions prior to September 11.

A Royal Public Relations Campaign

Since that time, the Saudi government has invested millions of dollars on an extensive public relations campaign to try to improve its image in the United States. Justice Department sources reported in the *New York Times* that the Saudis hired several public relations firms and spent more than $5 million in the first year after the terrorist attacks. Among the public relations firms employed were Patton Boggs, a firm known for its contacts among Democrats, and Akin, Gump, Strauss, Hauer & Feld, a firm headed by Robert Strauss, who once headed the Democratic National Committee. Lobbyists with Republican ties have also been employed, including James P. Gallagher, a former Senate staff member, and the media-buying firm of Sandler-Innocenzi.

Qorvis Communications is the public relations firm that produced the broadcast advertising campaign. It was being paid $200,000 a month for its services, garnering a reported $1.4 million from the Saudis from October 2002 to March 2003. The agency has prepared position papers that stress the positive relationship between the Bush administration and the Saudis. Reports said at least 10 other firms also had been hired to represent Saudi Arabia.

According to its Web site, Qorvis Communications is the largest independently owned public relations firm based in the Greater Washington, DC, area. Formed in August 2000, Qorvis has offices in Washington, DC, and McLean, Virginia, and provides services to its clients in investor and financial relations, public affairs, grassroots campaigns, public and media relations, marketing communications, and research and opinion surveys. The Washington, DC-based law firm of Patton Boggs is an investor in and strategic partner to Qorvis.

Michael Petruzzello, the managing partner of Qorvis, was interviewed by the Associated Press in February 2003. He said negative American opinions about the Saudis can be changed. "After a year of a lot of high-profile attention, positive and negative, people in the United States are asking, 'Who are the Saudis?' ... So now, what we are trying to do is reintroduce the Saudi people."

The advertisements stressed the long-standing ties between the two countries. One spot featured black-and-white photos of Saudi leaders with U.S. presidents from Franklin Roosevelt to George W. Bush. Its voice-over says: "We've been allies for more than 60 years. Working together to solve the world's toughest problems. Working together for a world of prosperity. Working together to bring peace to the Middle East. Working together to create a better future for us all."

Another ad features quotes from Bush and Secretary of State Colin Powell commending the Saudis for their cooperation in the war on terrorism.

The campaign utilized more than television and radio advertisements. Adel al-Jubeir, a Saudi adviser, said the strategy for improving the Saudi image would include increasing press accessibility, sending officials on speaking tours, polling American public opinion, and cultivating research. Prince Bandar Bin Sultan, the Saudi U.S. ambassador, has written op-ed pieces for the *New York Times*, the *Washington Post*, and the *Wall Street Journal*. The government has also purchased and run print ads in major magazines.

The Campaign Is Redesigned

But by December, *PRWeek* reported that the Saudis were displeased with the results of the campaign, and that it would be reshaped. Newly designed advertisements were to show a very modern Saudi Arabia. The royal family planned to travel to Washington and to meet with reporters, intending to discuss the common ideals of the United States and Saudi Arabia and to explain more about the Islamic faith.

An attack in Riyadh in May 2003 that killed 35, including 9 Americans, focused renewed attention on how the Saudi government was dealing with prospective terrorists. Results of the September 11 investigation released in summer 2003 led to more debate about the Saudi role and the public relations efforts concerning the country. The BBC reported that the 900-page report on the intelligence failings before the attacks said some Saudis had provided aid to the hijackers and had then failed to cooperate with the U.S. intelligence agencies. More than 20 pages were expunged from the report, leading to much speculation that it was the references to Saudi Arabia's alleged ties to terrorism that were omitted.

Referring to the secret section of the report, the Saudi Ambassador Prince Bandar bin Sultan told the BBC, "Twenty-eight blanked-out pages are being used by some to malign our country and our people." Saudi officials asked for 28 classified pages of a congressional report on the attacks to be made public, so the Arab kingdom can clear its name. But President Bush refused the official request on the grounds that it would compromise U.S. intelligence operations. Some argued this request was a public relations gesture, because the Saudis knew that Bush had already decided not to release the document. *USA Today* reported that Saudi foreign minister Prince Saud defended Bush from charges that his refusal to release the information was motivated by a desire to protect a longtime ally. Anyone suggesting that Bush was engaged in a cover-up "must be out of touch with reality or driven by ulterior motives," the foreign minister said. "It is an outrage to any sense of fairness that 28 blank pages are now considered substantial evidence to proclaim the guilt of a country that has been a true friend and partner to the United States for over 60 years."

QUESTIONS FOR REFLECTION

1. What are the most effective communication practices for a nation seeking to build and sustain a positive image with the citizens and government leaders of other nations?

2. Was the use of broadcast commercials the most effective strategy to support the apparent goals for this campaign?

3. Are there ethical considerations that should be examined when a public relations firm or counselor is asked to represent international clients?

Information for this case was drawn from the following: Associated Press. (27 February 2003), "When relations soured, U.S. and Saudi Arabia called in the PR professionals," *Jefferson City* (MO) *News Tribune* Online, www.newstribune.com; BBC News (25 July 2003), "Saudi Arabia denies terror links," at http://news.bbc.co.uk; De la Garza, P. (27 April 2002), "Saudi Arabia ads part of campaign to clean up image," *St. Petersburg Times* online, www.sptimes.com; Labott, E. (30 September 2003), "Saudi prince calls for end to U.S. tensions," CNN.com; Keen, J. (29 July 2003), "Bush refuses to disclose Saudi items in 9/11 report," *USA Today* at www.usatoday.com/news/washington.2003-07-29-saudis-bush_x.htm; Marquis, C. (29 August 2002), "Worried Saudis try to improve image in the U.S.," *The New York Times* online, www.nytimes.com; Murawski, J. (13 June 2003), "Saudi Arabia's TV ads out to polish image in U.S.," *The Palm Beach Post*, p. A12; Orris, M. (6 July 2003), "Saudis sell image to a skeptical U.S.," *The Atlanta Journal and Constitution*, p. A15; and Quenqua, D. (16 December 2002), "Saudis rethink PR as $3m 15-month campaign stalls," *PRWeek*, p. 11.

CASE 32. KICK ASH BASH SETS STAGE
FOR ANTISMOKING CAMPAIGN

Minnesota teenagers burned big tobacco companies with an antismoking program launched in April 2000 when 400 high school students from around the state gathered for a teen summit called the Kick Ash Bash. Organized by the Minnesota Department of Health (MDH) because of rising teen tobacco use, the summit decided to adopt the same tactics used by tobacco companies in attracting new customers to create a countereffort fighting the habit.

Just before the summit, the health department had completed a survey of 12,000 randomly selected students in middle schools and high schools. Results showed that nearly 40% of high school students and more than 12% of middle school students were currently using tobacco. A "current user" was someone who had used tobacco on one or more of the preceding 30 days. Though cigarettes were most popular, cigars and smokeless products like chewing tobacco were used by more than 10% of high school students. Gender made no difference in cigarette smoking; boys were more likely than girls to use other tobacco products.

The proportion of Minnesota high school students using tobacco was slightly higher than the national average (38.7% vs. 34.8%), and the middle school rate (12.6%) was almost the same as the national figure (12.8%).

Seventeen percent of high school students were frequent cigarette smokers, defined as individuals who smoked on at least 20 of the preceding 30 days. The rate of tobacco use, which climbed steadily from 6th through 12th grade, reached 45% among seniors.

Shaping and Reshaping Attitudes

The health department's survey showed that students understood the dangers of smoking. More than 90% acknowledged tobacco's power to addict users, its threat to the health of regular smokers, and its risk for nonsmokers exposed to secondhand smoke. In addition, most students did not believe that smoking for a year or two and then quitting tobacco would be safe.

Teenagers who attended the Kick Ash Bash heard how tobacco companies studied new smokers, their motivations, and their potential as continuing customers to understand how to attract them. The teens saw that the companies used special events, advertising, and sponsorships to connect with the natural interests of young people. And they were told that nearly 90% of the cigarettes sold in the United States under about 50 different labels are produced by four large companies.

After learning how Big Tobacco divides consumers into segments and identifies critical characteristics on which brand appeal can be based, the teens formed an antismoking movement and gave it a name designed to tell Big Tobacco: "We know how you really see us." The name they selected for their movement was Target Market. From the start, the teens and the organizers decided that Target Market would depend on youth leadership supported by adult guidance.

Source of Funds

Funding for Target Market and its anti-tobacco campaign came from an endowment that the Minnesota legislature set up, using a portion of the state's $6 billion settlement with the tobacco industry. The settlement stemmed from a lawsuit that the state had filed to recover some costs of tobacco's past harms. Endowment interest of $17 million in 2001 was earmarked for support of Target Media and other tobacco control initiatives, and the interest amount was expected to rise in succeeding years.

Teen interest in Target Market was strong from the outset, and membership reached 20,000 within a year. Looking for an organization to guide Target Market after its first year, the MDH issued a public request for proposals. The MDH request said that the selected organization would need significant experience in youth empowerment and grassroots organizing, knowledge of the state's youth market, and skill in motivating behavior change among the young.

The MDH said Target Market's mission was to "expose the marketing tactics the tobacco industry uses to target teens to become lifelong customers and to target the tobacco industry back with their own campaign."

A Specific and Measurable Objective

The objective of the endowment-supported programs was to reduce tobacco use among youth by 30% by the year 2005. The MDH was very explicit in spelling out this goal in its report on the Minnesota Youth Tobacco Survey (YTS).

"To meet the state's five-year goal, current tobacco use would have to fall from 38.7 to 27.1 percent among high school students and from 12.6 to 8.8 percent among middle school students when the YTS is conducted in 2005," the report stated.

In Minnesota, people under age 18 may not legally purchase tobacco products. Target Market's critical public included all individuals from age 12 through age 17—smokers and nonsmokers alike. The YTS specifically recommended that prevention efforts should focus on the 18% of middle school students and the 9% of high school students who had never smoked but had no firm commitment to avoid the habit.

Strategy for Action

The health department said studies had shown that teenagers resented adult control and attempts to manipulate them. Teens knew that tobacco use was harmful but didn't want to hear lectures or nagging on the subject. Although their familiarity with tobacco's dangers was high, knowledge of the industry's use of the social sciences to analyze and influence behavior was lower. Target Market's strategy was to open teenagers' eyes to the manipulation that lay at the heart of tobacco marketing and to give them the tools to create a campaign of their own to counter Big Tobacco.

Broadly, the tools included advertising, public relations, grassroots organizing, and an interactive Web site. In addition, Target Market had partners, also funded by the endowment, with whom it would need to coordinate its efforts. One partner's role was the creation of a media campaign—using television commercials, outdoor advertising, and more—that would carry the messages of Target Market throughout the state. Other partners included about 50 local coalitions addressing public health concerns.

The MDH established a $1.5 million annual budget for the organization chosen to guide Target Market in the second and third years of the program and indicated that the arrangement might be renewed for another 3 years if results were satisfactory.

Evaluation Based on Logic Model

Under contract terms, the organization would be required to apply 10% of the budget to the evaluation of results. The health department said that a "logic model" for the program was an essential precondition to development of an evaluation plan.

The department said in its request for proposals:

> Before you plan your evaluation, you need to develop a program *logic model*. The logic model lays out what the program is expected to achieve and how it is expected to work, based on an expected chain of events.

> The chain of events that links inputs to outputs to outcomes in response to a situation is your "logic model." It articulates what you hope to achieve and how. It is based on a series of ordered actions that are logically linked. All begin with a clear specification of the situation—the problem or issue—being addressed in order to indicate the most appropriate chain of events.

The department offered an example of a seven-part logic model:

1. Goals—What do you expect to achieve?
2. Strategies—What services and activities do you plan to use?
3. Intensity and duration—How often and for how long do you plan to use them?
4. Target group—Who will participate in and be influenced by the program?
5. Theory of change—How will the strategies produce the outcomes?
6. Short-term outcomes—What immediate changes are anticipated?
7. Long-term outcomes—What changes will occur over time?

Discouraging alteration of the original program, the department made its expectations clear: The selected organization would "continue the mission and momentum that is already underway at Target Market."

Tactics for Influence

In its first year after the Kick Ash Bash, Target Market had gained widespread visibility and thousands of new members through a variety of activities:

- A Web site at www.tmvoice.com went online in June 2000 to provide background on the movement and give teens an opportunity to exchange ideas.
- Special antitobacco teen events were scheduled at the Back-to-School Lounge at the Mall of America in Bloomington, 15 minutes from St. Paul and Minneapolis, and at the Minnesota State Fair.
- Sponsoring a statewide Battle of the Bands contest, the movement built awareness of its goals by associating Target Market with music popular among teens.
- A compact-disc compilation of emerging Minnesota musicians was conceived and created by movement members to promote Target Market.
- The TM Cruiser, a walk-in panel truck, traveled to Minnesota's beaches, festivals, parades, fairs, malls, and concerts to recruit the young into the movement.
- Members appeared in TV and radio commercials, produced by the movement's media campaign partner, offering unscripted comments on Big Tobacco.

To offer evidence of the industry's manipulation, Target Market took copies of tobacco marketing reports right to the schoolhouse. The TM Document Tour, a

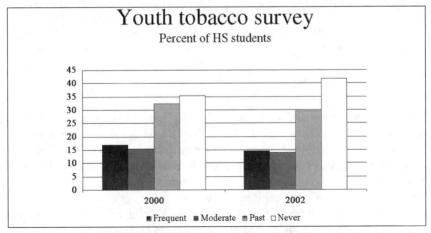

The use of tobacco among Minnesota high school students showed a decline after introduction of the Target Market antismoking campaign. (Source: Minnesota Department of Health. Chart by L. Lamb.)

traveling exhibit of tobacco industry documents, visited middle schools across the state. Installed in a tractor-trailer combination, the exhibit included examples of industry analysis and marketing reports. They contained statements like this 1981 excerpt from Philip Morris:

> Today's teenager is tomorrow's potential regular customer, and the overwhelming majority of smokers first begin to smoke while still in their teens. In addition, the ten years following the teenage years is the period during which average daily consumption per smoker increases to the average adult level. The smoking patterns of teenagers are particularly important to Philip Morris.

With the traveling exhibit and other tactics, Target Market not only attained a high profile in its first year but also earned a number of awards, including Silver Anvils from the PRSA and Bronze Quills from the IABC.

Comparison to Benchmark

In early 2002, the MDH repeated the survey of middle school and high school students that it had first conducted in early 2000. About 11,500 randomly selected respondents were represented, and the results showed solid progress over the 2 years.

The proportion of high school students who were currently using tobacco had dropped to 34.4% from 38.7%, and the middle school rate went down to 11.2% from 12.6%. In both categories, the number of current tobacco users per thousand students had dropped 11.1%. The number of frequent smokers per thousand students declined 40% in middle schools and went down 13% in high schools.

The department also published ad measurements provided by Target Market's media campaign partner. They indicated that 92% of teens had seen at least one of the movement's ads. Six of every 10 were able to recall specific details of the ad, and among this 60%, 8 of 10 indicated that they understood Big Tobacco's marketing approach.

Critics and Complaints

Despite the popularity and apparent success of Target Market, the movement had its critics, embarrassments, and scrapes. When it said that 40,000 teenagers had joined the movement, some observers said only 3,000 were active. The 2-year decline in teen tobacco use was welcome, but critics said it simply paralleled declines in national figures.

Minnesota legislators expressed concern about the lyrics and messages of a Chicago band that had performed at a Target Market concert. The lyrics referred approvingly to heavy drinking and used obscenities profusely.

For a few months, a Duluth teen named Matt Hannula maintained a Web site, www.antitargetmarket.com, questioning the tactics of Target Market and the organization's influence. A cross-country runner and nonsmoker, Mr. Hannula told the *Duluth News-Tribune*, "Skateboarding and rock concerts never helped anyone quit or kept them from starting."

Eventually, the major threat to Target Market came not from critics but from a $4.5 billion deficit in Minnesota's budget. When the state administration made its budget plan public at midyear 2003, the endowment funding Target Market was gone. Recessionary forces drained budgets not just in Minnesota but in most states and led many to reallocate tobacco settlement funds for essential government services.

Protests of Target Market teens and public health professionals could not overcome the arguments of those who said the tobacco prevention program was nice to have but not affordable.

~

QUESTIONS FOR REFLECTION

1. Organizations that submitted proposals to guide the Target Market anti-smoking campaign were required to outline their "logic model." What's a logic model?
2. How do the results of the Minnesota survey of teen smoking habits compare to your personal perceptions of your high school experiences?
3. Was the choice of the movement name, Target Market, a wise and effective choice?
4. Which Target Market tactics offered the best combination of creativity and potential effectiveness?

Information for this case was drawn from the following: the Minnesota Department of Health Web site at http://www.health.state.mn.us/; its teen smoking Web site at http://www.tmvoice.com/index.asp; (2002), Minnesota Youth Tobacco Survey, Center for Health Statistics, Minnesota Department of Health; Phelps, D. (9 May 2003), "Advocates criticize use of tobacco settlement money to fight deficit," *The Star Tribune*, p. B1; Stawicki, E. (31 March 2003), "Target Market targeted to disappear," Minnesota Public Radio; (2001), Target Market organization: Request for proposals, Minnesota Department of Health; (August 2000), "Teens and tobacco in Minnesota," Center for Health Statistics, Minnesota Department of Health; and (Accessed 11 July 2003), "What's TM been up to?" The Tobacco Initiative, http://www.mntobacco.net.

CASE 33.   "POWERFUL" CAMPAIGN SEEKS TO PROMOTE HEALTHY BONES

You care about your hair. You care about your clothes. You even care about your nail polish. Don't you think you should care about your bones? They need plenty of foods with calcium and lots of physical activity every day to stay strong. So, have some frozen yogurt or juice with added calcium. You know, girl, hairstyles come and go, but your bones are for life.

—Spokescharacter Carla

By age 20, the average woman has acquired 98% of her bone mass, so nutrition and exercise habits from childhood and adolescence are critical to developing bone density and strength. Yet The Institute of Medicine estimates that only 10% of girls 9 to 13 years are getting the recommended intake of calcium, and according to a National Youth Risk Behavior Study, nearly half of high school girls don't reach the recommended goal of engaging in vigorous physical activity at least three times a week.

Powerful Partners

To address this need, the U.S. Department of Health and Human Services's Office on Women's Health, the Centers for Disease Control and Prevention, and the National Osteoporosis Foundation have joined together to develop the 5-year National Bone Health "Powerful Bones, Powerful Girls" Campaign. The coalition also partnered with the Girl Scouts of the USA and with Girls Inc.

Public relations counselors from the Porter Novelli agency teamed with the coalition to develop the campaign. Porter Novelli International serves clients in 56 countries offering assistance in consumer, corporate/public affairs, health care, and technology practices. Its campaign won an honorable mention for 2003 Public Sector Campaign of the Year from *PRWeek*.

Their research found that girls associate good health with happiness, activity, energy, and self-esteem. Physical activity is believed to increase social interaction, strength, and energy. The goal for the multiyear campaign was to educate and encourage young girls to establish lifelong healthy habits, especially increased calcium consumption and physical activity. In addition to girls 9–12, the campaign targeted adults who influence girls, including parents, teachers, coaches, youth-group leaders, and health care professionals.

The campaign also used print and radio advertising aimed at girls and their parents. A seven-city tour was also held. The tour offered events such as the 1-day "Powerful Bones, Powerful Girls" sports day at the Navy Pier in Chicago where varied sports clinics for girls were held.

News releases during the 2001 winter holiday season offered tips on how girls could reach daily calcium goals by eating holiday treats such as roasted almonds with pudding made of low-fat milk; hot cocoa; cheddar-cheese cubes; broccoli with ranch dressing; and fresh fruit. Recommended "power-packed" presents included soccer balls, jump ropes, tennis rackets, or basketballs; sassy sneakers or workout gear; a set of dumbbells or hand weights; and gift certificates for dance or martial arts classes.

Carla Shows Powerful Girl Style

A major communication tool for the campaign was the Web site, at www.cdc.gob/powerfulbones, which featured the campaign's spokescharacter Carla, who appears on all materials. On the site, Carla identifies herself and the campaign:

> It's me—Carla. Like my name? Well, Carla means "strong," and I'm all about being strong. Not like a pumped-up body builder or anything, but being strong and powerful all the way around. You know, like doing your best in school and helping out your friends and parents.

> There's a lot to being a powerful girl. You need to have smarts and your own sense of style, and do your part to take care of yourself and others! A big part of that is making sure you have strong, healthy bones. That's right ... bones. Ya' know, the things that keep you from being just a big glob of skin! To be strong, bones need a lot of calcium and certain types of weight-bearing physical activity when they're growing. Hang with me to find out why and how to build strong bones. I promise you'll have fun with the cool games and info on this site. So, let's go!

The site explains that Carla loves low-fat or nonfat milkshakes, almonds, fruit, and grilled-cheese sandwiches. Along with snack recipes and ideas and list of fitness activities, it offers a variety of animated games, along with a pop-up tour of the human skeleton, and some poetry from Carla. A calendar and a journal that allow girls to track their calcium intake and physical activity can be downloaded through the Web site.

Working Out?

Porter Novelli is seeking to measure the impact of the campaign by tracking information dissemination and attitude change, although tracking the impact of a campaign that echoes messages girls may have heard in school, from their physicians, or from their parents for many years may be difficult. A baseline survey was conducted at the beginning of the campaign, and a follow-up survey will be administered at the end of the campaign. Through the advertising and media coverage, the campaign generated 8.5 million print media impressions and more than 540,000 estimated radio audience impressions by 2003.

Questions for Reflection

1. Identifying children and adolescents as key publics for campaigns may pose special challenges. Identify several of these challenges. Evaluate the use of the Web site as the primary communication tool with this public.
2. What are the advantages and disadvantages of using an animated spokes-character?
3. Evaluating the impact of a long-term public-information campaign may pose some challenges in isolating message source, source credibility, and short-term and long-term impact. How might these challenges be addressed?
4. What are the values in public/private coalitions for public-health or public-information campaigns?

Information for this campaign was drawn from the following: the Web sites at www.cdc.gov/powerfulbones; www.4woman.gov/owh/pr; www.girlpower.gob/adultswhocare/acrosscountry/eventdetail.asp; www.nof.org/powerfulbones/; www.porternovelli.com/PNWebSite/PNW; and http://content.health.msn.com/content; and Krause, C. (14 December 2001), "Powerful ones, powerful girls: Holiday snacks and gift ideas to help girls build strong, healthy bones," *U.S. Newswire*.

A Higher Ethical Standard for Nonprofits

James E. Moody, executive director,
Georgia Society of Association Executives

Because nonprofits enjoy tax-free status, we hold them to a higher standard. We expect them to operate in the public interest and to maintain the highest ethical standards. Yet nonprofits—charities, philanthropic organizations, and trade and professional associations—provide some of the most challenging ethical situations.

Some of these challenges arise simply because we expect them to be different than for-profit businesses. Although we may not think it's fair for the CEO of a large corporation to make an exorbitant salary and enjoy rich "trappings of office," it's not an issue many of us feel viscerally. Yet when it was disclosed that William Arimony of the United Way was earning millions of dollars and jaunting around in limousines, many people who had sacrificed to give part of their salary to the United Way were justifiably angry.

Sometimes the ethical challenges are less obvious but perhaps more significant. Trade and professional associations make public statements that are often held with high regard because we perceive them to come from an unbiased source.

The board of directors generally makes the final decisions on what the association will say on any given topic. Every board member has self-interests that may color the member's feelings about the topic. And the association itself will almost certainly have a bias toward the group it represents. Dealing with these potentially conflicting interests is the key to maintaining a high ethical standard.

For example, we assume that statements from a medical association are issued in the interest of public health. Would that still be your assumption if you knew that the majority of the association's board members received significant income for being spokespersons for a drug company?

Even when self-interest is not an issue, decisions can be ethically challenging. Many nonprofits struggle to make ends meet. Nonprofit doesn't mean your goal is to lose money! Sometimes endorsement deals are an attractive way to increase revenue. Is it ethical for an association to endorse a product or service in exchange for money? What about when the association is aware that the product it endorses is no better than its competitors?

Many associations have adopted codes of ethics to help draw the boundaries. Additionally, many boards have conflict of interest policies that require members to disclose potential conflicts prior to their service on the board.

Of course, no code of ethics or conflict of interest policy can describe every potential ethical dilemma a nonprofit may face. And truly unethical people will not be troubled by breaking a code of ethics or "forgetting" to disclose a conflict. Ultimately, it is up to those with high ethical standards to rid their organization's leadership of those who cannot put their own interests aside.

Jim Moody is executive director of the Georgia Society of Association Executives, the trade association for staff members of associations and other nonprofits in Georgia. He graduated cum laude with a bachelor's degree in communication from Berry College and earned the certified association executive designation from the American Society of Association Executives.

9

Stakeholders: Activists

Activists are saints, sinners, and sometimes both. It depends on your perspective of the public issue on which activists are focusing. Because issues seldom have only two sides, several activist organizations may get involved in a public discussion or controversy and try to influence its eventual outcome. Not only would the groups voice a range of viewpoints, but they also might use a variety of methods to grab attention and get support for their preferred outcome.

Activist groups generally adopt conventional behaviors, conforming to public expectations because there's little reward in intentionally annoying people. Some groups are more colorful or aggressive, especially if they have a hard time getting noticed. A small number are deliberately destructive and engage in illegal acts.

The SUV is a case in point. SUVs have accounted for about 25% of automakers' revenues and half of their profits in recent years. However, some activists have tried to reverse the vehicle's growing popularity through public relations campaigns that focused on SUVs' potential harms to the environment, highway safety, energy independence, and insurance-rate equity.

ACTIVISTS AGAINST SUVS

Groups advocating restrictions on SUVs have included Earth on Empty, Evangelical Environmental Network, Friends of the Earth, Sierra Club, and Union of Concerned Scientists.

Earth on Empty activists ticketed parked SUVs in 500 cities with notices that resembled parking violation envelopes. On the notices were statements such as "SUVs emit up to 5.5 times as much air pollution per mile as cars." Friends of the Earth sold bumper stickers with messages like "Support OPEC. Buy an SUV." The

192

Union of Concerned Scientists (UCS) offered plans on its Web site for design changes in SUVs that could make them safer, cleaner, and more cost-effective. UCS experts appeared on CBS-TV's "60 Minutes" news program to explain the proposal. In a handful of incidents, radical activists set SUVs afire on dealers' lots.

SUV OWNERS ORGANIZE

Responding to the SUV reform/reject movements, SUV proponents created the Sport Utility Vehicle Owners of America (SUVOA). SUVOA says it gives a voice to "the 24 million SUV owners whose freedom to choose is being threatened by a small, but vocal minority of fringe groups orchestrating a well-implemented campaign of misinformation and negativity."

When SUVOA advocates appeared on TV talk shows, they explained that SUV owners trust the vehicles to afford more protection for families in highway collisions and provide more room for household errands.

Ford Motor Company, General Motors Corporation, and other SUV manufacturers in the United States generally defended their SUVs. However, Ford and GM also joined CERES—the Coalition for Environmentally Responsible Economies, whose members include environmental, investor, and advocacy groups. CERES promotes dialogue on corporations' environmental and social practices.

By joining CERES, Ford and GM gained the opportunity to participate in the kind of discussions that a two-way symmetrical approach to public relations might favor. The automakers and activists could share ideas, learn more about the goals and limitations of each other, examine a range of solutions and adaptations, and identify answers that would satisfy—in some respects—everyone's interests. The prospect of a win-win solution could keep all sides engaged.

PURPOSES OF ACTIVISM

In democracies, activism contributes to the process of public life. Activists have influenced social acceptance of diverse lifestyles, social restraints on tobacco use, popular attitudes on animal rights, public debate on gun control, reproductive rights, alcohol consumption, and much more. So prevalent is the role of activists that a 322-page *Encyclopedia of American Activism: 1960 to the Present*, by Margaret B. Dicanio, was published in 1998.

Activist groups, often called special-interest groups or advocacy groups, usually try to:

- Influence popular opinion.
- Promote changes in public policy.
- Exert pressure on corporations.
- Remedy social problems.
- Affect personal behavior.

In the SUV controversy, some activists tried to cultivate a popular opinion that SUVs, despite their many benefits, cause more harm than good and that no motorist with a public conscience would own one. Other activists, trying to use public policy to address SUV problems, advocated changing federal regulations to apply the same fuel standards to SUVs that apply to passenger cars, which must travel farther on a gallon of gasoline. Activists directly pressured Ford, GM, and Daimler Chrysler to improve fuel economy of SUVs and abandon the largest models, such as the Ford Excursion and GM Hummer.

By owning shares in public corporations, activists gain the right to make statements and offer resolutions at annual meetings attended by investors. Shareholder resolutions proposed by activists not only draw public attention to the group's central concern but also affect corporate decision making on sensitive issues, even when the resolutions are voted down.

FOCUSING ON SOCIAL PROBLEMS

In big cities and small towns around the world, community activism has been used successfully to spotlight social problems and foster solutions. Activists have organized campaigns against drug abuse, teen pregnancy, neighborhood deterioration, domestic violence, and homelessness. They have formed programs to promote mass transit, historical preservation, youth activities, and fairness in hiring and housing.

The Annie E. Casey Foundation of Baltimore funded production of the *Making Communications Connections Toolkit* for community activists so that they could learn how to use strategic public relations in solving social problems. Since 1948, the foundation has been working to create better futures for disadvantaged children and their families through public policies, human services reforms, and community supports.

Written by the FrameWorks Institute, the kit's recommendations reflect research into more than 50 community campaigns that covered a range of issues and localities. The strategic approach is familiar to almost everyone who studies or practices public relations, beginning with a "clear definition of the problem" and ending with an "evaluation of the campaign's impact."

FRAMING A MESSAGE

In explaining message development, the toolkit offers advice on framing messages and suggests six elements of the frame—context, numbers, messengers, visuals, metaphors, and tone. The recommendations:

- **Context**—Include details about trends affecting the problem, and describe the broader social system in which the problem persists; focus on community efforts rather than individual or family responsibilities; present a solution.

- **Numbers**—Tell what your numbers mean; don't overwhelm narrative with numbers; state your message first, and then support it with numbers.
- **Messengers**—Use speakers whom the public will accept as knowledgeable and trustworthy; if possible, use unlikely allies.
- **Visuals**—Avoid conventional images already associated the issue; avoid close-ups of a child alone or with parents because it may suggest a family, rather than community, problem; use public and community situations.
- **Metaphors**—Check metaphors in language and visuals to confirm that they will support rather than undermine your message.
- **Tone**—Avoid rhetoric that polarizes; present the problem in human scale; don't over-dramatize a problem, making it appear beyond community control.

The kit also tells community activists that they should look for program partners in the local business community. Sympathetic businesses may include a group's messages in promotional materials or sponsor group events.

AN UNDEREXAMINED ROLE

Some public relations scholars have said that the study and practice of public relations have focused too much on examining the discipline from the standpoint of a practitioner working in or for a large organization. More work is needed, they've said, to understand relationships from the activists' perspectives and to listen to voices in the community at large that have been completely left out of discussions on public issues. In some circumstances, arriving at a win-win solution may simply mean that the quiet voices of small groups or unaffiliated individuals have been ignored.

In contrast, some critics have said that carefully orchestrated activist campaigns often distort the true dimensions of popular opinion. Some campaigns, critics say, hijack the public agenda by using conflict to lure the news media to a shallow pool of controversy and then claim it's the mainstream of public thought.

The chief executive officer of DaimlerChrysler's Chrysler Group said, "You might call it the difference between natural public opinion and synthetic public opinion."

ADDITIONAL READINGS

Alinksy, Saul. (1989). *Rules for radicals: A practical primer for realistic radicals*. Vancouver, WA: Vintage Books.

Best, Joel. (2001). *Damned lies and statistics: Untangling numbers from the media, politicians, and activists*. Berkeley: University of California Press.

Keck, Margaret E., & Kathryn Sikkink. (1998). *Activists beyond borders: Advocacy networks in international politics*. Ithaca, NY: Cornell University Press.

Shaw, Randy. (1999). *Reclaiming America: Nike, clean air, and the new national activism*. Berkeley: University of California Press.

CASE 34.   PASSIONATE ABOUT POLICIES
TO PROTECT POULTRY

Men and women in chicken costumes hobbled on crutches and hoisted signs outside KFC restaurants around the world in 2003 to protest the chain's animal welfare practices. Organized by People for the Ethical Treatment of Animals (PETA), the activists tried persuading KFC, once known as Kentucky Fried Chicken, to force its poultry suppliers to improve conditions in which chickens are raised and transported.

PETA contended that KFC purchased chickens from farms where the birds were mistreated and often injured through carelessness. KFC insisted it was a leader in adopting animal welfare standards.

The cast of characters in PETA's street theater at KFC restaurants varied from location to location. In Charleston, South Carolina, a large yellow chicken paraded with two companions, one of whom carried a sign depicting a deranged Colonel Sanders, icon of Kentucky Fried Chicken, attacking a chicken. In Bangalore, India, a seven-foot-tall white leghorn rooster, flanked by white-jacketed Indians bearing anti-KFC messages, held a sign that read "Go vegetarian." In Johnson City, Tennessee, a woman wore a revealing showgirl's chicken costume, replete with stack heels and fake-feather headdress, to attract the attention of pedestrians and passing motorists. She carried a sign that said "KFC Boils Chickens Alive."

In city after city from country to country, the scene was similar. Louisville received special attention from the animal rights group because the Kentucky city is KFC's corporate home. PETA scheduled an appearance by one of its "crippled chickens" in August at a restaurant less than five miles from the KFC president's office and within walking distance of Colonel Sanders' final resting place in Cave Hill National Cemetery.

PETA's Origin and Mission

PETA, founded in 1980 by Ingrid Newkirk and Alex Pacheco, is headquartered in Norfolk, Virginia. The organization says it "operates under the simple principle that animals are not ours to eat, wear, experiment on, or use for entertainment. PETA educates policymakers and the public about animal abuse and promotes an understanding of the right of all animals to be treated with respect."

PETA itself has earned respect from many individuals who give the organization credit for raising public awareness of animal welfare and lowering the level of mistreatment in the entertainment industry, research laboratories, livestock operations, and elsewhere. Even some managers in companies that have been PETA targets acknowledge that reforms would have been difficult without pressure from the activists.

However, some PETA campaigns also have stirred reactions ranging from ridicule to outrage. In early 2000, PETA targeted college students in its antimilk campaign and used the slogan "Got ... Beer?!" as a parody on the dairy industry's "Got Milk?" campaign. PETA says milk is not a healthful food, and beer is better for the body—from a nutritional standpoint.

A *Los Angeles Times* columnist complained, "People for the Ethical Treatment of Animals has reached a new low. The animal rights organization is asking college students to replace milk in their diets with beer."

Responding to Critics

Lighten up, the activists responded, saying, "PETA got a rise out of everyone from dairy farmers to Mothers Against Drunk Driving [MADD] with its tongue-in-cheek advisory to college kids that milk is so bad, nutritionally speaking, that *even beer* is better for you! MADD was mad, despite the fact that we made it clear that we only used beer for comparison purposes because no one thinks of beer as a health food."

New York Mayor Rudolph Giuliani was not smiling when PETA used his image, after adding a milk mustache, in another parody of the dairy industry campaign in 2000. On the billboard next to the mayor's image, PETA asked: "Got Prostate Cancer? Drinking milk contributes to prostate cancer."

Mr. Giuliani, who had been diagnosed with prostate cancer, said he was considering a lawsuit against PETA. An apology from Ms. Newkirk, the organization's president, soon arrived at the mayor's office. Separately, the American Cancer Society indicated that the cause of prostate cancer is not well understood.

The anti-KFC campaign also has its critics. Outside the South Carolina restaurant where PETA activists were on duty, a customer with KFC sack in hand told a *Charleston Post and Courier* reporter, "Chicken is born to be killed and eaten." Another heckler yelled from his car, "I love to skin chickens."

In Texas, the *Amarillo Globe-News* commented on a local activist who picketed in a chicken outfit, "These campaigns do little to advance PETA's agenda, but accomplish a lot in firing up the opposition."

KFC Is Top Chicken Chain

KFC is the world's leading restaurant in the chicken category. Established by Colonel Harland Sanders in 1952, it has more than 11,000 restaurants in 80 countries and territories and serves about 8 million customers each day. In the United States, it is four times the size of its nearest competitor.

KFC is one of five quick-service restaurant chains operated by Yum! Brands. The others are Pizza Hut, Taco Bell, Long John Silver's, and A&W All-American Food. In 2002, Yum!'s revenues exceeded $7.7 billion, and net income was $583 million. In total sales, only McDonald's was larger among quick-service restaurant corporations. KFC has been particularly successful outside the United States and accounts for about two thirds of Yum!'s international revenues.

The antagonism between PETA and KFC boiled up from what had initially been a polite exchange on animal welfare practices expressed in correspondence between the two organizations in April 2001. Five months later, KFC's newly formed animal welfare advisory council met for the first time. Through phone calls and letters, PETA continued to press KFC and its corporate parent, Yum! Brands Inc., for more changes and also provided information on chicken treatment to shareholders at the Yum! annual meeting in May 2001. The letters and phone calls continued, and PETA returned to the Yum! annual meeting in May 2002.

Over succeeding months, the tone of the exchanges turned sharper, and PETA announced in January 2003 that it was launching a campaign against KFC. It issued this news release (original punctuation and capitalization retained) under a heading that said:

PETA LAUNCHES WORLDWIDE KFC CAMPAIGN

COMPANY STONEWALLS ON ANIMAL WELFARE REFORMS

Louisville, Ky. — After nearly two years of failed negotiations and following victories over McDonald's, Burger King, and Wendy's—all of which bowed to PETA pressure to reduce cruel treatment of animals raised and slaughtered for food—PETA has declared its latest campaign target: KFC, owned by Yum! Brands, Inc. PETA will formally launch the campaign by unveiling new "Kentucky Fried Cruelty" posters, leaflets, stickers, and more and will show broadcast-quality footage of abusive animal treatment by KFC suppliers at a news conference on January 7 near the company's Louisville headquarters.

Date: Tuesday, January 7 / Time: 11 a.m. / Place: Seelbach Hilton, 500 Fourth St.

PETA attempted to negotiate with Yum! Brands executives for 21 months prior to the campaign launch, but despite assurances made long ago by Senior Vice President Jonathon Blum that KFC would "raise the bar" on animal welfare, the company refuses to eliminate the worst abuses.

Among the improvements that PETA wants KFC to implement are the following: replacing crude and ineffective electric stunning and throat-slitting with gas killing; phasing out the forced rapid growth of chickens, which causes metabolic disorders and lameness; increasing the space allotted per bird; adding minimal enhancements, such as sheltered areas and perches in order to provide chickens with some semblance of their natural environment; and implementing automated chicken-catching, a process that reduces the high incidence of bruising, broken bones, and stress associated with catching the chickens by hand.

"KFC has shortchanged the chickens, leaving us no choice but to turn up the heat," says PETA Director of Vegan Outreach Bruce Friedrich. "McDonald's, Burger King, and Wendy's responded to consumer pressure; KFC would do well to follow their lead."

News conferences are also planned in London and Toronto. For more information, please visit KFCCruelty.com.

The following day, KFC issued a short denial. It said that the restaurant chain was committed to the well-being and humane treatment of the poultry it purchases from suppliers. The company's statement said that its suppliers:

- Must follow guidelines set by KFC and its animal welfare advisory council.
- Must allow unannounced audits at poultry facilities throughout the year.
- Will face termination if they fail to remedy deficiencies uncovered by the audits.

PETA Rolls Out Reality TV Truck

On May 1, 2003, KFC announced that it would adopt comprehensive poultry farm standards developed by animal welfare experts under a commission from the National Council of Chain Restaurants and the Food Marketing Institute. It also said it was asking federal farm and labor authorities to examine PETA's suggestion for the use of gas in killing chickens as a replacement for existing methods.

The announcement included a reminder that KFC did not own or operate poultry farms or processing plants but purchased chickens from 18 different suppliers operating 52 facilities.

The following day, PETA said it was angered by KFC's hypocrisy and promised to park its "Reality TV" truck outside the home of the KFC president on Monday evening, May 5. PETA warned that it would use the truck's large screens to show video of the treatment chickens receive before they end up at KFC.

The activists repeated their demands for KFC suppliers to phase out rapid-growth practices, increase space for each bird, provide enhancements like shelter and perches, adopt automated chicken-catching technology, and replace the electric-stun and slit-throat death process with gas killing.

On Wednesday, the KFC president flew to Norfolk for a 3-hour meeting with PETA's Newkirk. KFC declined to provide details of the meeting to the news media, but PETA issued a news release on Thursday, May 9, indicating the adversaries were closer to agreement. It said that KFC had agreed to provide chickens with a 30% increase in living space and to install cameras in slaughterhouses to discourage abuse of chickens. In return, PETA promised to suspend protests in Louisville and halt some other campaign activities.

KFC Adopts New Policies

On the KFC Web site (www.kfc.com), the company published its farm-level welfare guidelines, spelling out standards for poultry suppliers in eight categories of activity that ranged from staff training to transportation.

To protect the chickens' welfare, the KFC farm-level guidelines required:

- Documented training for employees who handle live birds.
- Programs to assure monitoring of climate control systems.

- Proper diet and watering systems.
- Shelters with a clean and well-ventilated environment.
- Written health plans prepared in consultation with a veterinarian.
- Room for chickens to move freely to obtain feed and water.
- Twice-daily inspections of the birds and their environment.
- Measures to protect birds from injury or weather extremes during transportation.

In a parallel document, KFC published poultry welfare guidelines that included many of the farm-level standards but also addressed the birds' inevitable death. According to the guidelines, suppliers must ensure that chickens are stunned insensible prior to slaughter and that death itself is executed quickly.

A PETA representative attended the Yum! annual shareholder meeting on May 15 and spoke to commend the company for KFC's industry leadership. When the activist pushed for more changes, an unpleasant exchange of words with the Yum! CEO cooled the warm compliments.

PETA Files Suit Against KFC

Seven weeks after praising KFC, PETA filed a lawsuit in California, asking for a permanent injunction to prevent KFC and Yum! from making what the suit called false statements about animal welfare practices.

In the complaint filed with the Superior Court of California, PETA described its "international campaign to expose the intense suffering endured by these chickens" in the KFC supply system. The complaint said:

> The defendants have responded to PETA's campaign largely with public relations statements that are at best grossly misleading and, in numerous instances, entirely false. PETA brings this action to prevent the defendants from continuing their unlawful practices in deceiving consumers on factual issues about their methods of raising and killing chickens so that consumers will be able to make informed choices about whether to support these companies by purchasing from them.

PETA dropped its lawsuit 2 months later after KFC agreed to change the wording used to describe the treatment of chickens on its Web site and in telephone scripts of customer service representatives. Soon after, KFC's president resigned, and another was appointed to take her place.

As the seasons rolled along, men and women in chicken costumes hobbled on crutches and other activists hoisted signs outside KFC restaurants in Waco, Texas; Miami, Florida; Norman, Oklahoma; Frankfort, Kentucky; Rockford, Illinois; and other cities from coast to coast. They carried signs reading: "Kentucky Fried Cruelty ... We Do Chickens Wrong" and "The Colonel's Secret Recipe: Live Scalding, Painful Debeaking, Crippled Chickens."

Many of PETA's previous targets could confirm that the organization is patient, persistent and passionate about its causes. Pernicious is the adjective some would use.

QUESTIONS FOR REFLECTION

1. PETA has organized campaigns against Burger King, KFC, McDonald's, Whole Foods Markets, and others. Virtually all agreed to make some of the changes asked by PETA. In virtually all cases, the companies have insisted that they do not respond to coercion. Why do the companies make this apparently contradictory statement?
2. PETA has said that "animals are not ours to eat, wear, experiment on, or use for entertainment." The organization appears to want a vegetarian society. Should PETA have explicitly disclosed its goals in its KFC campaign?
3. A Texas newspaper said that PETA's tactics do more to energize its opponents than to win friends for its positions. Do you agree?
4. KFC does not own or operate poultry farms. Should consumers hold the company accountable for the practices of its suppliers?

Information for this case was drawn from the following: the PETA Web site at http://www.peta.org/; the KFC Web site at http://www.kfc.com/about/animalwelfare.htm; Becker, E. (6 January 2003), "Group says it will begin a boycott against KFC," *The New York Times*, p. A7; Becker, E. (7 July 2003), "Animal rights group to sue fast-food chain," *The New York Times*, p. A11; Becker, E. (2 September 2003), "Rights group for animals drops lawsuit against KFC," *The New York Times*, p. A2; (10 July 2003), "Editorial: Amarillo's animal magnetism continues to attract PETA," *The Amarillo Globe-News,* p. 18; Garber, A. (21 July 2003), "Fur flies as PETA sues KFC," *Nation's Restaurant News,* p. 1; Gartland, M. (16 March 2003), "PETA protests poultry purchases," *The Post and Courier,* p. 1; Howington, P. (8 July 2003), "Animal-rights group sues KFC," *The Courier-Journal,* p. C1; Moore, B. (14 March 2000), "PETA pushes beer to save cows," *The Los Angeles Times,* p. 2; and Rizzo, P. (3 September 2000), "PETA issues apology to Mayor Giuliani," *The Los Angeles Times,* p. 16.

CASE 35.   GREENPEACE PRESSURES CHEMICAL
PRODUCERS TO REDUCE RISKS OF CHLORINE GAS

Greenpeace environmentalists and American Chemistry Council (ACC) members have skirmished for a generation, but the terrorist attacks of September 2001 reshaped the dispute and sharpened anxieties.

Central issues have included the use or misuse of earth's resources, risks to human health near chemical plants, public access to information about plant hazards, and security against criminal intrusions and sabotage. In the debate, Greenpeace USA represents its 250,000 members, and the ACC speaks for chemical producers.

Seven months before al-Qaeda terrorists hijacked four airliners, Greenpeace activists organized a surreptitious visit to a Dow Chemical plant in Plaquemine, Louisiana, to test its security. They scaled an unguarded fence and entered an unlocked pump house, where they had access to a control panel regulating the discharge of wastewater into the Mississippi River. To provide journalists with proof of the unauthorized tour, the visitors took photographs and passed them out to news media in Baton Rouge upstream and New Orleans downstream.

The 1,500-acre Plaquemine operation, with nearly 3,000 workers at the site, produces 50 basic chemical products, including a large volume of chlorine.

The Dangers of Chlorine

Chlorine has been a chief concern of Greenpeace because the chemical is so common and so toxic. Most people are familiar with chlorine's beneficial uses—water purification, manufacture of pharmaceuticals, production of household bleach and PVC (polyvinylchloride) pipe, and more. However, it also is potentially dangerous.

Normally stored under pressure as a liquid, chlorine is a greenish yellow gas at standard temperature and pressure with a strong unpleasant smell. Because it's heavier than air, it stays near the ground and spreads when released. In the trench warfare of 1915 and later, Germans used the same gas to disable and kill British troops.

The rate at which it dissipates, or mixes with surrounding air, depends on whether there's a breeze. Lab tests indicate that concentrations of 900 parts per million may be lethal to animals. Human response to chlorine gas depends on duration of exposure and concentration of the gas. Because chlorine combines with water to form hydrochloric and hypochlorous acids, it attacks moist tissue first—the eyes and upper respiratory tract. Soon after exposure, people notice irritation in the nose, throat, and lungs, and tears flood the eyes.

In the United States, deaths from chlorine exposure have been rare—averaging fewer than one fatality per year in the 1990s. In most cases of exposure, the symptoms were uncomfortable but posed no threat of long-term damage. Some records indicate that about 1 in 10 incidents resulted in moderate or severe injury.

The Threat of Terrorism

Greenpeace has cited an elevated threat of terrorist attacks in insisting that companies producing and using chlorine should do more to lower the risks for communities near plant facilities. Safer substitutes exist for many applications that use the gas. For example, some water treatment facilities kill microbes with ultraviolet light.

Greenpeace also criticizes companies that store large quantities of the gas. The activist organization has said that releases, whether caused by sabotage or accident, could threaten the health and lives of hundreds of thousands.

To support its position, Greenpeace referred to disaster scenarios prepared by chlorine producers themselves under requirements of federal law. The Emergency Planning and Community Right-To-Know Act of 1986 compelled companies to account for the release of hazardous materials into the environment. It was enacted 2 years after 27 tons of methyl isocyanate spilled from a Union Carbide pesticide plant in Bhopal, India, killing 4,000 or more in neighborhoods surrounding the facility. Later, a 1990 amendment to the Clean Air Act obliged producers to describe worst-case scenarios of industrial accidents and their prevention plans. Summaries of the scenarios were made public.

Scaling Back on Access

In the months following the al-Qaeda attacks, the chemical industry persuaded the federal government to limit access to the accident scenarios, arguing that terrorists could use them in planning new attacks. Greater secrecy might deter or discourage terrorists.

Greenpeace countered that it was the producers themselves who were endangering communities by continuing to produce and store hazardous chlorine when substitutes were available. The environmentalists said that communities were entitled to know the risks imposed on them by industrial neighbors. Greater secrecy would relax pressure on the producers but handicap communities' power to protect the health and safety of residents.

To dramatize its concerns, Greenpeace sponsored a five-kilometer footrace— under the banner *Run for Your Life*—in Jersey City, New Jersey, in May 2003. The organizers distributed a news release that said the purpose of the race was to focus attention on the nation's vulnerability to a catastrophic release of toxic gas.

The environmentalists chose Jersey City for the race because it lies within the worst-case disaster scenario sketched out by Kuehne Chemical Company for its plant in nearby South Kearny. Kuehne (pronounced KEE-nee) stores chlorine at the facility for bleach production.

Worst-Case Scenarios

Greenpeace posted a map on its Web site showing cities and landmarks that lie within a 14-mile radius across which a chlorine cloud could drift if the Kuehne plant experienced a worst-case accident. Twelve million people live in the area and might face death or lung damage from exposure.

A year before the race, the *Wall Street Journal* reported that a Kuehne executive voiced concern about terrorism and criticized the activists' intention to publish the disaster map, saying, "I don't think someone who wants to do us harm has a right to know this."

In a subsequent letter, Greenpeace complimented Kuehne on steps it has taken since September 2001 to reduce the risks posed by chemicals at the New Jersey plant but suggested that more should be done:

> In practice, we see three stages of progress toward disaster-free, safer technologies. First are immediate and permanent steps to reduce storage. Second is the use of eas- ier, drop-in substitution of less hazardous chemicals. Third is the conversion to safer materials and processes that eliminate the production and use of chemicals, such as chlorine, which can be turned into a weapon of mass destruction. We think that is the wave of the future for smart "green chemistry" oriented companies.

Despite industry complaints, Greenpeace has published disaster maps not only for the Kuehne facility but also for plants operated by Dow Chemical, DuPont, and others in Michigan, Delaware, Texas, and West Virginia. Copies went to journal- ists as well.

Chemical industry representatives say that the worst-case scenarios fuel fears unnecessarily. In an imagined worst case, all safety systems would fail, and no one would try to flee the unfolding doom. In one of these nightmare scenarios, a 90-ton railcar loaded with chlorine would spill its entire contents within 10 minutes. A harmful cloud of gas then would roll along the ground for 14 miles in all direc- tions. Anyone who was near the accident and unprotected would die; those at the 14-mile-distant perimeter would suffer mild respiratory irritation.

A Spill in Missouri

In an actual accident that occurred in Festus, Missouri, in August 2002, the chlo- rine leak was slower, smaller, and less damaging. Workers were using two hoses to transfer chlorine from a railcar into 1-ton and 150-pound containers. One of the hoses burst, and an automatic shut-off valve failed to actuate. When a manual over- ride device also failed, employees evacuated the site immediately, and emergency response personnel went door to door in the surrounding neighborhoods, warning people to leave. U.S. Highway 61, adjacent to the facility's property, and nearby Interstate 55 were closed.

The chlorine continued to escape from the hose for 3 hours, discharging about 24 tons of gas. After donning protective equipment, hazardous-materials personnel entered the area near the railcar and measured lethal gas concentrations above 1,000 parts per million. They walked through a waist-high greenish yellow cloud and climbed the tank to close the valves.

Sixty-three people, workers and local residents, received medical treatment for nausea, respiratory distress, and coughing, and no one was seriously injured. Residents returned to their homes 7 hours later.

After the accident, activists said that the leak, its lethal concentration, and failure of safety systems underscored the need for public access to information on the chemical industry's use of hazardous materials. The industry's efforts to scale back its availability might raise risks to public health and lower trust in producers' operations.

Chemical Week magazine reported that the ACC's own random survey of Americans nationwide in early 2002—before the Festus leak—found that more than half were worried about chemicals or the chemical industry and that 48% described themselves as "distrustful" and 62% as "suspicious." The magazine said about two thirds of the respondents, when asked to indicate their overall assessment of the industry, held a largely neutral view, and the remaining third were almost evenly divided between positive and negative assessments.

QUESTIONS FOR REFLECTION

1. Greenpeace and chemical producers have quarreled about public access to information concerning health risks in neighborhoods surrounding chlorine plants. What is most convincing about the positions they have staked out?
2. Chlorine producers have said that they are concerned that terrorists might obtain and use the information that Greenpeace wants to publish. Should regulators restrict the availability of disaster maps?
3. *Chemical Week* magazine said that about half of all respondents to an ACC survey said they were "distrustful" of chemicals and the chemical industry. What might account for this response?
4. Greenpeace organized an unauthorized visit to an unattended chemical plant pump house in 2001. Was this entry unethical?

Information for this case was drawn from the following: the Greenpeace USA Web site at http://www.greenpeaceusa.org/; the American Chemistry Council Web site at http://www.accnewsmedia.com/; (October 2002), "Chlorine leak provokes fears," *Occupational Hazards*, p. 42; Cone, M. (17 April 2003), "Chemical plants said to pose risk," *The Los Angeles Times*, p. B1; Davis, A. (30 May 2002), "Toxic cloud: New alarms heat up debate on publicizing chemical risks," *The Wall Street Journal*, p. A1; (2 May 2003), "Investigators recommend steps to prevent future chlorine leaks," *The Jefferson City New Tribune*, p. 5; Pianin, E. (12 November 2001), "Toxic chemicals' security worries officials," *The Washington Post*, p. A14; (15 August 2002), "Rail car leak sends 28 to hospital in Missouri," *The Los Angeles Times*, p. A23; Schmitt, B. (3 July 2002), "Industry's critics make respect an elusive goal," *Chemical Week*, p. 42.

CASE 36. ACTIVIST CAMPAIGN IN INDIA EXAMINES SOFT DRINKS

India's Centre for Science and Environment (CSE) managed to unite the top rivals in the soft-drink industry as perhaps no one has done ever before. Coca-Cola and PepsiCo temporarily suspended the cola wars in August 2003 to stand shoulder-to-shoulder in condemning CSE laboratory tests that showed high levels of contaminants in beverages sold by the two companies in India.

CSE said that tested samples of 12 soft-drink brands sold in and around New Delhi contained pesticide residues that far exceeded limits adopted in the United States and European Union. The Coca-Cola Company and PepsiCo Inc. said the test results were just plain wrong.

The CSE is a nonprofit, nongovernmental organization that has functioned as a self-appointed public watchdog for the 1 billion people who live on the Indian subcontinent. Established in 1980, CSE aims to raise awareness of issues in science, technology, environment, and development that affect the lives of ordinary Indians. Here's how the center has described itself:

> Centre for Science and Environment is considered one of India's leading environmental NGOs [nongovernmental organizations] specialising in sustainable natural resource management. Its strategy of knowledge-based activism has won it wide respect and admiration for its quality of campaigns, research and publications. CSE promotes solutions for India's numerous environmental threats—of "ecological poverty" and extensive land degradation on one hand, and rapidly growing toxic degradation of uncontrolled industrialisation and economic growth on the other.

CSE Tackles Public Policy Issues

Through activist campaigns, CSE has focused attention on innovations in rainwater harvesting, protecting groundwater from pesticide invasion, air pollution caused by diesel fuels adulterated with kerosene and naphtha, and pure food regulations. In February 2003, the organization said it found potentially dangerous contaminants in most samples of bottled water sold at retail in Bombay and New Delhi.

In August 2003, CSE made headlines around the world when it announced that its lab tests had detected insecticides in Coca-Cola, Pepsi, Mountain Dew, and nine other popular soft drinks.

"All samples contained residues of four extremely toxic pesticides and insecticides: lindane, DDT, malathion and chlorpyrifos," the CSE news release said. "In all samples, levels of pesticide residues far exceeded the maximum residue limit for pesticides in water used as 'food,' set down by the European Economic Commission (EEC). Each sample had enough poison to cause—in the long term—cancer, damage to the nervous and reproductive systems, birth defects and severe disruption of the immune system."

Pesticide Levels Compared

According to CSE, the average pesticide levels in the Coca-Cola brands and the PepsiCo brands were similar—at least 30 times higher than acceptable European levels. The organization said that it also tested samples of Coca-Cola and Pepsi-Cola sold in the United States and found that they contained no pesticides.

Without excusing the soft-drink giants, the organization laid much of the blame at the doorstep of India's legislators and regulators, indicating that government has neglected its responsibility to protect public health and safety. CSE said that the rules governing bottled water were stricter than those applying to the soft-drink industry, which it described as "virtually unregulated."

Sunita Narain, director of CSE, acknowledged to the *Hindu Business Line* that milk and other foods in India often contain traces of pesticide. The country's environmental-protection laws generally do not match those in Europe or the United States.

Miss Narain told the financial daily that: "Just because others violate the law, it does not give the right to global corporates such as Coke and Pepsi to do the same. They are market leaders and need to set an example. Ground water here does contain pesticide, but companies should invest more in cleaning up the water, which is the raw material for soft drinks. Water accounts for more than 80 percent of the soft drink."

According to the *Washington Post*'s account of the controversy, Miss Narain said she was not trying to pick a fight with either of the soft-drink giants. The newspaper quoted her as saying: "Our battle is not with Pepsi or Coca-Cola; it is with the Indian government, whose norms are a vague maze of meaningless definitions."

Soft-Drink Executives Rebut Claims

On the same day that CSE disclosed its lab results, the chairman of PepsiCo's operations in India and the president of Coca-Cola India said that the quality of their companies' products is the same worldwide. They dismissed the CSE complaints as baseless and invited inspections by independent and accredited authorities. Appearing together at an unusual joint news conference, Coke and Pepsi executives said that any impurities in their soft drinks were well below the European thresholds of safety, which are stricter than those generally applied in the United States.

Despite the reassurances, the reaction in the Indian Parliament and on the street was immediate and harsh. In New Delhi, Parliament suspended sale of the soft drinks in its cafeteria, and demonstrators smashed bottles of the beverages on pavements in cities across the country. India's health minister promptly promised an investigation, as samples of the soft drinks were sent to government labs for independent analysis.

Soft-drink consumers reacted harshly, too. Within 10 days of the initial announcement, daily sales of Coke and Pepsi products had dropped about one third. The controversy represented a significant setback for the two companies because the soft-drink market in hot, humid, and huge India appeared to offer so much potential for growth.

Soft-Drink Market in India

India's annual per-capita consumption of soft drinks is nine 8-ounce servings. That's just nine per year for each person in India's population of 1 billion. The comparable figure for the United States is 848 per capita and for Germany is 341, according to *Beverage Digest* magazine's global profile for 2001. (Mexico is the world champion at 1,500 servings per capita per year.)

India's weather seems ideal for selling soft drinks. New Delhi's average daily high temperature in July is 101 degrees Fahrenheit (38 degrees Celsius) and in January is 68 degrees Fahrenheit (20 degrees Celsius).

In 2002, the total sales of all soft drinks in India reached about $2.3 billion. The Coca-Cola Company's brands together accounted for about 60% of the total, but the Coke brand itself, market leader almost everywhere else, is third in sales in India. Pepsi is No. 1, and Thumbs Up, a local cola that Coca-Cola acquired in 1993, ranks second.

Producers Fight Fears

The soft drink companies acted quickly to stem August's decline in sales. Giving consumers reasons to reject the fears stirred by the CSE report, the soft-drink companies talked with reporters, issued news releases, and created advertising that detailed their quality assurance programs.

Coca-Cola India created a special section on its Web site with individual pages describing its quality commitment, testing procedures, filtration systems, and more. It also included a section identifying what the company called false statements, or myths, that had been circulating since the CSE announcement and paired each myth with an explanation to refute it.

In the *Myths and Facts* section, Coca-Cola India addressed one of the statements that had inflamed passions the most and fired up indignation. Here is the pair from the Web site:

The myth: Coca-Cola has dual standards in the production of its products, one high standard for western countries and another for India.

The fact: The soft drinks manufactured in India conform to the same high standards of quality as in the USA and Europe. Through our globally accepted and validated manufacturing processes and quality management systems, we ensure that our state-of-the-art manufacturing facilities are equipped to provide the consumer the highest quality beverage each time. We stringently test our soft drinks in India at independent, accredited and world-class laboratories both locally and internationally.

Process for Purification

In a joint statement to editors, Coca-Cola and Pepsi described the multiple-barrier filtration process that both use to purify water contained in soft drinks. The four-step process is as follows:

1. Chlorination disinfects the water.
2. Filtration at the molecular level removes dirt, clay, suspended materials, microbial matter such as bacteria and virus, and heavy metals and compounds.
3. Activated carbon filters absorb organic compounds, which include pesticides and herbicides.
4. Finally, the water passes through a high-efficiency 5-micron filter that removes any trace of activated carbon.

The joint statement also explained that the companies buy high-grade sugar from mills in India and treat it to remove impurities before converting it into sugar syrup for use in soft drinks.

Health Minister's Report

On August 21, India's health minister gave Parliament a report on results obtained by government labs in their tests of soft-drink samples. She said that all 12 brands were safe to drink and met Indian standards for bottled water. However, she noted that several were not completely free of pesticide residue and some exceeded the limits set for contaminants by the European Union. Among the 12 brands, the labs found pesticide residue in 9 that were one to five times higher than European standards.

Soft-drink executives expressed delight that the government had declared the beverages safe to drink. The headline of a joint news release read: "Coca-Cola and Pepsi-Cola welcome Indian Government's endorsement on safety of soft drinks."

CSE officers also found some vindication in the health minister's report and continued their call for stricter regulation of bottled water, soft drinks, and the use of pesticides. The central government opened an inquiry into standards for soft-drink purity, and state governments began testing samples as well.

To some extent, individuals on all sides of the issue appeared to agree with some of the sentiments expressed in the *Myths and Facts* section of Coca-Cola India's Web site: "The situation calls for the development of national sampling and testing protocols for soft drinks, an end to sensationalising unsubstantiated allegations, and cooperation by all parties concerned in the interests of both Indian consumers and companies with significant investment in the Indian economy."

The Changing Role of NGOs

As the soft-drink controversy was unfolding in India, the *Economist* newspaper noted that the role of nongovernmental organizations (NGOs), such as the CSE, has been expanding beyond disaster relief campaigns and advocacy for human rights and environmental issues.

NGOs have performed better than government agencies in some poor nations and in areas of conflict such as Afghanistan and Iraq, the newspaper said. In other cases, NGOs' expanding role has produced mixed results:

> Campaigns against corporations often focus on the targets most likely to capitulate, rather than the worst offenders. The politicisation of many NGOs has led rich-world governments (such as that of Britain) to eschew them in favour of less effective governmental networks for delivering aid. The campaign against globalisation, which involves many NGOs, is a focus in the wrong direction (as some NGOs are coming to realise). In fact, measures such as water privatisation are likely to benefit the poor. And, the bullying of corporations pursuing compensation claims against poor countries may deter investment in the developing world.

QUESTIONS FOR REFLECTION

1. NGOs, such as the CSE, often tackle social problems when poor governments can't or won't. How can NGOs overcome claims that they are too political?
2. Why would CSE focus on brands like Coca-Cola and Pepsi-Cola when other foods in India, such as milk, contain pesticides?
3. Do you agree with the strategy adopted by Coca-Cola and Pepsi-Cola to combine efforts in refuting CSE's claims?
4. What advice would you give to the CSE concerning its future efforts to get chemicals out of India's food chain?

Information for this case was drawn from the following: the Centre for Science and Environment Web site at http://www.cseindia.org/; the Coca-Cola India Web site at http://www.myenjoyzone.com/ press1/; (5 August 2003), "Coke, Pepsi contain pesticide residues," *The Hindu Business Line*; (7 August 2003), "Non-governmental organizations," Economist.com, http://www.economist.com/background/ displayBackground.cfm?story_id1982550; Kripalani, J., & Clifford, M. (February 10 2003), "Finally, Coke gets it right," *Business Week*, p. 18; Lakshmi, R. (10 August 2003), "Soda giants battle public panic in India," *The Washington Post*, p. A17; Slater, J. (15 August 2003), "Coke, Pepsi fight product-contamination charges in India," *The Wall Street Journal*, p. B1; Slater, J. (22 August 2003), "Coca-Cola, Pepsi pass India's test on pesticides," *The Wall Street Journal*, p. B5; Slater, J., & Terhune, C. (25 August 2003), "Coke, Pepsi still face issues in India," *The Wall Street Journal*, p. B4; and Waldman, A. (23 August 2003), "India tries to contain a tempest over soft drink safety," *The New York Times*, p. A3.

CASE 37. ACTIVISTS KEEP NIKE ON THE RUN

Nike knows how to compete. It won its position atop the world's shoe industry a generation ago and remains the leader. It received acclaim twice as Advertiser of the Year—in 1994 and 2003—at France's Cannes Lion festival, sometimes called the Olympics of Advertising. It's the company whose 1996 ads said: "You don't win silver. You lose gold." Nike has repeatedly bested rivals like Adidas, New Balance, and Reebok in the athletic-shoe footrace. In the United States, its market share is 40%.

Yet, clear-cut victory has eluded Nike in its marathon contest with activists and media critics who have run the company ragged on the issue of worker abuse in overseas production facilities. Even when Nike asked the U.S. Supreme Court in 2003 to affirm the company's First Amendment right to speak publicly on the issue, the court refused to take a position on the question. No gold, no silver, no bronze.

Code of Conduct

Nike, headquartered in Beaverton, Oregon, doesn't own or operate shoe production plants overseas. Instead, it hires subcontractors in low-wage countries such as China, Indonesia, South Korea, and Vietnam to produce shoes to Nike specifications. To assure workers' rights there, Nike requires its subcontractors to adopt Nike's Code of Conduct and allow unannounced visits by inspectors chosen by Nike. Adopted in 1992, the code requires compliance in four areas of employee welfare:

- Health and safety.
- Pay and benefits.
- Terms of work.
- Management–workers relations.

Yet, some critics have said that Nike's worker-protection program is little more than window dressing for sweatshop operations, and others say that the company's public statements on the issue have been misleading and incomplete. Complaints about overseas labor abuse began plaguing Nike in the 1980s, and the reports reached a wide audience in the 1990s in media such as the *Economist* and the *New York Times*. CBS News reported in 1996 that workers making Nike shoes in Southeast Asia were poorly paid, exposed to hazardous chemicals, and mistreated by managers.

Columnist Provokes CEO Letter

In a single week in June 1996, *New York Times* columnist Bob Herbert twice used his commentary to take a swipe at Nike; its cofounder and chief executive, Philip

H. Knight; and the famous professional athletes making millions from Nike contracts. Citing Indonesia as an example, Mr. Herbert said thousands of workers producing Nike products earned $2.20 a day.

"Philip Knight has an extraordinary racket going for him," the columnist wrote on June 10. "There is absolutely no better way to get rich than to exploit both the worker and the consumers. If you can get your product made for next to nothing, and get people to buy it at exorbitant prices, you get to live at the top of the pyramid."

Four days later, Mr. Herbert added: "Nike is the most vulnerable to criticism of the athletic footwear corporations because it is the biggest, the most visible and by far the most hypocritical. No amount of charitable contributions or of idealized commercial images can hide the fact that Indonesia is Nike's kind of place. The exploitation of cheap Asian labor has been a focus of its top executive, Philip Knight, for more than three decades."

Mr. Knight, in a letter to the *New York Times* 1 week later, responded:

Nike has paid, on average, double the minimum wage as defined in countries where its products are produced under contract. This is in addition to free meals, housing and health care and transportation subsidies.

Underdeveloped countries must trade or see deeper declines in living standards. History shows that the best way out of poverty for such countries is through exports of light manufactured goods that provide the base for more skilled production.

Nike continued to answer its critics with information on its inspection and enforcement program as well as economic arguments about international trade, comparative advantage, and global competition.

Tongue-Tied Public Relations

The *Wall Street Journal*, under the headline "Nike Inc.'s Golden Image Is Tarnished As Problems in Asia Pose PR Challenge," asked in 1997: "How has Nike, a brand renowned for its global marketing finesse, found itself in this situation? It's because the athletic-shoe maker has remained tongue-tied, public relations experts say, in the face of a loose-knit but efficient attack that combines the speed of the Internet with good old-fashioned rabble-rousing."

On college campuses, student activists were questioning deals arranged by Nike and its competitors to provide big universities not just with footwear and apparel for varsity teams but also logo-licensed products for sale to the public. The activists said that, through the multiyear contracts, university administrators were complicit in the abuse of foreign laborers because universities assured a future market for goods produced under exploitation. To coordinate antiexploitation campaigns emerging on more than 100 college campuses, activists formed the United Students Against Sweatshops.

At the University of North Carolina (UNC) at Chapel Hill, student activists tried to persuade administrators to cancel a Nike contract in 1997 with a campaign featuring "Just Don't Do It" leaflets that accused the shoe company of unfair labor practices.

According to the *Wall Street Journal*, "In 1997, Nike signed an $11.6 million deal with UNC's athletic department to outfit most of its sports teams and to manufacture UNC-logo sweatshirts and T-shirts, which in turn would generate $6 million to $8 million in annual sales for the company."

Nike's Campus Visit

As the activist campaign gained attention at UNC, Nike responded with a combination of ads in the *Daily Tar Heel* student newspaper, campus visits by a public relations team, and personal contact by Nike representatives with the members of the activist group. Before the fall semester ended, the company had offered an expense-paid trip to Southeast Asia for a faculty member and three students, including a *Daily Tar Heel* reporter. Under the plan, the four would tour facilities to see for themselves the conditions in which Nike shoes were made.

The plan was scrapped when some UNC faculty members objected, and a regular undergraduate course on environment and labor in the global economy was established instead. Nike executives were invited to attend class, and one who did in April 1998 was Nike chief executive Philip Knight.

An Activist Sues

Marc Kasky, a San Francisco activist interested in humanitarian causes, watched the give-and-take between the company and its critics, and he grew angry over Nike statements that he considered misleading or downright false. At about the same time that Mr. Knight visited the Chapel Hill classroom, Mr. Kasky filed a complaint in California Superior Court, accusing the company of unfair business practices, negligent misrepresentation, fraud, and deceit.

In his lawsuit, Mr. Kasky cited nine instances in which Nike issued positive statements about its labor practices that conflicted with information from other sources. The nine instances included:

1. A letter from Nike to university presidents and athletic directors.
2. A 30-page brochure on Nike labor policies.
3. A news release on its labor practices.
4. Material on the Nike Web site concerning its code of conduct.
5. A document offering Nike's perspective on the labor controversy.
6. A news release responding to sweatshop allegations.
7. A letter from Nike to the YWCA of America.

8. A letter from Nike to the International Restructuring Education Network Europe.
9. Mr. Knight's letter to the *New York Times*.

Facts in Conflict

For example, Mr. Kasky challenged Nike's claim that it paid double the minimum-wage rate in Southeast Asian countries. He said that Ernst & Young, an auditing firm that Nike hired to inspect a Vietnamese factory, found that workers received an average wage of $45 monthly, $5 above the minimum wage. He called Nike's claim "deceitful."

Noting that Nike's Code of Conduct forbids the use of corporal punishment or harassment of any kind in worker discipline, Mr. Kasky said the CBS News "48 Hours" program reported that 45 Vietnamese workers were forced by supervisors to kneel with their hands held in the air for 25 minutes. The same program, he said, reported that a supervisor hit 15 Vietnamese women on the head as a penalty for poor sewing.

Nike's letter to university officials included assurances of compliance with health and safety regulations, according to Mr. Kasky, but the Ernst & Young inspection found that thousands of women between the ages of 18 and 24 were exposed to high levels of toluene fumes and chemical dust in a Vietnamese plant.

In his lawsuit, Mr. Kasky said a central purpose of Nike's Code of Conduct was "to entice consumers who do not want to purchase products made in sweatshop and/or under unsafe and/or inhuman conditions." He said that the letters and other communications were marketing tools used by the company to attract customers.

Public Debate or Commercial Speech?

Nike disagreed. The company told the court that it was engaged in a public discussion of controversial issues, such as globalization and international trade, that had sparked comment in a number of quarters. The letters, news releases, web pages, and other communications represented the company's voice in an open debate on matters of public policy, according to Nike, and its participation in public discussion was protected absolutely by the First Amendment.

The decision of the California Superior Court favored Nike. When Mr. Kasky appealed to the California Court of Appeal, his argument was rejected again. Mr. Kasky persisted, and the California Supreme Court reversed the earlier decisions in May 2002.

"Because the messages in question were directed by a commercial speaker to a commercial audience, and because they made representations of fact about the speaker's own business operations for the purpose of promoting sales of its products, ... [Nike's] messages are commercial speech," the California judges said.

The court did not say that Nike had misled anyone, deceived consumers, or misrepresented its practices. In fact, such an evaluation had not been attempted by the lower courts because they judged that Nike's statements were entitled to full protection of the First Amendment.

Breathing Space in Public Debate

In public policy discussions, the courts generally say that the First Amendment protects the expression of views, even if incorrect or exaggerated, as long as they contain no deliberate or reckless falsehoods. Full and robust debate flourishes when speakers have the liberty to voice ideas, however unconventional or unpopular, without fear that they may be hauled into court to explain errors, misstatements, misinterpretations, or shades of meaning.

Commercial speech is a different animal, the courts say, and the First Amendment affords it limited protection because its fundamental purpose is to promote a transaction rather than to contribute ideas to public debate.

The California Supreme Court explained, "Our holding in no way prohibits any business enterprise from speaking out on issues of public importance or from vigorously defending its own labor practices. It means only that when a business enterprise makes factual representations about its own products or its own operations, it must speak truthfully."

Five months after the California court ruled that Nike's statements were commercial speech, the company filed an appeal with the U.S. Supreme Court, asking it to review the decision. Nike's attorneys said the California verdict would curtail businesses' participation in public discussion and deprive the general public of a full spectrum of views.

U.S. Supreme Court Accepts Case

In January 2003, the high court agreed to hear Nike's appeal. Many First Amendment scholars, news organizations, and others supported Nike and filed friend-of-the-court briefs to oppose California's apparent expansion of the commercial-speech umbrella. Among the briefs was one filed by the PRSA.

"Those of us who assist companies in gathering and disseminating information related to their businesses have always relied on the same First Amendment protections as those who openly criticize Nike and other corporations," PRSA President Reed Byrum said. "Without that protection, there will be a serious impact on all aspects of corporate communications from business, to corporate crisis communications and even to philanthropic and community-outreach programs."

Sonia Arrison, a First Amendment Fellow of the National Press Club, wrote a newspaper commentary that said, "Laws that were meant to stop false claims such as 'orange juice cures cancer' should not be distorted and used as political weapons. And surely in an established democracy, the government does not allow one side in a debate to summarily stifle its opponents' viewpoints."

A Mix of Debate and Marketing

When the Supreme Court justices heard attorneys for Kasky and Nike in April 2003, several seemed to see elements of both commercial speech and noncommercial speech in the Nike communications.

According to a *New York Times* account of the hearings, Justice Stephen G. Breyer told the attorneys, "The truth of the matter is, I think it's both," and later he added, "I think the First Amendment was designed to protect all the participants in a public debate, and a debate consists of facts. Once you've tied a party's hands behind his back with respect to the facts, you've silenced him."

The Supreme Court handed down its order in June 2003 and left many who looked forward to a landmark ruling in stunned silence or heated indignation. "Improvidently granted," said the court, meaning that it had changed its mind about taking the case. Six voted to dismiss, and three would have rendered a verdict.

Nike faced the prospect of returning to the California court system, where it would have to defend its communications as commercial speech. The company would be going back in 2003 to the future it had first faced in 1998.

Settlement Reached

Less than 3 months after the U.S. Supreme Court decided not to decide, Nike and Marc Kasky settled their differences out of court. Nike agreed to give $1.5 million to programs of the Fair Labor Association (FLA). With the funds, the FLA planned to support:

- Improvements in independent monitoring of workplace conditions in manufacturing countries.
- Worker development programs that focus on education and economic opportunity.
- Collaboration to formulate a global standard for measuring and reporting corporate responsibility performance.

The FLA was formed in 1999 by a diverse group, including Nike and other apparel manufacturers, colleges and universities, human rights organizations, and activists. It promotes its code of conduct, monitors practices in factories that make products for Nike and other brands, and coordinates public reports on monitoring results.

In the Bloomberg news service reports on the settlement, a law professor at George Washington University said Nike's payout was a sensible alternative to further litigation.

The professor, Jonathan Turley, said, "Any trial in this case would have been a bloody nightmare—the type of press that a company like Nike would never welcome."

Attorneys for Mr. Kasky issued a statement saying that their client was "satisfied that this settlement reflects Nike's commitment to positive changes where factory workers are concerned."

QUESTIONS FOR REFLECTION

1. In what ways did Nike's communications focus on marketing and sales? In what ways did they focus on public debate about international trade and economic growth?
2. Nike doesn't operate shoe production facilities in the United States or elsewhere. Why would some consumers hold the company responsible for working conditions in facilities where its shoes are made?
3. Most footwear companies hire subcontractors in developing countries to make their shoes. Why would Nike attract a lion's share of the criticism?
4. Nike has said it will refrain from public debate about overseas working conditions in the future. Is this a good idea or a bad idea?

Information for this case was drawn from the following: the Nike Web site at http://www.nike.com/nikebiz/nikebiz.jhtml?page=0; Arrison, S. (22 January 2003), "Letting Nike speak," The *News & Observer*, p. A25; Carter, R. (30 April 2002). "ABC: Athletics, business & Carolina," *The Daily Tar Heel*, p. 1. (20 April 1998), Complaint, *Kasky v. Nike*, Superior Court of the State of California; Herbert, B. (14 June 1996). "In America: Nike's bad neighborhood," *The New York Times*, p. 25; Herbert, B. (10 June 1996), "In America: Nike's pyramid scheme," *The New York Times*, p. 27; Knight, P. (21 June 1996), "Letter: Nike pays good wages to foreign workers," *The New York Times*, p. A29; Marshall, S. (26 September 1997), "Nike Inc.'s gold image is tarnished as problems in Asia pose PR challenge," *The Wall Street Journal*, p. B1; McCarthy, M. (15 June 2003), "Wake up consumers? Nike's brash CEO dares to just do it," *USA Today*, p. B1; (26 June 2003), Opinion, *Nike v. Kasky*, U.S. Supreme Court; (3 March 2003), "PRSA presses Supreme Court to protect free speech right for American business," PRSA news release; Savage, D. (11 January 2003), "Justices to hear Nike free-speech claim," *The Los Angeles Times*, p. C1; Stancill, J. (15 November 1997), "Nike offers tour of Asian factories to UNC critics," *The News & Observer*, p. B1; Tkacik, M. (10 January 2003), "High court may decide to hear whether Nike's PR statements to media, others are protected," *The Wall Street Journal*, p. B1.

CASE 38. "WALKING THE TALK"—DUPONT'S LAND LEGACY PROGRAM DONATES 16,000 ACRES TO THE CONSERVATION FUND

In August 2003, Dupont announced it would donate 15,985 acres of land adjacent to the Okefenokee National Wildlife Refuge in southeast Georgia to the Conservation Fund. The Conservation Fund then was to transfer ownership of the 16,000 acres to federal and state agencies or to local community groups, which would manage the land as a protected area. Some 5,000 of the acres became part of the Okefenokee refuge. The donation was the largest in the history of the DuPont Land Legacy program—and may reflect the corporation's response to what the *Atlanta Journal-Constitution* called a "national uproar" of protests about its original plans for using the land.

Dupont Chairman and CEO Charles O. Holliday, Jr. said in an Aug. 27, 2003, press release:

> We believe that our donation of DuPont land in and near Okefenokee National Wildlife Refuge is a concrete example of "walking the talk" with regard to our company's commitment to sustainable growth and social responsibility. The refuge is an ecological treasure. Through the good work of our partner, The Conservation Fund, we are confident that the land we are donating will be properly and permanently protected. We are also grateful to all the stakeholders who participated in the collaborative process that helped us reach this very positive outcome.

Collaborating on Land Management

The 396,000-acre Okefenokee National Wildlife Refuge was established in 1937 to protect the 438,000-acre swamp. In 1974, the interior 353,981 acres of the refuge were designated a National Wilderness Area.

International Paper holds the land's wood fiber and recreational rights, which it will retain through 2080. International Paper will maintain a working forest on the property. The corporation cooperated with DuPont to protect the land by relinquishing acquisition rights permanently, which will prevent mining of the property in the future.

Responding to the announcement, Georgia Gov. Sonny Perdue told the *Atlanta Journal Constitution*, "This is a great gift for Georgia, the local community and the entire nation."

Plans for a Titanium Mine Arouse Protests

The corporation had purchased the land in 1991 and 1996 in order to mine titanium ore from the site. Titanium is the key ingredient in titanium dioxide, a white pigment used in paint, plastics, and paper. In 1997, DuPont announced plans to mine a

30-mile, 3-mile-wide ridge that bordered the Okefenokee, the world's largest and purest freshwater wetlands. It contains more than 1,000 species of plant, bird, and aquatic life and connects to the headwaters of the Suwannee and St. Mary's rivers.

Almost immediately after the mining plan was announced, protests began. Environmentalists said the ridge, the site of native American burial grounds and a remnant of a prehistoric seashore, acted as a natural dam that causes rain to flow into the Okefenokee. U.S. Interior Secretary Bruce Babbitt visited the land site to announce his opposition, and Georgia Gov. Zell Miller also protested the proposed mining activities. The Georgia Board of Natural Resources passed a resolution opposing the mining unless DuPont could demonstrate "beyond a reasonable doubt" that the operation would be safe for the swamp.

In response, DuPont announced it would suspend its plans and would instead form a collaborative to discuss the project. DuPont established a Collaborative Process Core Group of landowners, mining, tourism, and wood-fiber interests, local community officials and politicians, local NGOs, landowners, and Native Americans. The corporation agreed to accept the recommendation of the collaborative.

At its shareholder meeting that April, a proposal to bar the company from mining at the site was voted down, although enough votes were cast to require bringing the resolution back up at the next year's shareholders meeting. About 3.4% of the shareholders, representing about 50 million common shares, voted in favor of the resolution. The proposal had come from a coalition of shareholders and environmentalists, including the Sisters of St. Francis of Philadelphia, the Missionary Oblates of Mary Immaculate in Silver Spring, Maryland, the Community of the Sisters of St. Dominic of Caldwell, and Jean A. Reisman of East Boston, Massachusetts, part of a nationwide network of about 300 institutions belonging to the Interfaith Center on Corporate Responsibility.

The second shareholder consideration would not be needed. In 1999, the collaborative group endorsed a "no mining"option and recommended that public and private funding be sought to reimburse DuPont and others for their anticipated profit if the mining had been allowed.

DuPont then sought $90 million in compensation, for the actual cost of the land and estimated profits it might have earned over the 40-year life of the mine. The *Atlanta Journal Constitution*, in a February 11, 1999, editorial, opposed the compensation, arguing that the price was too steep and that recovering $20 million in actual costs of the mining project and the collaborative would be a more equitable settlement. However, the newspaper reported on August 27, 2003, that DuPont's title to the land was being transferred to the Conservation Fund without compensation except for a tax write-off.

DuPont Establishes a Land Legacy Program

DuPont had been involved in land management for more than 200 years, but has been offering this type of protection to certain lands for about a decade. Since

1802, DuPont has owned property that has been used for plants and offices, but some land holdings were undeveloped or were no longer in use by the corporation. The undisturbed lands became prime areas for preservation, and DuPont's Land Legacy Program has placed nearly 18,000 other acres of company land into protected status since 1994.

In 1994, DuPont donated the 1,000-acre Willow Grove Lake property to the Nature Conservancy of New Jersey. In 1997, DuPont gave 7,700 acres near Brevard, North Carolina, to the Conservation Fund to create what is now North Carolina's DuPont State Forest. Monds Island in the Delaware River estuary near Gibbstown, New Jersey, was donated to the New Jersey Audubon Society in 1998 and is now part of Twin Islands Sanctuary, a nesting site for great blue herons and bald eagles. In 2002, DuPont gave 855 acres in Louviers, Colorado, to the Conservation Fund and Douglas County to offer a habitat for such species as elk and black bear.

The Wildlife Habitat Council, a Maryland-based nonprofit dedicated to increasing the quality and amount of habitats on corporate, private, and public lands, has certified 23 DuPont sites in Mexico, Ireland, Spain, Luxembourg, and the United States where the corporation has developed or protected such wildlife-friendly habitats as wetlands, tree and wildflower plantings, and nesting platforms for various bird species.

Mr. Holliday explained the corporation's environmental philosophy in a statement on DuPont's Web site:

> At DuPont we are proud of a decade of reducing our environmental footprint. We have come a long way, certainly in reductions of waste and emissions, but also in recognizing the impact of our operations on global issues such as climate change. However, there are still enormous challenges .... As a company that is owned by thousands of investors, our challenge is to address these issues in a way that makes business sense. We define this direction as sustainable growth—the creation of shareholder and societal value while decreasing our environmental footprint along the value chains in which we operate.

DuPont operates in more than 70 countries, offering a wide range of products and services in agriculture, nutrition, electronics, communication, safety and protection, home and construction, apparel, and transportation.

QUESTIONS FOR REFLECTION

1. Activists in this case included private and public environmentalists and politicians. How did DuPont seek to establish communication with the stakeholders represented here?

2. What does this case illustrate about the benefits and risks of building public and private coalitions?

3. How do DuPont shareholders benefit from its environmental philanthropy?

Material for this case was drawn from the following: the DuPont Web site at www.Dupont.com; Editorial (11 February 1999), "Mining buyout looks like gouging," *Atlanta Constitution*, p. A22; Mack, M. (1 January 1998), "The State of Georgia: The environment. On the edge of the Okefenokee," *The Atlanta Journal-Constitution*, p. A16; Reuters (11 April 1997), "DuPont suspends Georgia mine plan," *Reuters Business Report*; Seabrook, C. (30 April 1998), "Mining proposal still alive: DuPont shareholders leave the door open for extracting titanium dioxide from land next to Georgia's Okefenokee Swamp," *The Atlanta Journal-Constitution*, p. D1; Seabrook, C. (27 August 2003), "16,000-acre gift to swamp," *The Atlanta Journal-Constitution*, pp. A1, A12; Sissell, K. (17 February 1999), "DuPont will forgo mining to protect Okefenokee Swamp," *Chemical Week, 161;* and Spangler, T. (29 April 1998), "DuPont shareholders reject proposal to retire Okefenokee mining rights," *AP Online*.

10

Stakeholders: Global Citizens

China has been the biggest market outside the United States for KFC fried chicken and has sometimes produced more profit for the restaurant chain than its U.S. operations. KFC has more than 900 stores in China.

The world's busiest McDonald's restaurant is on Pushkin Square in Moscow, a 10-minute walk from the Kremlin. McDonald's operates about 100 restaurants throughout Russia.

Globalization of American institutions creates new challenges for public relations practitioners. For example, McDonald's has about 100 restaurants in Russia, including this one on Prospekt Mira in Moscow.

More than 70% of the Coca-Cola Company's income comes from outside the United States. Coca-Cola is available in more than 200 countries.

Evidence of globalization is visible within the United States, too. Most of the U.S. market for super-premium ice creams, such Haagen-Dazs and Ben & Jerry's, is controlled by two European companies—Nestlé SA of Switzerland and Unilever of the Netherlands. Americans think first of Japan's Sony in consumer electronics and use more cell phones from Finland's Nokia than from any other producer.

PRACTITIONERS' ROLE IN A GLOBAL MARKET

As markets for products and services connect countries and cultures around the world, organizations with multinational operations need public relations practitioners who can manage communications programs across borders, who can understand the risks of dynamic situations, and who can adapt quickly to either opportunities or problems.

Most public relations professionals in the United States take for granted the predictability and convenience of life in a free-market economy with political stability. Of course, several nations match the U.S. standard of living, and a few others are rapidly closing the gap. Many are far behind.

Where living standards approach America's norm, differences in culture and media may complicate a public relations process that would seem simple in the United States. Even nations that share as much as the United States and Great Britain still contain remarkable differences.

Language is one example. Though English is spoken by almost everyone in both countries, the meaning of the same word may differ depending on where it's said. In Great Britain, businesspeople commonly use the word *turnover* to mean total revenues for a financial period, but Americans use the word *sales* to express the same idea. Americans often expect the noun *scheme* to mean a cunning or devious plot, but in Great Britain it's commonly used as a synonym for plan or program (or programme, as it would be spelt in London).

CULTURAL DIFFERENCES

Almost as variable as language, attitudes toward the use of time vary widely from culture to culture. To many, Americans appear to rush everything—even leisure. A business dinner that might last 75 to 90 minutes in a United States restaurant could take twice as long in some European cities.

The meals themselves—the food, when it's eaten, how it's eaten—also change from country to country. An English breakfast is large and varied, and afternoon tea remains a tradition. In Italy, the first meal of the day may be a bun and espresso, and other meals are likely to include pasta as a side dish but not a main dish. In Russia, breakfast foods—meats and cheeses—resemble what some Americans eat for lunch. Evening meals in many nations are later than they would be in the United States.

For public relations professionals, arranging media receptions or special events that feature food involves meticulous planning and selection to please guests. In an unfamiliar culture, only local expertise can ensure that an important event will succeed rather than embarrass.

GET LOCAL HELP

Respected authorities in international public relations strongly advise practitioners working in cultures other than their own to:

- Avoid the ethnocentrism that overvalues American habits and methods.
- Get advice and assistance from established public relations consultants in the locations where goodwill is needed.

Americans sometimes believe that what works at home will surely work in other countries. Adapting tactics that have worked famously in U.S. cities, they plunge ahead, expecting similar results. Sometimes they are lucky and get what they want, but often they confuse, mystify, or offend their target publics or miss them altogether.

Local consultants can provide help with language, customs, regulations, media contacts, local transportation, and last-minute supplies or modifications. They can identify stakeholders and opinion leaders whose views will count the most. By including on-site consultants in early planning for an international program, practitioners can save time and money and also achieve a better outcome.

OVERCOMING LANGUAGE BARRIERS

In international efforts, language often represents the single most troublesome challenge. Not only are the words and sentence structure different, but also the alphabet may be entirely unfamiliar or—just as bad—misleadingly similar. In Russia, the Cyrillic alphabet is used, and the letters *BP*, the name of the petroleum giant, would sound like *VR* if strict pronunciation were used.

Sometimes, the problem is a common phrase in one language that conveys the wrong message when spoken in another. According to the *New York Times*, an expensive Italian restaurant gave Shanghai residents reason to smile when it opened under the name Va Bene, which means "go well" in Italian. In Shanghai dialect, it sounded like "not cheap."

Translation is essential, but it often slows things down. When a speaker and translator take turns, the speaker's remarks double in length, risking both boredom and misunderstanding. To avoid the need for clumsy sequential translation of a speaker's remarks through a translator, a practitioner might team up with a local consultant who learns the intricacies of a public relations program's platform and key messages well enough to handle media interviews and similar tasks independently.

Some multinational corporations are large enough to have full-time public relations professionals in countries where they operate, or they train managers in other departments to handle public relations as needed. In either case, the staffers should come from the local population.

Executives at corporate headquarters also should listen carefully to public relations advice they get from consultants or qualified staff working in another country and adjust plans or responses to issues accordingly. Listening to local voices is essential regardless of where the headquarters might be.

PARALYSIS OR HUBRIS?

In 2000, *Business Week* reported that Firestone's public relations crisis in the recall of 6.5 million tires resulted, in part, from executive paralysis at its parent, Bridgestone Corporation, in Tokyo.

"Bridgestone's behavior speaks volumes about the huge gaps that still exist between U.S. and Japanese management," the magazine said. "All the Tokyo executives ... seem unable or unwilling to respond to pleas from investors and the media for explanations and reassurance."

A year earlier, the Coca-Cola Company suffered a series of embarrassing recalls in Europe that seemed to cascade from one country to another. First, about 200 consumers in Belgium and France complained of illness after drinking Coke products. Critics said the company was slow to respond to the concerns, and authorities in Belgium, France, and Luxembourg ordered 65 million cans of Coke products off the shelves. Days later, Coca-Cola issued a small recall of soft drinks in Portugal when specks of charcoal from a filtration system were found in cans. A week later, the company recalled bottled water in Poland because of the presence of mold.

In Coca-Cola's hometown, an *Atlanta Business Chronicle* columnist said Coke's "combination of marketing and legal muscle has made the company extraordinarily successful and perhaps left it feeling a tad omnipotent. Enter the dust-up in Belgium and France over supposedly contaminated Coca-Cola products. The company's culture didn't allow it to respond as quickly as it should have, and the result was a crisis."

CRITICS OF GLOBALIZATION

Although globalization probably ranks as the leading economic force of the new century, it has attracted its share of critics. Some say globalization is a movement that exploits poor workers in weak and underdeveloped countries to provide inexpensive consumer goods for individuals who are privileged to live in prosperous countries.

Activist groups like the Mobilization for Global Justice have held rallies and marches to draw attention to the poverty of many workers in Latin America and

Asia. The groups have performed street-theater skits outside offices of Citibank, the International Monetary Fund, Monsanto, Occidental Petroleum, and the World Bank. Radical protesters resorted to violence and vandalism at demonstrations in Seattle and Geneva.

Business Week pointed out that "Anti-globalization groups speak in the name of Third World countries, but democratically elected governments in countries such as Mexico and India often disagree with them. They want more corporate investment, not less; freer trade, not more restricted markets; and the enforcement of local labor laws, not the imposition of foreign ones."

ADJUST TO GLOBAL THREATS

The global practice of public relations has gained new urgency with the increase in geopolitical tensions between the United States and other nations. Fears of terrorism and anti-American violence have caused U.S. companies to add more security at overseas operations, reexamine relationships in vulnerable locations, and rely more on operational leadership chosen from local populations.

Reviewing the anxious situation, *PRWeek* magazine said that multinational companies should:

- Step up employee communications activities for workers in stressful regions.
- Emphasize long-term relationships and high-ranking local managers.
- Focus on the company's local history, employment, and contributions.

"Stick to talking about who your company is and what its products offer," the magazine recommended, "and don't get caught up in political issues or side-taking."

ADDITIONAL READINGS

Tilson, Donn J., & Emmanuel C. Alozie. (2004). *Toward the common good: Perspectives in international public relations*. Boston: Pearson Education.

Casmir, Fred L. (1997). *Ethics in intercultural and international communication*. Mahwah, NJ: Lawrence Erlbaum Associates.

Higgins, Richard. (2000). *Best practices in global investor relations*. Westport, CT: Greenwood.

Kruckeberg, Dean, & Katerina Tsetsura. (2003). *A composite index by country of variables related to the likelihood of the existence of "cash for news coverage."* Gainesville, FL: Institute for Public Relations.

CASE 39.   BAYER DRUG RECALL STRAINS INTERNATIONAL RELATIONSHIPS

The Bayer name means aspirin to most consumers, but production of the pain reliever represents a small fraction of the German company's global business. Headquartered north of Cologne in Leverkusen, the Bayer Group is a chemical industry giant, producing products in four business areas: health care, crop science, polymers, and chemicals. Its worldwide 2002 revenues exceeded €29 billion (about $32 billion), and employees numbered more than 117,000.

The company's health care products include over-the-counter medications such as Bayer aspirin and Alka-Seltzer tablets as well prescription drugs such as Cipro antibiotic. Cipro gained attention in 2001 when it was used to treat U.S. Postal Service workers and others who had been exposed to anthrax in acts of bioterrorism. Other Bayer pharmaceuticals treat blood disorders and cardiovascular disease.

Fighting High Cholesterol

In 1997, the U.S. FDA approved a new Bayer drug, Baycol, that physicians could prescribe to help patients lower the level of cholesterol in their blood. High cholesterol levels can cause the formation of plaque in arteries and lead to heart attacks.

In Europe, the same drug, under the name Lipobay, received approval in 1997 from the British Medicines Control Agency, whose licensing authority is accepted by countries in the European Union through a process called mutual recognition.

Baycol was a member of a class of drugs called statins, a popular therapy for individuals with high cholesterol. Other pharmaceutical companies, such as Merck and Pfizer, already were producing statin drugs.

Because heart disease is the leading cause of death in industrialized nations and high cholesterol contributes to heart disease, the market for drugs that lower cholesterol has attracted pharmaceutical companies. It is a big and profitable category.

Though four or more therapies are available, the statin class of drugs is widely used. According to some sources, the number of individuals using statins exceeds 8 million in the United States alone. Depending on an individual's prescription, a 1-month supply of Baycol might cost about $75.

Bayer was pleased with the results of its new drug from the outset. The number of physicians prescribing it grew rapidly, suggesting that it had the potential to reach blockbuster status—generally regarded as annual sales of $1 billion.

Bayer Issues Warnings

However, problems began to mount 2 years after the Baycol's approval. Bayer told the FDA in December 1999 that it had detected a troubling rate of rhabdomyolysis among Baycol users in the United States. Rhabdomyolysis (often called "rhabdo") is a disorder involving the release of toxins from muscle deterioration into the bloodstream. Symptoms include muscle pain and weakness. In some cases, rhabdo can lead to kidney damage and even death.

Baycol users were more likely to develop rhabdo if they were taking the prescription in combination with Lopid—a cholesterol drug made by Pfizer—or were using the highest approved Baycol dosage (0.8 milligrams). In January 2000, the first rhabdo death of a Baycol user in the United States was reported.

Bayer changed Baycol's label to warn against concurrent use with Lopid and sent a letter to physicians outlining the risk. In June 2000, Bayer changed the label again to limit use of the highest approved dosage. About 1 year later, Bayer shared information on rhabdo reactions to Lipobay with European regulators, and they acted in June 2001 to require the same warnings adopted earlier in the United States.

Deaths From Side Effects

On August 8, 2001, Bayer announced that it had decided to voluntarily withdraw Baycol from the market in the United States and Europe. By that date, Bayer had learned of 31 deaths among Baycol's 700,000 American users.

Lipobay users had died in Europe as well, but no tally was immediately available because no single European agency was responsible for monitoring the safety of drugs once they were licensed for use. In Spain, health officials said that three people had died from rhabdo; in Germany, the total was five. Later in August, Bayer confirmed 52 deaths worldwide and 1,100 cases of rhabdo side effects. In Japan, the drug remained available until September because Pfizer's Lopid was not distributed there.

Some European government officials were highly critical of Bayer's procedures for sharing information on the discovery of risks linked to Baycol/Lipobay. Seven weeks before withdrawing the drug, Bayer had given the British Medicines Control Agency (MCA) a study on severe side effects in Baycol users who also took Lopid. After the drug's withdrawal was announced, the German health ministry complained that it had not received the study given to the MCA. It called Bayer's information policies unacceptable.

A *New York Times* article quoted an official at the Federal Institute for Medicine and Medical Products, Germany's counterpart to the FDA, as saying: "It isn't the job of the MCA to be postman for the European Union."

When journalists raised questions about the year-long delay in warning European healthcare authorities about the risks, a Bayer spokesman explained that Europeans were less likely to combine the cholesterol drugs, and fewer problems were detected.

Reactions to the Withdrawal

In the United States and Europe, the withdrawal of the Bayer drug triggered three distinct reactions:

1. Pharmaceutical companies promptly produced public relations programs to assure physicians and patients that the statin class of drugs was safe.
2. Public policy advocates called for improvements in systems to track drug safety and alert health care officials and their patients to problems.
3. Plaintiffs' attorneys began seeking compensation for Baycol/Lipobay users who suffered the side effects of rhabdomyolysis.

As cardiovascular patients learned about the Baycol withdrawal, competing pharmaceutical companies feared that their statin drugs would lose users to other types of medication. With Bayer's drug out of the picture, the makers of Lipitor, Pravachol, Zocor, and other statin drugs acted to protect their existing statin business and to appeal to Baycol users. According to *Pharmaceutical Executive* magazine, Pfizer teamed up with the American Heart Association and *Prevention* magazine in a public relations campaign to reassure statin users and their physicians about safety and efficacy, and Bristol-Myers Squibb offered Baycol users a month's supply of its statin drug.

Some individuals and organizations were alarmed that drug safety problems could go undetected for years and unresolved for an even longer period. Baycol was on the market for more than 4 years and had millions of users worldwide. Advocates called for changes in the systems used in the United States, Europe, and other nations to find pharmaceutical problems more quickly. Commenting on the issue, *Business Week* said:

> The system for tracking the safety of prescription drugs after they hit the market is inadequate. The FDA spots those problems mainly through voluntary reporting by physicians when patients have bad reactions. But by the FDA's own estimate, no more than 10 percent of these reactions ever get reported. "We know how many suitcases were lost last year by the airlines," says Dr. Raymond L. Woosley, vice president for health sciences at the University of Arizona. "But, we don't know how many people have been harmed by prescription drugs."

For Bayer, the biggest immediate threat following the withdrawal announcement came from a flood of litigation filed by plaintiffs' attorneys on behalf of Baycol users who said the drug had caused them to suffer rhabdomyolysis. By the time the first case came to trial in February 2003, the number of lawsuits had reached 7,800. A Bayer attorney insisted that most of the plaintiffs had not experienced any adverse effects from using Baycol.

Even so, investors' fears about the potential liability had helped push the price of Bayer common stock down to $13.37 on February 25, 2003, as the trial began. The price had been $33.09 on January 24, 2002, when Bayer shares first began trading on the NYSE as American depository receipts (securities issued in the United States to represent shares of a foreign company).

The First Trial Begins

The initial case—heard in Nueces County Court in Texas—involved an 82-year-old resident of Corpus Christi and began with Bayer committing an embarrassing public relations faux pas. On the day before jury selection was to begin, the public relations vice president for Bayer's U.S. health care operations sent a letter about the impending proceedings to 2,100 local residents. The letter reminded residents that Bayer employed 2,000 people at its Texas operations.

"As you hear and see reports of the trial," the letter said, "I hope that you will keep an open mind to the efforts that Bayer made to give fair redress to this gentleman and, on a much broader scale, the tremendous contributions that our company has and continues to make to the health and welfare of millions of people worldwide."

A Bayer attorney told the Nueces County judge that the letter had been intended for members of the Corpus Christi Chamber of Commerce, and its wider distribution was a mistake that resulted from miscommunication within Bayer. At least one prospective juror received the letter. The district attorney considered filing jury-tampering charges against the Bayer public relations executive but decided against it.

At trial, the plaintiff's attorneys tried to show that Bayer had known about the risks of Baycol long before withdrawing it and failed to adequately warn physicians and patients of the dangers. The plaintiffs suggested that the drug's success and profitability interfered with the corporation's conscience. At the time of withdrawal, Baycol was Bayer's third-best-selling drug.

Bayer countered that it met its responsibilities to the regulatory authorities, health care professionals, and patients. It pointed out that it forwarded data on side effects to the FDA promptly, strengthened the warnings in the prescribing information, and eventually withdrew the drug voluntarily.

Jury Clears Bayer

The jury verdict cleared Bayer in the Corpus Christi case on March 18, 2003. The company had been working to resolve other cases out of court and had already paid $125 million to settle about 450 of these when it received the verdict.

Following the decision, the company issued this statement from its headquarters in Leverkusen:

> Bayer said it is pleased that the jury in the Corpus Christi, Texas, USA, Baycol trial reached a verdict in its favor. The verdict validates Bayer's assertion that the company acted responsibly in the development, marketing and voluntary withdrawal of Baycol.

Bayer will now turn its attention to the other pending Baycol cases to analyze the specific circumstances of each case and the nature of the claims. It is Bayer's intention to pursue its policy of seeking to fairly compensate anyone who experienced serious side effects from Baycol, regardless of whether we have valid legal defenses to such claims. At the same time, where an examination of the facts indicates that Baycol played no role in the patient's medical situation, or where a settlement is not achieved, Bayer will continue to defend itself vigorously as it did in the Corpus Christi case.

QUESTIONS FOR REFLECTION

1. Bayer notified government regulators in the United States and Europe about unexpected reactions to its high-cholesterol drug, but the company provided the warnings at different times. How would you justify the difference?
2. In Europe, no single agency has been responsible for monitoring a new drug's safety after it's licensed for use. How does this situation affect a pharmaceutical company's risk profile?
3. Bayer's competitors scrambled to attract Baycol users once the Bayer drug was withdrawn. What public relations methods would you have recommended to reach former Baycol users?
4. A Bayer public relations executive's letter to the Corpus Christi Chamber of Commerce accidentally got wider distribution. How would you explain the purpose of sending the letter to its originally intended audience?

Information for this case was drawn from the following: the Bayer Web site at http://www.press.bayer.com/News/News.nsf/id/010005; Andrews, E. (22 August 2001), "Drug's removal exposes holes in Europe's net," *The New York Times*, p. C1; Barrett, A. (10 September 2001), "Commentary: Drug safety needs a serious overhaul," *Business Week*, p. 61; (8 August 2001), "Bayer voluntarily withdraws Baycol," Bayer news release; (4 September 2001), "Bayer faces Baycol probe," Cable News Network; Breitstein, J. (October 2001), "Baycol fallout," *Pharmaceutical Executive*, p. 96; Fuhrmans, V., & Harris G. (9 August 2001), "Bayer withdraws major cholesterol drug," *The Wall Street Journal*, p. B2; Fuhrmans, V., Harris G., & Winslow, R. (10 August 2001), "Bayer recall spurs Europe to wide review," *The Wall Street Journal*, p. A3; Fuhrmans, V. (19 March 2003), "Jury rules Bayer isn't liable in closely watched drug case," *The Wall Street Journal*, p. B2; Petersen, M. (22 February 2003), "Judge criticizes letter from Bayer," *The New York Times*, p. C14; and Simmons, M. (21 August 2001), "Left holding the pill bottle," *The Washington Post*, p. F3

CASE 40.   HELIOS? A GREEK GOD WITH A BRITISH ACCENT FOR A GLOBAL COMPANY

Work crews on ladders and aerial lift trucks started stripping Amoco and BP markings from service stations around the world in late 2000, signaling the start of a 4-year program that would visibly unify the operations under a new global brand.

Down came Amoco's torch-and-oval symbol and BP's green shield with yellow initials. In their place, the crews raised a new symbol—a sunburst of green, white, and yellow. Accenting the symbol, like an exponent, were the lowercase sans serif letters bp.

The program rebranded a handful of stations the first year, about 4,600 the second year, and thousands more in subsequent years as the conversions progressed.

"Put simply, we have adopted a single brand to show our customers around the world that, wherever they see the BP sign, they can consistently expect the highest quality of products and services," said John Browne, BP chief executive, in the July 2000 news release announcing the rebranding program.

BP plc will replace the torch-and-oval symbol at Amoco service stations with BP's new sunburst logo, the Helios mark.

Building a Global Giant

Development of a new corporate identity system and its use on retail stations came as a predictable climax to a series of acquisitions that propelled BP to the top ranks

A green shield with the letters BP in yellow has served as the petroleum and refining company's symbol for more than 70 years.

of the petroleum supermajors. In 1998, British Petroleum had acquired Amoco in a $57 billion deal. In early 2000, it purchased ARCO for about $27 billion and, soon after, paid almost $5 billion to acquire Burmah Castrol, producer of one of the world's leading motor oils.

A tally showed that the new BP plc, as it was named, operated almost 27,000 retail service stations around the world, pumping about 160 million gallons of fuel each day. The BP group also was selling natural gas in 24 countries, operating 55 petrochemical sites worldwide, handling $3 billion in annual convenience stores sales, and more. Annual group sales in 2001 exceed $174 billion, and employees numbered about 100,000 in more than 100 countries.

With customers and employees in every corner of the globe, BP needed a single new identity to erase even the hint of ethnocentrism in its heritage and also to better control the communication costs of maintaining a multiplicity of brands.

Costs and Risks of Remarking

Adopting a new corporate identity system—with changes in name, symbol, color, and theme—can be expensive and time-consuming. BP said it spent some $7 million to research and prepare the new brand and expected to spend another $25 million a quarter to support the change through nonretail signage and additional advertising. These figures do not include the costs of remarking the service stations, which had been scheduled for refurbishing before creation of the unified brand.

Applying a new identity to predecessor companies requires managerial sensitivity because many employees, forced to accept the eclipse of a brand for which they've labored, will find the change unsettling. They may question whether a break with the past will marginalize them and their careers, bring new opportunity, or create a cloud of transitional uncertainty. Companies usually try to move quickly through a period of major change to minimize the risks of distracting employees and confusing consumers.

British Petroleum considered a number of designs proposed by Landor Associates, a branding consultantcy, before settling on the sunburst and naming it the Helios mark, a nod to the ancient Greek god of the sun.

BP's choice of the Helios mark was influenced management's desire to:

- Clearly distinguish the company's new identity from its predecessors'.
- Symbolize energy in all its forms, from fossil fuels to solar.
- Avoid confining the company to its existing businesses.
- Show its commitment to the environment.

BP plc will update its service stations with BP's new sunburst logo, the Helios mark. (Photo by A. Sleeth.)

Accolades and Brickbats

Some graphic designers and brand consultants gave BP accolades for the new corporate identity system and its environmental emphasis. A post to the Viridian Web site, which offers commentary on design and culture, said that BP "is the only Big Oil major with a lick of common sense about the Greenhouse Effect."

Others were not so complimentary, faulting not only the pace of the company's efforts in developing solar energy but also its new advertising theme. In ads, the company had extended the meaning of BP to include "Beyond Petroleum."

BBC News reported that environmentalists at Greenpeace said: "This is a triumph of style over substance. BP spent more on their logo this year than they did on renewable energy last year.... BP doesn't stand for Beyond Petroleum. It stands for Burning the Planet."

External and Internal Appeal

A BP executive acknowledged, in an interview published on ceoforum.com.au, that some people may experience cognitive dissonance in associating a petroleum refiner with environmentally sensitive policies.

"Externally, the issue is often one of suspended disbelief," said Greg Bourne, who was BP's regional president/director for Australia and New Zealand at the time the Helios was adopted. "Changing your logo won't change society's mind. It is only by exhibiting changed behavior and attitudes over a long period of time that you will slowly but surely differentiate yourself."

Mr. Bourne told ceoforum.com.au that BP employees, after some initial hesitation, enthusiastically embraced the new brand and the four succinct company values that it represents—performance-driven, progressive, innovative, and green: "On the green and progressive attributes, I would say that inside the company there is a stronger environmental push than most people imagine. By saying you are going to be green and progressive, employees start feeling that 'you are playing my song; let's do it together.' It is actually very liberating in terms of generating energy and drive within the company."

Like most global companies, BP recognized that its visual communications and its reputation had to appeal to people in many cultures who use an array of languages. Strong distinctive markings, divorced from language and even from an alphabet, offer the potential to convey organizational purpose, reputation, and values among people everywhere.

Identity and Image

Strategic communication consultants tell clients to distinguish between identity and image and to pay attention to the cultivation of both. Kenneth J. Roberts, CEO of Lippincott & Margulies, offers this differentiation: "Simply put, your identity is who you really are, and your image is how much of that reality people understand."

Mr. Roberts said that *identity* comprises organizational vision, strategy, goals and objectives, products and services, and employee behavior and spirit. Everything that's done to create value in the marketplace and in financial markets constitutes an organization's identity, he said.

In comparison, Mr. Roberts said that *image* is the sum of all associations and impressions that target publics build up from an organization's communications as well as from actual experiences with its products and services. He points out that the activities and programs that shape image are usually under the organization's control. The programs include public relations, advertising, Internet sites, visual identity system, and more.

"Effective management of the corporate image is essentially the only way to ensure that your organization is building the reputation it wants," Mr. Roberts said.

Tips for Visual-Identity Programs

Visual branding consultants note that organizational names, logotypes, and colors make countless impressions every day on individuals within a target public, and global visual identifiers should have certain properties. They say that logos, for example, generally should:

- Avoid colors or shapes that would have an offensive or unacceptable meaning in any culture where they might be used.
- Avoid nationalistic overtones that might stir resentments or appear insensitive.
- Adopt timeless colors and classic type styles to convey stability and trust.
- Look as appealing in black-and-white as well as they do in color because communications are often faxed and photocopied.
- Use a functional shape, such as a circle, square, triangle, or rectangle, so that they are adaptable to a variety of layout and design plans.
- Appear legible and distinctive in a variety of sizes because they may appear on the side of a truck or the barrel of a ballpoint pen.

Too often, business executives minimize the importance of visual identity, describing it as cosmetic or superficial. Yet, visual-identity systems affect consumer behavior and preferences, support and extend advertising, influence employee spirit, and integrate internal processes with external outcomes.

At BP, Lord Browne described the importance of the new marking system: "In a global market place, branding is crucially important in attracting customers and business. It is not just a matter of a few gasoline stations or the logo on pole signs. It is about the identity of the company and the values which underpin everything that you do and every relationship that you have."

QUESTIONS FOR REFLECTION

1. Some critics say that global rebranding efforts like BP's are simply exercises in corporate vanity. Is that viewpoint valid?
2. Greenpeace contended that BP should spend more on development of solar energy and other renewable sources than on rebranding. How would you respond?
3. The Lippincott & Margulies CEO made a distinction between identity and image. Some people say an organization that focuses on the substance of its identity will earn a good image as a result. Would public relations professionals agree?
4. Why are some employees fearful of mergers and acquisitions? How would you deal with their worries?
5. BP wants people to think of the company as a petroleum producer that's sensitive to environmental concerns. What problems will it encounter in this effort?
6. What public relations programs could you recommend to BP to improve its environmental reputation?
7. BP sells petroleum products such as gasoline around the world and has been working to combine its many brands under one name and one symbol. What are the attractions and risks of this globalization effort?
8. From an employee's standpoint, is the program to consolidate the BP identity appealing or threatening?

Information for this case was drawn from the following: the BP plc Web site at http://www.bp.com/centres/press/index.asp; (24 July 2000), "BP Amoco unveils new global brand to drive growth," BP news release; (24 July 2000), "BP goes green," BBC News; (August 2001), "CEO dialogue," ceoforum.com.au, http://www.ceoforum.com.au./200108_ceodialogue.cfm#jump1; Guyon, J. (5 July 1999), "When John Browe talks, big oil listens," *Fortune*, p. 116; and Roberts, K. (accessed 5 November 2003), "Managing image in a dynamic corporate environment," http://www.lippincott-margulies.com/publications/a_roberts03.shtml.

CASE 41.   PUBLICIS AND THE EUROPEAN CENTRAL BANK INTRODUCE "THE EURO—OUR MONEY" TO THE WORLD

Money talks, or so the cliché says. Imagine if the money in question has to speak at least 12 different languages, be accepted by citizens used to different currencies and conversion rates, and be "heard" within a few months. In essence, this was the task faced by the European Union (EU) nations who moved in January 2002 to adopt the euro as their official currency as they phased out their traditional bill and coin systems. Introducing the new bills and coins to members of the public so they would be familiar enough with their values for them to be used in daily commerce would require a coordinated communication campaign across the 12 EU nations that had adopted the euro.

Adopting the Euro

The euro became the official banking currency of 12 EU nations, Austria, Belgium, Denmark, Finland, France, Germany, Greece, Ireland, Italy, Luxembourg, the Netherlands, and Spain, on January 1, 1999. By January 2002, the national currencies were to be phased out and the euro was slated to become the united currency. After the initial creation of the euro notes, member nations continued to use their traditional national currencies such as the marks, francs, and lire. Converting to the new single currency, among those nations that had chosen to do so, was no simple task, involving more than designing and printing new bills and minting new coins.

The value of the euro had to be fixed against the national currencies of the participating nations. Prices within stores and calculations within registers and ATMs had to be converted to euros.

By January 2002, more than 14.5 billion euro banknotes were printed and ready for distribution. Then, the national notes and coins of the participating countries had to be withdrawn before they became illegal some 2 months after the introduction of the euro.

A European Central Bank (ECB) news release from December 28, 2001, described the adoption process:

> On 1 January 2002, the 306 million citizens of the euro area will begin to use the euro banknotes and coins. The euro cash changeover operation has been advancing according to plan, thanks to the thorough preparations and firm commitment of the hundreds of thousands of people directly involved in the cash changeover process.

> As a complement to the euro-related information activities conducted by the governments, the European Commission and other private and public entities, the European Central Bank (ECB) and the 12 national central banks of the euro area have conducted the Euro 2002 Information Campaign in order to familiarise citizens with their new money.

Over the last few weeks of 2001 some 200 million copies of a leaflet providing information on the euro banknotes and coins, their security features and the changeover modalities in the eleven official Community languages have been distributed to European households. This leaflet has also been translated into 23 other languages, in co-operation with the respective national central banks.

To keep the media and the general public informed of the progress of the euro cash changeover, the ECB will publish daily updates on its website from 2 January to 11 January 2002, and weekly updates on 18 and 25 January 2002.

More than 15 billion euro banknotes, worth more than EUR 630 billion, have been produced, as have well over 51 billion coins worth almost EUR 16 billion. Of these 15 billion euro banknotes, less than 10 billion will enter circulation initially. The rest will be held as logistical stocks to accommodate any changes in demand.

Celebrating the Euro

So, who would help make the new currency "talk" by designing and coordinating the cross-national communication campaign? Some 40 firms initially sought the account. After the list of agencies was narrowed, the ECB chose Publicis, a French-based firm, to manage the multimillion "Euro 2002" campaign over J. Walter Thompson/Hill & Knowlton, and Young & Rubicam/Burson Marsteller. Publicis is a full-service agency, with units offering advertising, media relations, direct marketing, and consultancy. Joanna Baldwin, head of business development at Publicis Worldwide, was quoted in the November 11, 1999, *Marketing Week*: "We aim to make people feel good about the euro—that it is a cause for celebration."

Publicis worked with the European Commission, the executive body for the EU. Publicis was charged with "gradually preparing the general public for the introduction of the euro banknotes and coins, so that they are favorably received," according to the ECB. The agency faced some major challenges: different languages, different cultures, differences among the traditional currencies used, and the vast numbers of people who needed to be informed, ranging from the 302 million residents of the euro-using nations to the millions outside the EU who needed to understand the currency. It chose the theme, "The euro—our money," to introduce the euro as the official currency of the participating 12 EU countries.

The total budget for the campaign was estimated at between $30 million and $50 million. The campaign had two phases: one designed to build recognition for the new currency, and a second designed to teach cashiers and clerks how to recognize counterfeit currency. This second phase spread beyond the immediate EU nations into the United States, Japan, and eastern Europe.

Understanding the Currency

The saturation campaign was launched in September 2001 in order to prepare for the launch of the euro in January 2002. The strategy was based on the belief that the public would be more receptive to information about the notes and coins right before they were issued. A survey conducted in February 2001 suggested that about half the public might not receive or understand the messages about the euro. Therefore, the campaign's messages were designed to be simple and clear.

ECB president Wim Duisenberg told the *Financial Times* of London in March 2001: "We aim to provide very broad access to information, to communities and individuals, to old and young, to people in towns and the countryside, to the disabled and the able-bodied."

The campaign was launched simultaneously with the unveiling of the look of the new currency. Television commercials, newspaper ads, posters, and leaflets were used in the campaign. The initial television ad, in an appeal to unity, stressed that the euro would be used by 300 million people across the continent. Three more commercials announced the seven different denominations of the notes and stressed their security features. The fourth advertisement listed the coins' denominations. The advertisements were produced in all the languages of the countries involved in the euro conversion.

The ECB and the European Commission worked together to distribute 28,000 kits with dummies of the euro banknotes for use with trainers of those with physical or learning disabilities. The ECB set up a Web site with extensive information on the currency and how it was developed. The site added a "children's zone" where children could play games using the euro.

QUESTIONS FOR REFLECTION

1. What obstacles might be faced when planning a multilanguage information campaign?
2. What obstacles might be encountered when asking key stakeholders to change nationally accepted symbols such as currency?
3. What obstacles might be encountered when your key stakeholders groups are composed of a variety of age groups?

Information for this case was drawn from the following: (31 October 2000), "Ad campaign aims to ease euro's arrival," *The Wall Street Journal*, p. B24; Barber, T. (2 March 2001), "Euro publicity blitz to be launched in September," *Financial Times London*, p. 7; Barber, T., & Brown, K. (30 August 2001), "Design of euro banknotes unveiled today," *Financial Times London*, p. 8; Bentley, S. (11 November 1999), "Publicis lands GBP30m euro task," *Marketing Week*, p. 11; Geary, J., & Sautter-Bonn, U. (16 March 1998), "Europe: The euro as child's play," *Time International*, p. 27; (5 November 1999), "Publicis wins $30M–$50M account to launch the euro," *Euromarketing via E-mail*, *III*(6); and (6 December 2000), "Publicity campaign in Italy to take the sting out of the euro," *European Report*.

CASE 42.   RED, WHITE, AND BLUE—AND GOLDEN?
MCDONALD'S RESPONDS TO INTERNATIONAL PRESSURES

The golden arches of the McDonald's logo may help make it the most recognizable company in the world. The company, which has operated about 30,000 company-owned and franchised outlets in more than 120 countries, has found in recent years, however, that the arches may just as well have been depicted as red, white, and blue as the company has become the focus of anti-American sentiment or animosity toward its international economic power in many locations around the world.

McDonald's expanded rapidly internationally during the 1990s and early 2000s, even opening a franchise in 1994 inside Mecca, Saudi Arabia, the most sacred site for Muslims, who are required to visit Mecca on pilgrimage at least once during their lives, if able. The *International Herald Tribune* said it had opened as many as 1,000 restaurants a year worldwide during the boom. In 2001, it reported international system sales of $7.8 billion. Its Web site says its vision is "to be the world's best quick service restaurant experience."

Violence and Protests Rock the Arches

The *Toronto Star* reported that since 1990, franchises in France, Belgium, Mexico, London, Chile, Serbia, Columbia, South Africa, Turkey, and Greece have been bombed. Violence against the fast-food chain has escalated. In December 2001, a restaurant in China was bombed, and in September 2001, a McDonald's in Istanbul was destroyed. In September 2002, a restaurant in a suburb of Beirut was bombed, and a month later, a Moscow restaurant was bombed. On November 20, 2002, a franchise in Riyadh, Saudi Arabia, was burned. Then, in December 2002, a bomb killed at least three in a McDonald's in Makassar, Indonesia. French farmer Jose Bove led protests against "mal bouffe," or what he called junk food, that destroyed a McDonald's under construction in Millau in 1999. A new McDonald's in Grenoble, France, was burned in November 2002 following protests.

Although there may be no link, the corporation announced in late 2002 that it was closing 175 of its overseas restaurants and all its outlets in Bolivia and two Middle Eastern countries it did not identify. In four international markets in the Middle East and Latin America, ownership would be transferred to licensees. At the same time, some 200 to 250 jobs were cut in the United States, and another 200 to 350 jobs were eliminated internationally. The fast-food chain had seen its earnings drop in the previous seven quarters.

Harvard anthropology professor James Watson, who studies McDonald's, told the *Toronto Star:* "In many parts of the world if people can't reach the embassy, there's always McDonald's.... McDonald's represents an entire packaged cultural system. The fact that it's food makes it even more dangerous and more powerful—there's nothing more powerful than food in any society as a symbol of identity."

Benjamin Barber, author of *Jihad vs. McWorld*, agreed. He told the newspaper: "Attacking McDonald's is not a surrogate for attacking America's foreign policy. They're attacking McDonald's because it directly stands for things they oppose."

Growing evidence suggests that Barber's assessment is accurate. McDonald's and other American corporations such as Starbucks and Coca-Cola that either operate in or support Israel have faced boycotts. Some Muslim fundamentalists have called for attacks on McDonald's, according to reports in *Salon.com*, which said that in October 2001, an article in the online Islamist magazine *Khilafah* identified McDonald's and McDonnell-Douglas as "two devices that are used for ensuring American global reach.... The fast food chains have become imperial fiefdoms, sending emissaries far and wide."

Sometimes, it is not anti-Americanism that leads to conflict, however, but other issues of culture and faith. The corporation was sued in 2001 by a group of Hindu vegetarians and others who charged in a class-action lawsuit that McDonald's French fries had used beef extract not listed in the ingredients. When in 1990 the company replaced beef fat in its deep fryers with 100% vegetable oil, it didn't reveal that it added beef essence to the oil. McDonald's paid a $10 million settlement, apologized, and altered the way it reports ingredients in its foods.

The Corporation Seeks to Adapt

McDonald's CEO Jack Greenberg participated in a panel discussion at the February 2002 World Economic Forum with the secretary general of the League of Arab States, Amr Moussa. Moussa said there were "deep grievances" against U.S. policies around the world. Greenberg said his restaurants offered a "model of how a corporation has to behave—through dialogue, facts and solutions," the *New York Times* reported.

McDonald's has responded to protests by trying to stress that its golden arches are grounded in local soil. It has allowed employees to close for prayers during the day, to alter its menu to meet religious requirements, and to separate male and female diners, according to *Franchise Times* magazine. *Salon.com* reported that McDonald's has incorporated other local and cultural requirements into its menu, offering a vegetarian McNistisima menu in Cyprus, a kosher McDonald's in Israel, and wine in France. In Brazil, McDonald's outlets have in-store Internet access, and in Japan, the children's playgrounds have been replaced by computer play centers.

Reuters described the McDonald's in Jakarta, Indonesia, in an October 2001 article, as an example of an adapting restaurant. Customers are served by women in veils and men in prayer caps. Islamic posters inside point out that "McDonald's Indonesia is owned by an indigenous Muslim Indonesian." Some posters are in Arabic, and others are in English. Some of the restaurants play religious music.

Its *2002 Social Responsibility Report*, the first issued by the corporation, pointed to its international charitable works. Posted on the company Web site, the report gave information about the $5 million UNICEF grant to support immunization projects in Africa and efforts to work with environmental and conservation groups. The report grew out of an internal social-responsibility audit carried out by the Business for Social Responsibility NGO based in San Francisco.

A Golden Day for Children

A major public relations campaign was launched in 2002 to support the November 20 World Children's Day at McDonald's, which sought to raise millions in support for the Ronald McDonald House Charities and other children's services such as support for orphanages in Russia, Estonia, and Kuwait, for children's hospitals, and for children's health organizations. The event commemorated the 100th birthday of McDonald's founder Ray Kroc and was timed to commemorate the anniversary of the Convention on the Rights of the Child, which had been held on November 20, 1989. A portion of the proceeds from all sales on November 20 were donated to the causes.

Golin/Harris International coordinated public relations for the event, but McDonald's also worked with local agencies. Internal communication support began in April, and public announcement of the World Children's Day came in July after CEO Greenberg met with the secretary general of the United Nations and the executive director of UNICEF.

International musicians Celine Dion and Enrique Iglesias and 125 Olympic athletes were recruited to serve as spokespeople for the day. International events included a daylong concert in Mexico City where more than 40 celebrities were slated to appear. In Auckland, New Zealand, the prime minister made an appearance. In Hong Kong, a local musician was to cook breakfast for area children, and in Moscow, a McDonald's hosted orphans.

Cathy Nemeth, senior director for worldwide communications with McDonald's, told *PRWeek*, "It's a global public relations program that is community based."

QUESTIONS FOR REFLECTION

1. What principles should characterize community relations and social responsibility practices on an international scale?
2. Discuss the role of research in the development of public relations campaigns and programs for multinational corporations.

3. How might corporations such as McDonald's and Starbucks differentiate themselves from their home country? What possibilities and what dangers does that differentiation pose for practitioners and managers?

Information for this case was drawn from the following: Associated Press (15 December 1994), "New mecca for burger with fries," *Newsday*, p. A22; Chabria, A. (22 April 2002), "McDonald's shows off CSR credentials in debut report," *PRWeek*, p. 3; Elam, S. (23 October 2002), "McDonald's pledges to refocus on core locations," *National Post*, p. FP18; Frank, J. N. (11 November 2002), "McDonald's starts PR push for global kids fundraiser," *PRWeek*, p. 9; Goldberg, M. (6 December 2002), "Falling arches," *Salon.com*; Goldberg, M. (8 December 2002), "Fires of anti-Americanism burn McDonald's," *The Toronto Star*; Jung, H. (19 April 2003), "Starbucks risks a backlash with international growth; overseas dissent is reminiscent of some of the problems faced by McDonald's," *London Free Press*, p. C5; Pfanner, E. (20 November 2002), "Diet awaits the giant of fast food; McDonald's to trim its expansion plans," *International Herald Tribune*, p. 11; Prewitt, M. (18 February 2002), "Chains look for links overseas," *Nation's Restaurant News*, p. 1; Schmemann, S. (2 February 2002), "Forum in New York; workshops; where McDonald's sits down with Arab nationalists," *The New York Times*, p. A10; Soetjipto, T. (12 October 2001), "U.S. icon McDonald's embraces Islam in Indonesia," *Reuters Business Report*; Valkin, V. (9 November 2002), "McDonald's to close 175 overseas outlets," *The Financial Times*, p. 19; and Weiss, J. (8 July 2002), "McDonald's fries fracas simmering," *The Dallas Morning News*, p. A1.

CASE 43. MARITIME TRAGEDY COMPOUNDED
BY CULTURAL DIFFERENCES

People throughout Japan angrily condemned the U.S. Navy when a submarine accidentally rammed and sank a Japanese fishing vessel in the open ocean off Hawaii on Friday, February 9, 2001. Over the weekend, anger over the collision and relief at the rescue of 26 aboard paled beside anxiety over 9 still missing, including 4 teenagers.

As Navy officers and Japanese survivors provided more details, people everywhere were astonished to learn that the sub's maneuvers had been arranged to impress 16 civilian guests on board and that some guests had handled critical controls before the accident.

"It's outrageous and unforgivable," one resident of Uwajima, the fishing vessel's home, told BBC News. "It sounds like they were fooling around. It's very upsetting for the people in this town."

Additionally, Japanese survivors said the submarine had rescued no one but instead waited for the U.S. Coast Guard to arrive and lift them from their life rafts. Confirming their tale, the Navy said waves had been too high to risk opening the sub's hatches or approaching the small rafts.

The Navy began investigating the collision immediately and relieved the sub's commanding officer. As he prepared for a court of inquiry, he asked to testify under immunity and initially declined to speak publicly about the incident.

U.S. Navy divers swim alongside the *Ehime-Maru* during recovery operations off Honolulu. (USN photo by Andrew McKaskle.)

The *Yomiuri Shimbun*, Japan's largest daily newspaper, expressed disapproval: "In Japan, the person responsible for such an accident would be bound to personally apologize for their actions and accept full responsibility."

In the United States, high rates of litigation and gigantic jury awards have conditioned people to proceed cautiously as the facts of an accident are collected and assessed, especially when criminal charges might result.

Eventually, investigators pieced together events that led to the collision.

Pieces of the Puzzle

The *Ehime-Maru*, a 180-foot trawler, was heading south at 11 knots on February 9 with the open Pacific ahead and the coastline of Oahu just visible 9 miles off the stern. It had departed Honolulu 90 minutes earlier, at noontime, carrying a crew of 20 as well as 13 students and 2 teachers from the Uwajima Marine Products High School.

Skies were overcast, and haze made visibility no better than fair; but it was a warm day—the air was 78 degrees and the ocean was 77. The surface was choppy, rolling with swells of 4 to 6 feet.

Built in 1996 and weighing 500 tons, the *Ehime-Maru* functioned as a floating classroom, with accommodations for up to 45 students, where Japanese teens could learn the skills they'd need in the maritime trades. The trawler was bound for a fishing area 435 nautical miles distant. High above the white hull and bridge, surface search radar scanned the vicinity for traffic.

Four hours before the trawler left Honolulu, the *USS Greeneville* had put to sea at 8 a.m. from the Naval Station at Pearl Harbor, just a few miles to the west. On board were 106 officers and enlisted men.

Distinguished Civilians Aboard

Also on the *Greeneville* were 16 civilians, men and women who were the Navy's guests for the day, expecting to return to port before nightfall. The Navy arranged such visits to the *Greeneville* and other ships as part of its community relations program. The purpose was to demonstrate:

- The Navy and Marine Corps team as a unique and capable instrument of national policy.
- Resource requirements for the nation's maritime security strategy.
- Prudent stewardship of taxpayer investments in naval platforms and systems.
- The proficiency, pride, and professionalism of sailors and Marines and the need to recruit and retain them.

"The *Greeneville*'s sole mission on 9 February," according to a Navy document, "was to conduct a public affairs 'distinguished visitor' (DV) embark for 16 civilian guests."

Assigned to a large operations area south of Oahu, the 362-foot sub proceeded on the surface for the first 2 hours, with the commanding officer taking groups of guests up to the bridge. Then, the *Greeneville* submerged at 10:17 a.m. During this maneuver, guests operated some of the dive controls under close supervision of the crew, and the sub continued south until noon and then reversed course.

The sub's sonar array first detected the *Ehime-Maru* at about 12:30 p.m. Due to error, initial calculations showed that the distance between the two vessels was increasing rather than closing.

Demonstration of Maneuvers

As the *Greeneville* continued north, the commanding officer put the 6,000-ton submarine through a series of up-and-down angles and high-speed turns to demonstrate its tactical maneuverability. He also planned to execute a rapid dive to a depth of 400 feet as well as an emergency surfacing drill.

Navy rules require a submarine to rise to periscope depth before an emergency surfacing maneuver so that officers can look in all directions to eliminate any danger of collision. Only after this inspection is complete will a submarine descend to practice the rapid ascent.

As prescribed, the *Greeneville* scanned the surface through its periscopes, but the officers and crew saw nothing. The seas were high; a white haze reduced visibility; the trawler's hull was white; its angle of approach reduced its profile; and the sub's surface search procedure was short.

At the time, the *Ehime-Maru* was less than 2 miles away from the *Greeneville*, and the sub's detection equipment confirmed the trawler's presence, its distance, its speed, and its course. Because of earlier miscalculations and inadequate crew communications on the sub, the danger went unnoticed.

Approaching the Fatal Moment

After 66 seconds at periscope depth, the *Greeneville* began its dive and reached 400 feet about 2 minutes later. The commanding officer invited one visitor to sit at the helm, another to operate ballast actuator valves, and a third to sound a klaxon during the emergency drill. All three guests were under close crew supervision. The *Ehime-Maru*, unnoticed and unsuspecting, was less than a mile away.

It took the *Greeneville* less than a minute to get from 400 feet to the surface. As it shot out of the waves, its rudder sliced the *Ehime-Maru* from starboard to port. The trawler captain gave immediate orders to get everyone on deck for a headcount. Even before the count could be completed, waves washed across the deck and began sweeping people into the sea. The vessel was gone in less than 10 minutes.

The trawler's life rafts deployed automatically, and the crew and students struggled through waves and diesel fuel and flotsam to reach them. Within minutes, the

USS *Greeneville* sits atop blocks in dry dock at Pearl Harbor Naval Shipyard following a collision at sea with the Japanese fishing vessel. (DoD photo.)

rafts held 26 survivors. Missing were four 17-year-old students, three crew members, and both teachers.

On the *Greeneville*, the officers and crew were surprised by the noise and shudder caused by the collision. Using the periscopes, they examined the surroundings and were surprised to see a fishing vessel sinking and its people tumbling into the water. The sub itself had suffered some damage but nothing that would threaten its seaworthiness.

The *Greeneville* immediately called the U.S. Coast Guard for rescue assistance, but the high seas prevented the submarine itself from taking survivors on board. Water washing across the deck would have poured into any open hatch as the cylindrical hull rolled with the waves. The officers also were concerned that the sub's rolling motion might swamp or capsize the rafts if the vessel got too close.

Survivors Evacuated to Honolulu

Coast Guard watercraft arrived at the scene about 1 hour later and by 4:15 p.m. had moved all survivors to Honolulu. Surface vessels and aircraft from the Coast Guard and Navy continued to search for the nine missing Japanese for days but had no success.

Tragic as the collision was, the Navy's embarrassment grew as it acknowledged over succeeding days, first, that the sub was impotent in the rescue efforts; second, that a sizeable guest contingent was aboard; third, that civilians handled controls in the drills; and then, that the sole purpose of the cruise was public relations.

U.S. Defense Secretary Donald Rumsfeld (center) confers with Japanese Senior Vice Minister of Foreign Affairs Seishiro Eto (right), Ambassador to the U.S. Shunji Yanai (left) and Chief of Naval Operations Vern Clark. (DoD photo by R.D. Ward.)

By Sunday, apologies and condolences had been extended to Japan by the commander in chief of the U.S. Pacific Fleet, the Ambassador to Japan, the Secretary of State, and the new U.S. President, inaugurated less than a month earlier. The Japanese Prime Minister lodged an official protest and warned that the United States might have to raise the trawler from the ocean floor, 2,000 feet beneath the waves, if the missing nine were not found.

In Japan, people were far from satisfied by the expressions of regret, and the news media there kept insisting that the United States and the submarine's commander should extend "sincere" apologies.

A Contrast in Cultures

Japanese writer Shin'ya Fujiware, commenting in the *New York Times*, said: "The nonappearance of the commander of the *Greeneville*—his failure to meet the families of the victims to express his feelings of apology and mourning—is shocking, even incomprehensible to a people whose culture stresses decorum and form. Such decorum is not merely 'formal' in the American sense; it is the shape in which common humanity finds expression."

One month after the accident, the sub commander arranged to meet face to face with relatives of the victims who were lost. In a closed-doors gathering in March, he bowed formally before them and tearfully expressed his regrets.

In June, the Navy acceded to the wishes of the missing victims' families and began a salvage effort to lift the trawler from the ocean floor and move it to shallower waters where divers could search the vessel's interior for bodies. All but one of the missing nine were found by November.

Navy Gets Cultural Guidance

During the salvage operations, the Navy turned to a professor of religion at the University of Hawaii for guidance in observing cultural norms to show proper respect in the recovery of remains.

Professor George J. Tanabe, Jr., reflecting on the entire episode for the *New York Times*, said: "You couldn't have constructed a better scenario for the uncorking of the darker side of Japan's love–hate relationship with the United States.... It was one humiliation after another for Japan, a reinforcement of deeply resented stereotypes of the relationship between the two countries as tough guys versus wimps."

Cultural differences represent more than the manners and preferences of peoples. They represent perceptions of what is right and wrong, what deserves respect and how to show it, the power of symbols, the need for dignity, and the expectation of truth revealed promptly and thoroughly.

During final ceremonies for the *Ehime-Maru* aboard *JDS Chihaya*, representatives from three families threw flowers into the sea to honor their lost relatives. (USN photo by Keith W. DeVinney.)

QUESTIONS FOR REFLECTION

1. Some reporters said that the Navy's slow release of details in the first week after the accident provided a steady flow of damaging news. What were the alternatives?
2. Was the Navy obligated to shield the "distinguished visitors" from the media's intrusiveness?
3. What steps were available to the Navy to address the anger in Japan and make sincere apologies?
4. How would you balance the concerns about litigation in the United States with demands in Japan for full accountability and openness?

Information for this case was drawn from the following: the U.S. Navy Web site at http://www.cpf.navy.mil/greeneville; Cushman, J. (11 February 2001), "Sub in collision was conducting drill, Navy says," *The New York Times*, p. A1; French, H. (5 November 2001), "U.S. makes amends to Japan for sinking of ship," *The New York Times*, p. A6; Jehl, D. (12 February 2001), "Clues sought in sub accident; some Japanese fault rescue," *The New York Times*, p. A1; Kakuchi, S. (7 March 2001), "Apologies do little to ease grief over sea tragedy," *Asia Times*, p. 7; Marquis, C. (10 February 2001), "9 are missing off Pearl Harbor after U.S. submarine collides with Japanese vessel," *The New York Times*, p. A16; Shin'ya, F. (17 February 2001), "In Japan, waiting for the captain to appear," *The New York Times*, p. A17; (16 February 2001), "Sub tragedy leaves Japanese town bitter," BBC News, http://www.bbc.co.uk/1/hi/world/asia-pacific/; and (13 April 2001), Transcript of USN Court of Inquiry into circumstances of collision.

Index